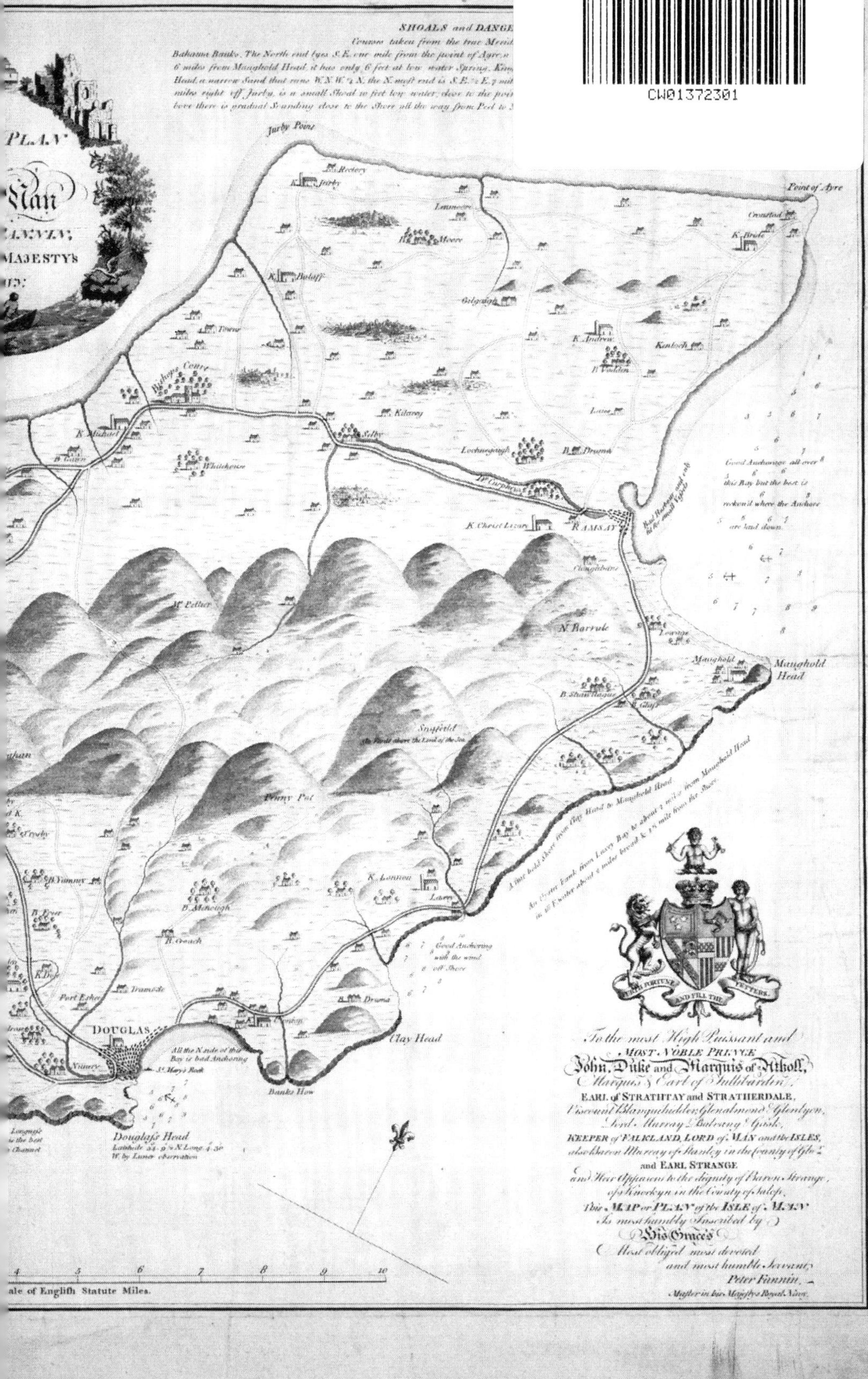
SHOALS and DANGE
Jurby Point
Point of Ayre
Rectory
K. Jurby
K. Bride
Moore
K. Balaff
Bishops Court
K. Michael
Whitehouse
Kilarey
Selby
K. Andrew
Lochneguyh
B. Druma
K. Chrest Lezar
RAMSAY
N. Barrule
Maughold
Maughold Head
Snæfeld
Penny Pot
K. Lonnon
Laxey
Good Anchoring with the wind off Shore
Clay Head
Banks How
DOUGLAS
St. Mary's Rock
All the N. side of this Bay is bad Anchoring
Douglass Head
Good Anchorage all over this Bay but the best is reckon'd where the Anchors are laid down.
Port Esher
Nunery
B. Druma
Scale of English Statute Miles.
To the most High Puissant and
MOST NOBLE PRINCE
John, Duke and Marquis of Atholl,
Marquis & Earl of Tullibardin,
EARL of STRATHTAY and STRATHERDALE,
KEEPER of FALKLAND, LORD of MAN and the ISLES,
and EARL STRANGE
This MAP or PLAN of the ISLE of MAN
Is most humbly Inscribed by
His Grace's
Most obliged most devoted
and most humble Servant,
Peter Fannin,
Master in his Majesty's Royal Navy.

Favourite of Fortune

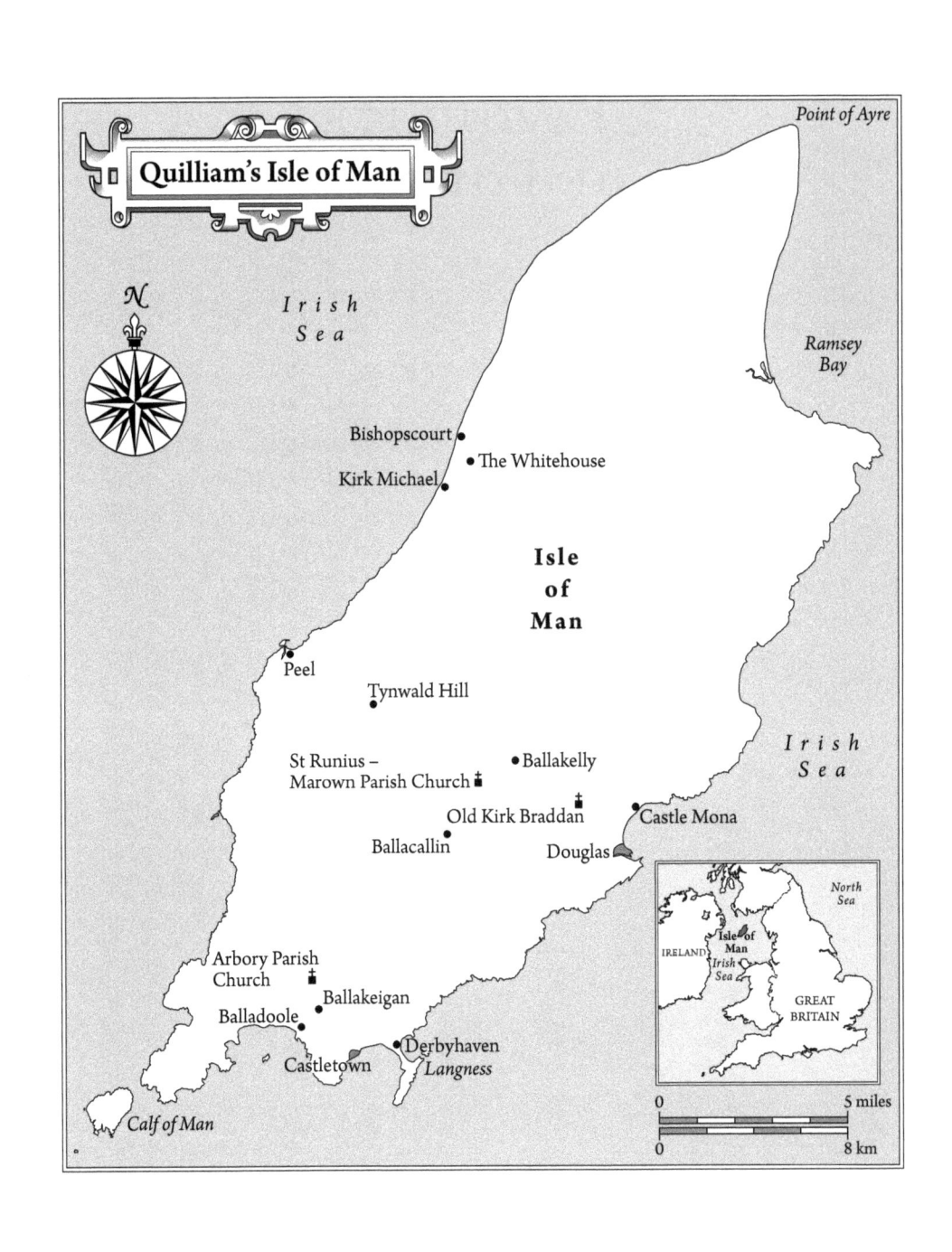

Quilliam's Isle of Man

Point of Ayre

Irish Sea

Ramsey Bay

Bishopscourt
• The Whitehouse
Kirk Michael

Isle of Man

Peel
• Tynwald Hill

St Runius – • Ballakelly
Marown Parish Church
Old Kirk Braddan • Castle Mona
Ballacallin
Douglas

Irish Sea

Arbory Parish
Church
• Ballakeigan
Balladoole
• Derbyhaven
Castletown *Langness*

Calf of Man

North Sea
IRELAND — Isle of Man — *Irish Sea* — GREAT BRITAIN

0 — 5 miles
0 — 8 km

FAVOURITE OF FORTUNE
Captain John Quilliam, Trafalgar Hero

ANDREW BOND, FRANK COWIN
AND ANDREW LAMBERT

Published with the support of the Quilliam Group,
Robin Crellin and Hamish Ross

Seaforth
PUBLISHING

Endpapers: 'A CORRECT PLAN of the Isle of Man By PETER FANNIN, MASTER in His MAJESTY's ROYAL NAVY'. Dedicated to the Duke of Atholl and published in 1789, Fannin's map includes a view across Douglas harbour from the Duke's house and a plan of the harbour showing the damaged precursor to the Red Pier. Fannin had been master of HMS *Adventure* on Captain Cook's second expedition to the South Seas in 1772–5 and subsequently established a school of navigation in Douglas.

Copyright © Andrew Bond, Frank Cowin and Andrew Lambert 2021

First published in Great Britain in 2021 by
Seaforth Publishing
An imprint of Pen & Sword Books Ltd
47 Church Street, Barnsley
S Yorkshire S70 2AS

www.seaforthpublishing.com
Email info@seaforthpublishing.com

British Library Cataloguing in Publication Data
A CIP data record for this book is available from the British Library

ISBN 978-1-3990-1270-6 (Hardback)
ISBN 978-1-3990-1271-3 (ePub)
ISBN 978-1-3990-1272-0 (Kindle)

All rights reserved. No part of this publication may be reproduced or transmitted in any form or by any means, electronic or mechanical, including photocopying, recording, or any information storage and retrieval system, without prior permission in writing of both the copyright owners and the above publisher.

The moral rights of the authors have been asserted.

Pen & Sword Books Limited incorporates the imprints of Atlas, Archaeology, Aviation, Discovery, Family History, Fiction, History, Maritime, Military, Military Classics, Politics, Select, Transport, True Crime, Air World, Frontline Publishing, Leo Cooper, Remember When, Seaforth Publishing, The Praetorian Press, Wharncliffe Local History, Wharncliffe Transport, Wharncliffe True Crime and White Owl.

Typeset and designed by Mac Style
Printed and bound in the UK by CPI Group (UK) Ltd,
Croydon, CR0 4YY

Contents

Authors' Preface		vii
List of Illustrations		ix
Introduction		xiii
1	Land of his Birth	1
2	Ship Keeper	5
3	China	7
4	War	15
5	Quartermaster's Mate	19
6	Master's Mate	24
7	Camperdown	28
8	Lieutenant Quilliam	32
9	Spanish Gold	35
10	Shipwreck	39
11	HMS *Amazon*	43
12	Copenhagen	50
13	Mediterranean	58
14	The Chase	66
15	Quilliam's Trafalgar	74
16	Captain Quilliam	86
17	Flag Captain	89
18	Frigate Captain	94
19	'A Very Fast Ship'	101

20	Newfoundland	110
21	Damnation to the Captain	120
22	Courts Martial	126
23	West Indian Swansong	133
24	Manx Worthy	138
25	An Honest Man, the Noblest Work of God	146

Notes 148
Glossary 166
Bibliography 173
Index 177

Authors' Preface

Frank Cowin and Andrew Bond both grew up aware from an early age of a connection with 'the man who steered the Victory at Trafalgar'. In Frank's case, that connection manifested itself in a three-quarter length portrait of 'Captain John Quilliam R.N.', which dominated the main room of the family home. Family legend had it that Frank's great, great grandmother, Jane Quilliam, was Captain Quilliam's sister. That suggested that she might be the captain's youngest sibling whose paternity was queried at her baptism but who subsequently disappeared from the records. In fact, what the records do show is that she was claimed in a deed as 'the beloved child' of another member of the Quilliam family, so the direct connection remains unproven.

Andrew Bond's connection is that the captain's wife, the former Margaret Christian Stevenson, was his four times great aunt. Andrew's grandmother, born Alice Woods, was a direct descendant of Margaret's sister Charlotte, the chatelaine of the family seat, Balladoole, and would regale the family with tales of visits to the house where, when the wind blew, 'the carpets rose from the floor'.

Frank's mother researched John Quilliam's naval career both locally in the Isle of Man and in London at the Public Record Office in Chancery Lane and later at Kew. With the bicentenary of Quilliam's birth approaching, however, she handed her material over to Frank who, after further research, presented it in a paper to the Isle of Man Natural History and Antiquarian Society, which they published in 1972. Frank subsequently continued to research Quilliam's later life, greatly assisted by his brother, Noel.

Andrew Bond's interest was triggered by another bicentenary, that of Trafalgar itself in 2005, which prompted both a visit to HMS *Victory* at Portsmouth and a subsequent trip to the Island. When retirement some years later freed up the time to pursue Quilliam in more detail, that 1972 paper soon led to Frank and regular contacts followed. At the National Archives and elsewhere, Andrew was able to track Quilliam's career day by day through dockyard records, muster, pay and log books, court martial papers and correspondence.

Meanwhile, in 2015, the Quilliam Group, which had been formed on the Island to commemorate and promote wider interest in Quilliam's life, had invited Andrew Lambert, the Laughton Professor of Naval History at King's College, London, to deliver its annual lecture at Arbory church. Each year the lecture forms part of Trafalgar Day observances, which include contributions from pupils at the local primary school and members of the British Legion. On that occasion it also saw the dedication of the stained glass window commissioned by the Group depicting Captain Quilliam.

Following the success of his lecture on Quilliam's service after Trafalgar, the Group approached Professor Lambert with a view to his expanding his paper into a full-length biography. However, already well aware of both Frank's and Andrew's researches, he very generously suggested that the project would be best approached as a tripartite enterprise. The end result combines his unrivalled knowledge of Nelson's navy with Frank's deep understanding of all things Manx and Andrew's forty years as a journalist and editor.

Illustrations

Endpapers

A CORRECT PLAN of the Isle of Man By PETER FANNIN, MASTER in His MAJESTY's ROYAL NAVY, 1789. © Manx National Heritage P.1275/2 (P.XX 3L).

Between pages 14 and 15

1. *Captain John Quilliam RN, HK* by Henry Barber, 1826. © Manx National Heritage 1979-0162.
2. *The Death of Nelson, 21 October 1805* by Benjamin West. Photo: Bridgeman Images.
3. *Douglas Town and Bay, November 1805* by Edward Meredith. © Manx National Heritage P.6632 (DPG.44.M).
4. *The Royal Dockyard, Portsmouth, 1790* by Robert Dodd. © British Library Board Maps K. Top. 15.46.a.
5. *View of the City of Ten-cheou-fou, 21 July 1793* by William Alexander. © British Library Board. All Rights Reserved/Bridgeman Images.
6. *View of the Entrance of St John's Harbour, Newfoundland, From Fort Townshend, 1823* by P C Le Geyt. © National Maritime Museum, Greenwich, London PAD2012.
7. *Admiral Sir Erasmus Gower (1742–1814)* by Richard Livesay. Photo: Amgueddfa Cymru – National Museum Wales.
8. *Captain Edward Riou* by Samuel Shelley. © National Maritime Museum, Greenwich, London MNT0216.
9. *Vice-Admiral Horatio Nelson, 1st Viscount Nelson* by Sir William Beechey. © National Maritime Museum, Greenwich, London, Greenwich Hospital Collection BHC2892.

10. *Admiral Sir James de Saumarez, 1st Baron de Saumarez* by Samuel Lane. © National Maritime Museum, Greenwich, London, Caird Fund BHC3166.
11. *Lord Bridport's action off L'Orient, 12 June 1795* by an unknown artist, British School. © National Maritime Museum, Greenwich, London PAD8507.
12. *The Battle of Camperdown, 11 October 1797* by Thomas Whitcombe. © National Maritime Museum, Greenwich, London, Caird Fund BHC0505.
13. *The Battle of Copenhagen, 2 April 1801* by Nicholas Pocock. © National Maritime Museum, Greenwich, London, Caird Collection BHC0529
14. *The Battle of Trafalgar, 21 October 1805* by J M W Turner. © National Maritime Museum, Greenwich, London, Greenwich Hospital Collection, BHC0565
15. *George Murray, Lord Bishop of Sodor and Mann* by an unknown artist. © Manx National Heritage L21815.
16. The Quilliam window in St Columba's church, Arbory. Photo: Frank Cowin.

Between pages 62 and 63

17. St Runius church, Marown. Photo: Frank Cowin.
18. Warrant for John Quilliam's examination for lieutenant, National Archives, ADM 107/22. Photo: Andrew Bond.
19. *The frigate HMS Amazon (1799) pursuing an unnamed French ship (possibly the Belle Poule), 1806* by Nicholas Pocock. © National Maritime Museum, Greenwich, London PAD8878.
20. *Rear-Admiral John Pasco* by an unknown artist, British School. © National Maritime Museum, Greenwich, London BHC2284.
21. Captain John Quilliam's uniform coat. © Manx National Heritage 1954-0933b-c.
22. *Lieutenant Governor Cornelius Smelt* by Thomas Barber. © Manx National Heritage 1954-1689.
23. *Vice-Admiral Sir Richard Gordon Keats* by John Jackson. © National Maritime Museum, Greenwich, London, Caird Collection BHC2975.
24. *Captain Peter Heywood* by an unknown artist. © Manx National Heritage 1963-0175.
25. Plot from Quilliam Court Martial papers, National Archives, ADM 1/5445. Photo: Andrew Bond.

26. Balcony House, The Parade, Castletown. Photo: Frances Coakley.
27. Quilliam's 'Memorandum of Service', National Archives, ADM 9/2/321. Photo: Andrew Bond.
28. *George Quayle HK* by an unknown artist. © Manx National Heritage PG/3634.
29. Isle of Man Bank One Guinea note. © Manx National Heritage 1956-0130.
30. Castletown Lifeboat House. © Manx National Heritage PG/4027/75.
31. Quilliam memorial, St Columba's church, Arbory. Photo: Andrew Bond.
32. HMS *Quilliam*. © Imperial War Museum FL 1378.

MAPS

1. Quilliam's Isle of Man	ii
2. HMS *Lion* 26 September 1792–7 September 1794	8–9
3. North Sea	20
4. Western Approaches	25
5. North Atlantic and Mediterranean: HMS *Victory* 18 January–21 October 1805	68–9
6. Baltic Sea	96–7
7. Newfoundland and Nova Scotia	111

Introduction

Of the three senior officers on the quarterdeck as HMS *Victory* closed on the combined French and Spanish fleet off Cape Trafalgar on the morning of 21 October 1805, one, already a national hero, would become the iconic embodiment of British naval power. Another would go down in history as the archetypal faithful subordinate and friend, immortalised in his chief's dying words: 'Kiss me, Hardy.' The third, *Victory*'s first lieutenant John Quilliam, is barely recognised outside his native Isle of Man. However, there he is the hero, celebrated in statuary, stained glass, museum exhibits and a re-enactment by school children each Trafalgar Day. Every Manxman and Manxwoman has a story of Captain Quilliam, and some of them may even be true.

That Quilliam is so little known in the wider world is all the more remarkable, given his extraordinary career, which can be compared with those of the great heroes of naval fiction, Hornblower and Aubrey. He began with a voyage halfway round the world, conveying Britain's first ambassador to China, and continued through all twenty-three years of the Revolutionary and Napoleonic Wars. Almost uniquely, he took part in no fewer than three major fleet actions before Trafalgar including Camperdown and Copenhagen, when only a tiny proportion of the thousands who served at sea over the period saw even one. Nevertheless, the histories and biographies of the period allow him barely a mention and are often factually incorrect. Local accounts have challenged some of the Quilliam mythology, but this is a life that belongs on a larger stage.

Fortunately, Quilliam's naval *curriculum vitae* can be traced through original documents. Muster books, pay books, log books, professional correspondence and court martial papers provide an almost unbroken paper trail, illuminating a life more extraordinary than any of the local myths and legends. Triumph alternates with disaster as shipwreck follows Spanish gold and command of the Navy's latest frigate leads to prosecution for obeying secret orders. Quilliam emerges as a consummate professional, a man whose talents were recognised and rewarded by Nelson and a host of other captains and admirals.

Quilliam in Context

This book examines the career of an exceptional naval officer; quite how exceptional becomes obvious when we look at the career patterns of his contemporaries. Eighteenth-century naval officer careers were shaped by patronage, the unequal friendship between the powerful and the aspiring, in which the former rewarded the latter for diverse reasons.[1] Patronage introduced the personal factor into careers. The sons of senior naval officers, or their nephews in Nelson's case, had an advantage. By the mid-eighteenth century the naval officer corps was marked by continuity and inter-marriage, and linked to patronage networks. However, it was also shaped by a constant cycle of wars in which able men could advance through observed merit. In wartime, admirals had powerful inducements to promote successful officers, good seamen and effective leaders. Such men secured victories, prize money and prestige, adding to the reputation and wealth of the patron.

Patronage worked. Nelson's career was shaped by his maternal uncle, Captain Maurice Suckling, a fine fighting seaman, successful administrator and exemplary patron. His early death left Lieutenant Nelson two steps from captain's rank; Suckling's friends finished his work in his memory. It was up to Nelson to justify their decision. As an admiral, Nelson would use his own patronage opportunities with skill and discretion; Thomas Hardy was an obvious example of merit rewarded. And so was John Quilliam.

Older studies of officer careers tended to emphasise the number that came from aristocratic and landed families, and underestimate those from the lower middle-class world of trade and business.[2] Recent work has shifted that emphasis, however. The stable analytical core is that between 45 and 50 per cent came from the professional classes, which included naval officers. The variations are at the upper and lower levels: around 25 per cent came from lower middle-class backgrounds, rather than a mere 5 per cent as previous studies suggested, and 20 per cent from titled and landed families, rather than 35 per cent.

The key to the new figures has been access to more complete data sets, which removed the tendency of officers from higher-status backgrounds to be better represented in older print literature, including the naval biographical dictionaries of the era. While Quilliam made his way into those dictionaries, he did so as a successful post captain, not the son of a Manx farmer. This reality only adds emphasis to Evan Wilson's observation that: 'The most common drivers of officers' careers, though, were nepotism, merit, and timing.'[3] While Quilliam lacked the first of these assets, exceptional skill and the fortune of circumstance combined to overcome a late start.

In order to secure his place on the quarterdeck, Quilliam also needed the education and social skills of a 'gentleman': his education more than met the necessary standards, while a man of his intelligence would have found it easy to absorb any specific social mores in the close proximity of long voyages in a wooden world that valued his professional competence.[4] Professional military organisations have always tended to establish standardised social codes as a bonding mechanism, something that can be observed in every entry-level officer training academy around the world. While the uniform comes complete with a professional persona, exceptional officers rise to the challenge of going beyond, of mastering their complex and demanding calling, as seamen, leaders and warriors. Having earned the patronage and praise of great sea officers, with Nelson, James de Saumarez and Richard Keats as his unequal friends, there can be no doubt that John Quilliam possessed skill, judgement and perseverance of the highest order. Nelson, a post captain at twenty-one, recognised his merits, and despite his late start Quilliam's career prospered down to the peace. To be chosen by Nelson, and then to command a crack frigate under such a master of the business as James de Saumarez, was the highest accolade for any naval commander.

The Royal Navy's domination of the seas between 1793 and 1815 reflected the reality that it rewarded exceptional men like Quilliam. It did so without checking for noble lineage, or suitable political principles, obsessions that compromised the fleets of France, be it Royal, Republican or Imperial, along with those of Spain and Russia. The sea cares nothing for birth and politics.

A Short Note on Logs and Original Documents

Quilliam and his contemporaries were far less concerned about spelling, punctuation and grammar than subsequent generations. Ships' records or log books were written up with virtually no punctuation and a seemingly random distribution of capital letters, so that it can be difficult for readers to distinguish where one sentence ends and the next begins.

Because of the constraints of time and space, they also made extensive use of abbreviations, but these were neither standardised between different writers nor necessarily consistent, even within the same entry. Where there is consistency, it is often consistently different from modern usage, for example 'chace' as in 'chace guns' and 'in chace' or 'too' as in 'brought too' and 'came too'. Nor had modern naval conventions, for example of referring to ships by name without the definite article – '*Lion*' rather than 'the *Lion*' – or of being 'in' rather than 'on' a ship, been established, neither had that of recording ships' names in italic script.

Other documents including letters and even court martial records exhibit similar characteristics. Place names, proper names and even ships' names may all be spelled differently and often phonetically, not only by different writers but also by the same writer, even within the same document. Although some allowance might be made for logs being written up by young, often very young, midshipmen or other petty or warrant officers, the same idiosyncrasies appear in documents produced by or for more senior individuals. Quilliam's and Sutton's various spellings of Valletta are just one example, while Nelson and his clerks and secretaries were similarly creative, not least with Quilliam's own name. Interestingly, towards the latter stages of Quilliam's career there are indications of increasing consistency, which may reflect the growing proportion of midshipmen who had passed through the Royal Naval Academy, after 1806 the Royal Naval College, at Portsmouth, where standards were higher.

In order to retain their contemporary flavour, we have as far as possible quoted verbatim from all the contemporary documents that tell Quilliam's story. If the reader occasionally finds it necessary to reread a quotation in order fully to understand its meaning, we hope that will be seen as a small price to pay to hear authentic contemporary voices.

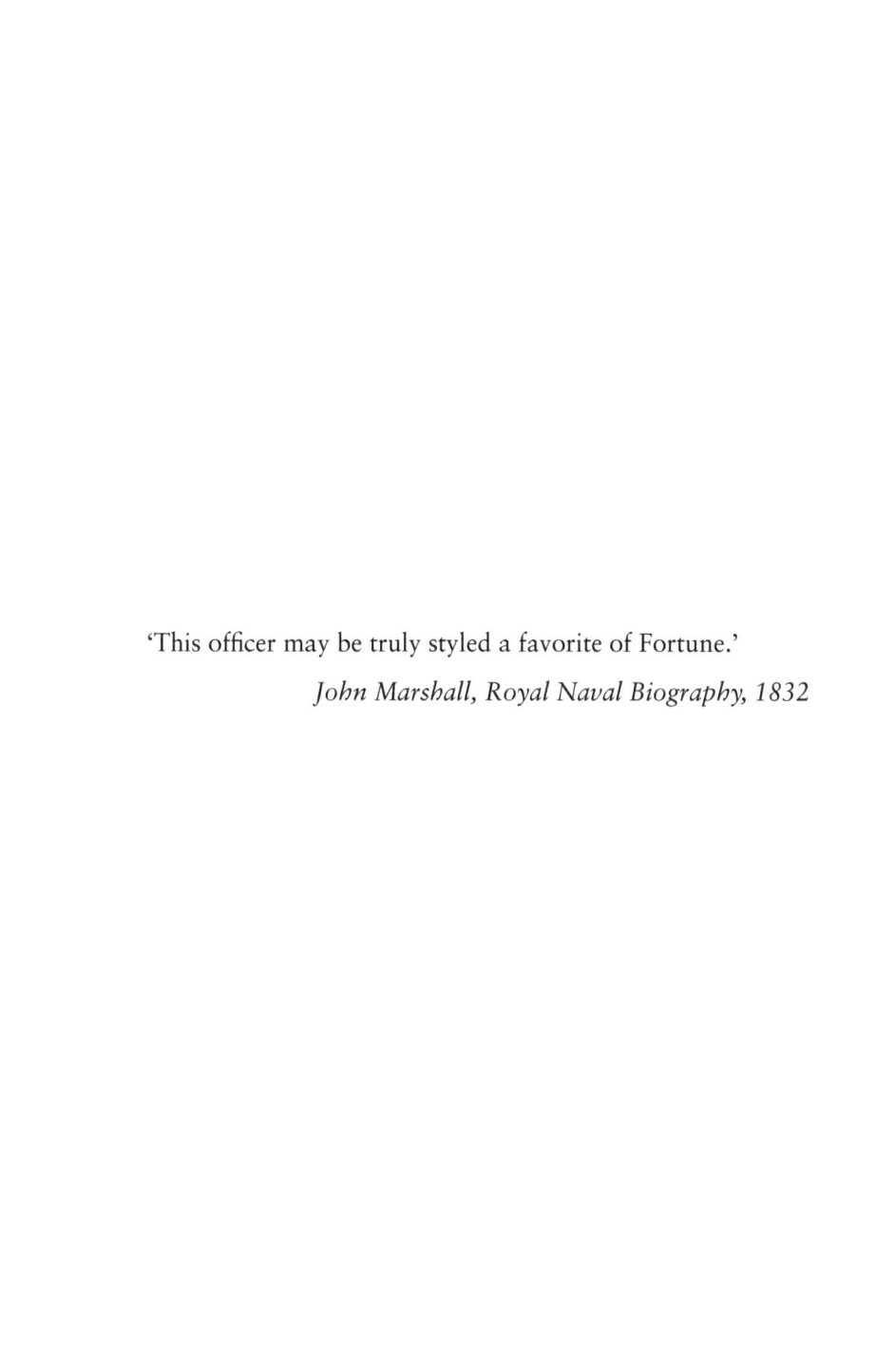

'This officer may be truly styled a favorite of Fortune.'

John Marshall, Royal Naval Biography, 1832

1

Land of his Birth[1]

We don't know when John Quilliam[2] was born but we do know that he was baptised on 29 September 1771[3] in St Runius church, Marown, the only one of the Isle of Man's seventeen ancient parishes that has no sea coast.[4] He may therefore have been born on the 28th and certainly within the previous week at the family property, Ballakelly, in Marown parish. His father was also John and his mother Christian, née, or in then current Manx usage, alias Clucas. John's grandfather, another John,[5] still held the property and lived with the family at Ballakelly, as he would until his death in December 1779[6] when it passed to Quilliam's father.

Quilliam's mother was the daughter of Thomas Clucas and Isabel Kelly of The Garth, a substantial farm, and the Clucas family were prominent members of the community. By contrast, the Quilliams' Ballakelly property was only part of the Ballakelly quarterland. More a small holding than an adequate farm, its income would have been supplemented by fishing, seafaring and other related occupations. Quilliam's father may well have spent some time at sea since he appears in the church registers on at least one occasion as Captain Quilliam.

Young John Quilliam was the oldest of what would eventually be seven siblings, although the paternity of the last two was queried by the church. Quilliam's mother answered the first query in 1789, by which time Quilliam had already been 'off island' for four years, on the grounds that she had a husband and that he was the father of the child. However, the second query in 1792 was not resolved and the child, a girl, disappeared from the records. The property at Ballakelly had been sold in 1783 to a Thomas Crane, a significant name in view of later events, and the proceeds used in part to discharge the associated mortgages.[7] As a result, the family seems to have broken up and by the 1790s Quilliam's mother appears to have been living in Douglas and his father probably in Liverpool.

No contemporary record of the young Quilliam exists for his first fourteen years, although plenty of myths have tried to fill the gap. These variously have him working on the farm, running away to sea and being taken by the press gang. Some may have an element of truth, since he never denied any of them, but the impressment certainly isn't.[8] Nor is the story that, as an apprenticed stonemason, he worked on the Red Pier in Douglas harbour before running away to sea. The Pier wasn't started until 1793,[9] when he was 6,000 miles away off the coast of China.

What is clear is that he must have received at least a basic education. In 1703/04 Tynwald, the Isle of Man parliament, had promulgated a law making it compulsory for all children to be sent to a 'petty' school for children aged from five to seven.[10] By 1736 each of the Island's seventeen parishes had a petty or parish school and the four main towns each had grammar schools. Two surviving exercise books indicate that at least some of the parish schools taught navigation, one of them being from Marown School, which Quilliam would have attended.[11] This unrivalled level of basic education made Manx seamen, whether volunteers or pressed, very attractive to both the Royal Navy and the merchant service. At the height of impressment during the Revolutionary and Napoleonic wars, the Governor in Chief, complaining to the government in London that the quota for the Island had been set at 162 men, claimed that nearly 3,000 men, or a fifth of the male population, were serving in the Royal Navy.[12]

By Quilliam's time a number of specialist mathematical and navigational schools had also been established, including Moore's Mathematical School in Peel, and in Douglas, a school of navigation run by Peter Fannin, master of HMS *Adventure* on Captain Cook's second expedition to the South Seas in 1772–75.[13] Had Quilliam attended Fannin's School, a fellow student and near contemporary would have been Peter Heywood. As a midshipman on HMS *Bounty,* Heywood was found guilty of mutiny and condemned to hang, only to be pardoned by the King, resume his naval career and cross Quilliam's path again nearly thirty years later.

When the fourteen-year-old Quilliam left the Island in 1785 to embark on a career that would eventually lead him to join the Royal Navy, he followed a trend that had been accelerating for twenty years. Over the centuries, the 'seabourne' community of the Island had developed an extensive international trade, enhanced prior to 1765 under the Lordship of Mann held by the Dukes of Atholl by setting its own customs duties. Goods subject to high levels of duty in Great Britain and Ireland could be imported entirely legally into the Isle of Man. Once transhipped and moved further than 3 miles off shore, however, they became illegal contraband, suspected of being smuggled into England, Wales, Scotland and Ireland.

Not only did this combination of a legal trade and an illegal 'running trade' provide handsome profits for both respectable local and 'stranger' merchants and a more motley mixture of Manx and foreign adventurers, but it supported and trained a disproportionately large cohort of highly skilled seamen. It also provided the opportunity for others to hone a range of skills, among them Scot John Paul Jones, the 'Father of the American Navy', who went on to raid Whitehaven in 1778,[14] and Captain Yawkins, who set up home on the Island and became the model for Dirk Hatterick in Sir Walter Scott's novel, *Guy Mannering*.[15] Yawkins was eventually taken by the Navy, 'forcibly entered' and later acted as a pilot for Nelson at Flushing.[16] On the other hand, the sloops and cutters of the Royal Navy's Irish Sea Station gave many a distinguished officer his first taste of command as a lieutenant. Some leased properties on the Island for their families, others married locally and many returned in their retirement, earning the caustic comment from one observer that 'they wanted their shilling's worth for sixpence'.[17] As a result, many well-known naval names appear in Manx records including Admiral Sir Thomas Pasley,[18] who commanded HM Sloop *Ranger* on the Irish Station in the 1760s; George Dundas, who commanded HM Cutter *Pygmy* on the same duty in 1783 and moved his family first to Strangford in Braddan parish and then to Douglas;[19] and William Bligh.[20]

In an attempt to bring the illegal trade under control, the British government passed the Mischief Act in 1765 'for more effectually preventing the mischiefs arising ... from the illicit and clandestine trade to and from the Isle of Man' and, in order to enforce it, purchased the Lordship of Mann, though not its manorial rights, for the Crown for £70,000. It then passed the Revestment or Isle of Man Purchase Act, transferring control of the Island to the British Crown.[21] Thereafter, the running trade continued on a very different footing with the stranger merchants moving out to overseas bases such as Dunkirk while Manx traders transferred their attention to the African trade, and Manx seamen worked out of other ports. Goods were now transferred offshore by armed vessels to the smaller boats of the 'onshore traders' and there were numerous clashes with naval and revenue patrols. The two Acts also gave the Navy and the revenue the power to stop and search on both the Island and its surrounding waters. With opportunities in the legal trade declining and the hazards of the running trade growing, by the time Quilliam left the island a growing number of Manx seamen were following the same path, taking their skills to the Royal Navy and the British merchant marine.

2

Ship Keeper

Portsmouth harbour was jammed with ships in the summer of 1785. The treaty ending the American Revolutionary War had been ratified the previous year and the Navy progressively run down. No fewer than eighty-nine ships were laid up 'in ordinary' without topmasts, rigging or guns and each required a skeleton maintenance crew of 'ship keepers'. How John Quilliam came to be one of eleven on the frigate *Fox,* which he joined on Tuesday, 2 August,[1] is not clear. Although he was immediately rated 'ab' or able seaman,[2] suggesting that, far from being a novice, he had already spent time at sea, it could equally imply that he had 'interest', that is the support of someone in authority. That could have come from any of the naval officers living near the Quilliams on the Island but the most likely candidate is John Crane, already in the Dockyard service and for many years from 1791 onwards Master Attendant at Portsmouth Dockyard.[3] Crane may have been related to the Thomas Crane who bought the Quilliams' Ballakelly property in 1783, and had other connections with the family.

In his first full quarter, Quilliam was paid £3 17s 1d,[4] and was stopped 3s 1d 'Chest' or pension contribution and 1s 8d 'Hospital', a rudimentary form of health insurance.[5] Over the next seven years he served on three other ships at Portsmouth. However, in September 1791 a 64-gun battleship, HMS *Lion,* arrived at Portsmouth from Barbados[6] and on 15 September the Commissioner was rowed out to pay the ship off. *Lion*'s Muster Book lists the seven men of the 'Portsmo Commisser Boats Crew' as 'Supernumeraries for victuals only' who joined and were discharged the same day, one of whom was 'Jn°. Quilliam'.[7]

Quilliam remained on the dockyard staff for another eight months, until 22 May 1792, when he officially joined *Lion.*[8] Her new Muster Book lists his 'Entry' and 'Appearance' on the same day. As 'Quillin' he was again rated 'ab', setting his rate of pay at 24 shillings per twenty-eight-day month.[9] Every future officer had to start his career 'before the mast' as a rating and spend six years at sea, two of them as either a midshipman or a master's mate,[10] before sitting the examination to become a commissioned officer, a lieutenant. What is unusual about Quilliam is the age at which he joined. Many near contemporaries, including his future captain on HMS *Victory*, Thomas Masterman Hardy, had joined at twelve or even younger and were already lieutenants.[11] Nor was his background unusual for a future officer. Hardy's father, for example, was a Dorset gentleman farmer.

Quilliam's opportunity to join *Lion* arose when the British government decided to send a trade mission to China. Heading up the venture was Anglo-Irish peer George Macartney, a former Governor of Madras.[12] He was to be accompanied as Secretary to the Mission by his old friend Sir George Staunton. *Lion* would be Macartney's personal transport, the East Indiaman *Hindostan* would carry gifts for the Emperor and the brig *Jackall* would act as tender.

Commanding the expedition was forty-nine-year-old Captain Sir Erasmus Gower. Having gone to sea at the age of thirteen, Gower had already been round the world twice by the age of twenty-four. His subsequent career had included service in the West Indies under Rodney, the East Indies and Newfoundland.[13] Gower needed to get his ship ready for an early departure, and the man best placed to help him was John Crane, now Master Attendant of the dockyard. Crane may have mentioned the capable young Manxman with dockyard expertise that would be invaluable on such a venture. A long peacetime voyage provided an ideal opportunity for Quilliam to make the transition to officer candidate under the guidance of an experienced leader.

Lion remained in Portsmouth harbour, setting up her rigging and taking in her guns and powder, until Saturday, 28 July, when she moved to the fleet anchorage at Spithead. Days later, Quilliam had his first sight of naval discipline when seaman John Kelly received a dozen lashes for theft. Most of August was spent drilling the ship's company and by mid-September she was ready for Lord Macartney and his retinue. The Ambassador didn't travel light. His entire staff of over ninety, under Comptroller of the Household and future Secretary to the Admiralty John Barrow, included secretaries, scientists, artisans, musicians, soldiers and domestic servants. Finally, on Wednesday, 26 September 1792 *Lion*, *Hindostan* and *Jackall* 'at ½ past 11 weighed and made sail'.[14]

3

China

Two weeks out from Portsmouth, having lost contact with *Jackall* in a storm in the Channel, *Lion* and *Hindostan* dropped anchor in Funchal road, Madeira, on 11 October 1792. While the Ambassador's party explored the island and were entertained at the Portuguese Governor's residence, the ship's company loaded water and fresh provisions on to the boats and ferried them out to the ship. Then, on the afternoon of Thursday, 18 October, with no sign of *Jackall,* the two ships 'at ½ past five weighed and steered for the South'.[1]

Reckoning the wine at Madeira of inferior quality, Gower decided to call at Tenerife less than 300 miles to the south where substantial quantities of better-quality wine were obtained at a keener price. Some of the Ambassador's party made an unsuccessful attempt to climb Mount Teide and, during their absence, the two ships had to ride out a storm in which *Hindostan* lost two of her anchors. It was therefore a relief when on 27 October they again weighed and made sail, setting a course for Santiago, known to the British as St Jago, the largest of the Cape Verde Islands a further 1,000 miles south-west.

Once under way, Quilliam for the first time heard the captain read the Articles of War, drawing the crew's attention to the twenty-two separate offences that could incur the death penalty. He also confirmed that they were bound for China and Japan and would be unlikely to see England again for another three years.

Enjoying the benefit of the north-east trade winds, on Friday, 2 November they dropped anchor in Praya Bay, St Jago, again having seen no sign of the missing *Jackall*. With the island in the grip of famine having had no rain for three years, they stayed only five days before setting course for Rio de Janeiro some 3,000 miles away. *Lion* and *Hindostan* completed the passage in just twenty-two days, crossing the equator eleven days out

HMS *Lion* 26 September 1792 – 7 September 1794

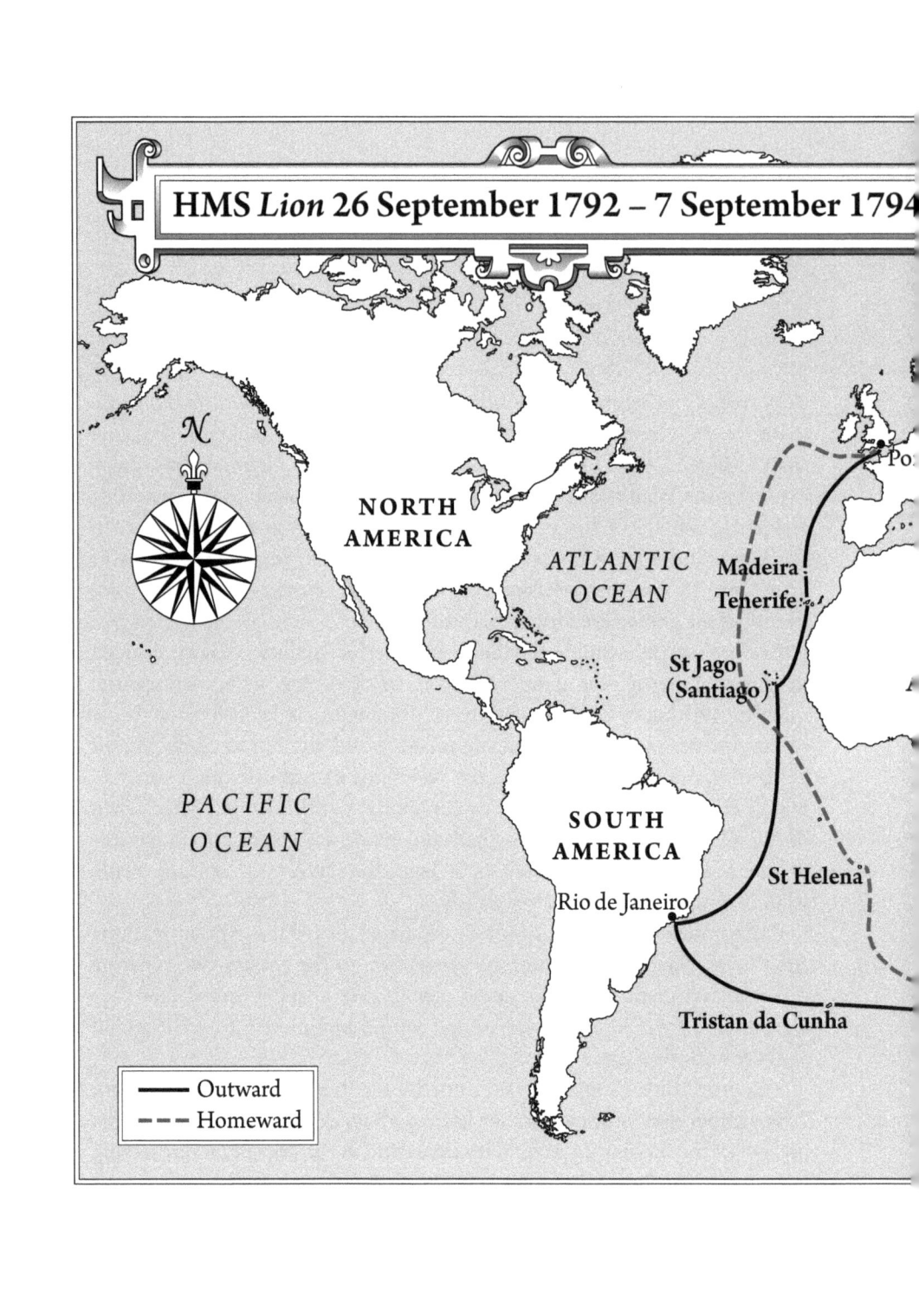

NORTH AMERICA

ATLANTIC OCEAN

Madeira
Tenerife
St Jago (Santiago)

PACIFIC OCEAN

SOUTH AMERICA
Rio de Janeiro

St Helena

Tristan da Cunha

— Outward
--- Homeward

RUSSIA

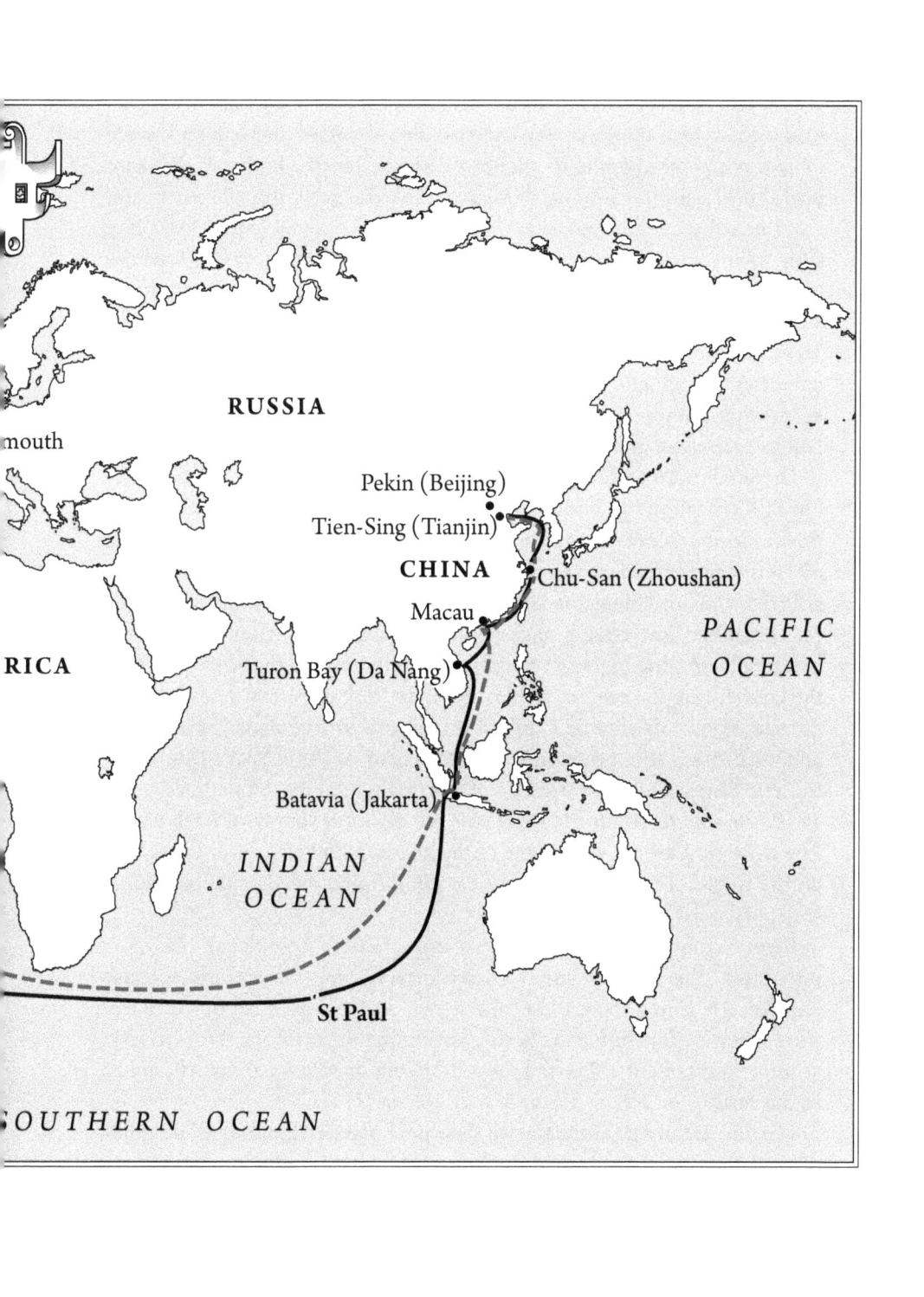

Pekin (Beijing)
Tien-Sing (Tianjin)
CHINA
Chu-San (Zhoushan)
Macau
PACIFIC OCEAN
Turon Bay (Da Nang)

Batavia (Jakarta)

INDIAN OCEAN

St Paul

SOUTHERN OCEAN

with what Gower described as 'the usual ceremony in shaving & ducking' to which first timers like Quilliam were subjected.

On Friday, 30 November the 1,300ft mass of Sugarloaf Mountain was sighted and the next day the two ships crossed the bar and made their way up the channel to anchor in Rio de Janeiro harbour. Quilliam was almost certainly among those given leave ashore, though not one of the nine subsequently punished for various offences including 'breaking their leave', perhaps as a result of encounters with the local ladies whose 'fine dark eyes' and 'animated countenances' caught Staunton's attention. While the Ambassador and his party were entertained by the Portuguese Viceroy, Quilliam and his shipmates gave *Lion* a full refit before taking on water, wood and provisions 'in such quantities as to supersede the necessity for stopping at the Cape of Good Hope',[2] thereby avoiding the Dutch anchorage at a time when Anglo-Dutch relations were strained.

On Sunday, 16 December 1792 *Lion* and *Hindostan* worked their way out of Rio harbour with their next port of call 8,500 miles away. Heading down the South American coast, they picked up the westerlies in latitude 37° south and turned to 'run their easting down', driven by what Staunton referred to as the 'unchangeable gales' of the high latitudes. By Sunday, 30 December, just twelve days and 1,800 miles out from Rio, Gower recorded in the log 'many of the people of the opinion that they had seen the land during the evening and as we had a very imperfect knowledge of the situation of Tristan da Cunha I brought to for the night. Saw whales and albatrosses about the ship.' Two days later, on New Year's Day 1793, the two ships anchored a mile off the main island. Uninhabited until 1810, the sole reason for landing was the plentiful supply of fresh water. The party sent ashore were some of the first human beings ever to set foot on the island. Those who remained on board marvelled at the sea lions, seals, penguins and albatrosses.

Before resuming their easterly course, Gower completed the most important objective of the visit by establishing the islands' precise position. He found them to be 'about two degrees eastward of the place, where they are laid down in charts', attributing the previous errors to less-accurate instruments.[3] He had moved Tristan da Cunha about 100 miles to the east.

Leaving Tristan da Cunha, with their next planned landfall 4,000 miles distant, the two ships pushed down into the Southern Ocean, eventually reaching 41° south. They had sighted only one other vessel in the 2,000 miles between Rio de Janeiro and Tristan da Cunha and they didn't see another in the next 4,000 miles. Despite it being the southern summer, the Roaring Forties lived up to their name with the wind continually 'blowing strong' and the weather alternating between fog and rain and cold and clear, although 'birds and fish were seen in considerable numbers; whales almost every day'.[4] Hundreds of miles south of Mauritius, then Île de France, they encountered their only serious Southern Ocean storm. Gower rewarded his exhausted, soaked and chilled crew in the traditional way: 'Served grog to the ship's company – four water to one of spirit.' Three weeks later he brought them north again and by the end of the month sightings of 'a penguin and some seals' suggested they were close to land. Sure enough, on 1 February 1793, the day on which, thousands of miles away, revolutionary France declared war on Great Britain, they 'saw the land bearing ENE'.[5] This was St Paul Island, the more southerly of two tiny specks in the middle of the Indian Ocean known today as Île Amsterdam and Île Saint-Paul, part of the French Southern and Antarctic Lands.

As the two ships sailed up the coast, two men were seen wildly gesticulating on what was thought to be an uninhabited island. They eventually anchored a mile offshore and, when a party went ashore, they found a group of seal hunters who had come from Île de France five months earlier to collect seal skins for subsequent export to China. They had already killed 8,000 seals and expected their ship to return to collect them after another ten months. Seals were by no means the only wildlife. Crayfish were so abundant they could be pulled out by the basket load and an 11ft shark was caught by sailors from *Lion* in which was found a whole penguin. However, with no fresh fruit or vegetables to be had, there was little incentive to linger once the water casks had been filled and on 4 February they headed north-north-east for the Sunda Strait between Java and Sumatra.

As the two ships made their way into the tropics, they moved further apart to increase the chance of sighting a homeward-bound Indiaman and *Hindostan* eventually lost contact. However, on 26 February *Lion* sighted Java Head, the eastern side of the entrance to the strait, and the following day passed Krakatoa Island, before the eruption of 1883 a spectacular conical mountain rising 800m straight out of the sea. That day they sighted the first ships, other than *Hindostan*, they had seen since leaving Tristan da Cunha nearly two months earlier.

The Sunda Strait provides the most direct route from the Indian Ocean to the Java Sea, the East Indies and the South China Sea. Today it is generally ignored by large ships, but in the days of sail it was a busy thoroughfare. Partially blocking it at its narrowest point is Thwart-the-Way Island or, to give it its Indonesian name, Pulau Sangiang. Here on 28 February *Lion* found *Hindostan* and joined her at anchor. Having checked that *Jackall*, last seen off Portland the previous September, had not beaten them to the pre-arranged rendezvous at North Island, a little further up the east coast of Sumatra, on 6 March 1793 they finally dropped anchor in the great natural harbour of Batavia. Now known as Jakarta, Batavia was the Dutch colonial capital and an important commercial centre. *Lion*'s log recorded 'found riding here a huge fleet of Dutch Indiamen & several ships of other nations' together with large numbers of junks, giving a flavour of their final destination 3,000 miles away.

Despite its importance, Batavia was plagued by malaria and other tropical diseases; life expectancy for Europeans was measured in months or even weeks. They only stayed eleven days but, as they left on Sunday, 17 March, *Lion* ran aground on an uncharted rock and they had to shift the guns and carry the kedge anchor out to haul her off. Fortunately, there was no damage to her hull or copper sheathing, but the experience convinced Gower and Macartney that, having given up all hope of seeing *Jackall* again, they needed another tender capable of sounding ahead of the two ships. Next day an officer was sent to Batavia to procure a brig, which was christened *Clarence*.[6] The growing flotilla then set off once more for the original rendezvous at North Island where, shortly after their arrival, 'Jackall brig came in sight & made the signal.' Having had to put back into Portsmouth for repairs and missing the other ships by a few days at Madeira and St Jago, she had come on non-stop to North Island in four months. With 'her lower masts sprung & sides & decks in want of caulking', she was soon alongside *Lion* to be put back in order.[7]

The next leg of the journey lay through the Banca Straits and out into the South China Sea. The flotilla had to wait until the wind associated with the monsoon had swung round from north-easterly to south-westerly and it was not until 28 April that the four ships entered the straits with *Clarence* and *Jackall* sounding ahead. By now the effects of their short stay at Batavia were beginning to show themselves in an alarming increase in sickness and the first deaths since leaving England. Nevertheless, by the middle of May they had reached the island of Puloe Condore off the coast of what is now Vietnam and on 26 May they anchored in Turon Bay, the huge natural harbour on which stands the modern city of Da Nang. Here they were 'visited by one of the Mandarines',[8] who arranged for fresh supplies to be provided and for the sick to be put ashore, but not before three more of *Lion*'s seamen 'departed this life'.[9]

They finally got under way again on Sunday, 16 June and four days later 'anchored off the Great Ladrone', the name then given by Europeans to Lantau Island, the largest island of modern-day Hong Kong.[10] Macartney was eager to press on to their final destination, Tien-Sing, thought to be the nearest port to Pekin, so the squadron paused just long enough for *Jackall* and *Clarence* to go into the Portuguese enclave of Macao[11] on the other side of the mouth of the Pearl River delta to recruit pilots for the next stage of the journey through the Yellow Sea. They returned with the news that the Emperor had ordered pilots to be provided at Chu-San – modern-day Zhoushan – some 700 miles up the coast.[12] Their route now took them up the 90-mile-wide Straits of Formosa between the mainland and modern-day Taiwan, where they encountered some of the worst weather of the entire outward journey. Gower's reaction to a succession of split sails and sprung spars was as ever eminently practical: 'Served a dram of rum apiece to the ship's company having been fatigued and very wet.'

Once clear of the straits they set a course for the Chu-San islands, their progress impeded by huge numbers of boats carrying curious onlookers. After *Clarence* had collected the pilots, on 9 July the squadron stood out into the Yellow Sea, where they met the East India Company's brig *Endeavour*, which had been instructed to join the expedition. The newly expanded fleet made its way up the west coast of 'Corea' (Korea) and on 17 July rounded the eastern extremity of the Shan-tung (modern-day Shandong) peninsula into the Gulf of Pekin. Turning westward along the coast with 'vast crowds of people … assembled on the rising grounds to see the European Vessels pass', on 28 July 1793, exactly ten months to the day after leaving Portsmouth, they reached their final destination, the mouth of the Pei-Ho river leading to Tien-Sing city.[13]

A bar across the mouth of the river meant that there was no safe anchorage for *Lion* and *Hindostan,* so the Ambassador's baggage, including his own four-wheeled travelling coach and the presents for the Emperor, had to be transferred to vessels suitable for the journey to Pekin on the Grand Canal.[14] Among the presents were scientific and astronomical instruments; artillery pieces and small arms; a scale model of a 110-gun battleship, the ultimate symbol of British power; and a wide range of examples of British manufactures. The Ambassador and his suite were conveyed to Tien-Sing in *Clarence*, *Jackall* and *Endeavour* for onward travel by 'yacht' along the Grand Canal, before transferring to land for the final few miles into the capital.

Macartney planned to spend ten months in China, over wintering in Pekin and re-joining *Lion* in Canton in May 1794. In the meantime, while *Hindostan* stayed behind in the hope of obtaining a cargo, Gower would take *Lion* either to Ki-San-Seu or, failing that, Chu-San to establish a camp on shore where the invalids could recover while the ship was undergoing a refit. Then he would follow an ambitious itinerary visiting Japan, the Philippines, the Moluccas, the Celebes and Borneo, identifying safe anchorages and potential centres for trade and establishing contact with local rulers. The project reflected Britain's focus on global trade in the years following Cook's opening of the Pacific and the loss of the American colonies: skilled seamen and accurate instruments were the key to new commerce.

In the event Ki-San-Seu proved unsuitable and on Sunday, 1 September *Lion* moored in Chu-San harbour. A hospital was established on shore for the sick and the ship began a full refit. Although there were further deaths, the majority of the sick recovered rapidly. By the beginning of October the ship's company had 'finished painting the outside,' all 159ft of her, and 'stay'd the lower masts and set the lower rigging up' and on 13 October *Lion* 'weighed and made sail for Roundabout Island'. Before beginning his 7,000-mile grand tour of the East Indies, Gower decided to return to Macao to obtain additional supplies of medicines[15] which the Chinese had been unable to supply. Consequently, ten days after leaving Chu-San *Lion* was back off the Bocca Tigris, the narrow strait in the Pearl River Delta leading to Canton, where she 'anchored Macao town WSW 7 or 8 miles'.

1. Captain John Quilliam RN, HK. Henry Barber painted the fifty-five-year-old Quilliam in his captain's uniform in 1826, nine years after he came ashore on half pay and just three years before he died.

2. The Death of Nelson. Benjamin West placed Nelson's death on the quarterdeck of *Victory* rather than in the cockpit where he actually died. The then thirty-five-year-old Quilliam is at the right-hand end of the row of five officers standing behind the kneeling Hardy. West is said to have taken the portraits of the fifty leading figures from life, in which case Quilliam must have sat for him shortly after his return to England in the prize *Ildefonso* in June 1806 and before the painting was first exhibited the same year.

3. Douglas Town and Bay. Meredith's etching, dated November 1805, shows the Red Pier and its Light Tower, completed in 1801, on which legend had Quilliam working as a young man at a time when he had in fact long left the Island. The large building left of centre was in the mid to late 1700s occupied by the family of *Bounty* mutineer and Quilliam contemporary Peter Heywood. Lieutenant, later Captain, Bligh's family lived for a time on The Parade, seen to the right opposite the right-angled offset in the Quay wall. Mutineer Fletcher Christian's family lived in Fort Street, close to the sea beyond the Heywood house, while the large property in the centre on the sea front is Castle Mona, island home of the Dukes of Atholl.

4. The Royal Dockyard, Portsmouth. Robert Dodds' aquatint is dated 1790 when Quilliam had been employed there as a ship keeper for five years and the year before HMS *Lion* arrived back from Barbados. Quilliam was one of the seven-strong boat crew that rowed the Commissioner out to pay her off.

5. View of the City of Ten-cheou-fou, July 21st 1793. William Alexander's watercolour from the deck of the anchored *Hindostan* shows *Lion* under sail. Also at anchor is one of the brigs, almost certainly *Clarence* since *Jackal* had at this time been sent ahead to reconnoitre the mouth of the Pei-Ho river, their final destination, which they reached just five days later.

6. View of the entrance to St John's Harbour, Newfoundland. *Crescent* spent the winter of 1813–14 here until Quilliam took her back to sea in late March 'because of a disturbance among the officers which … would soon be among the ship's company'. Le Geyt's 1823 coloured lithograph shows how the narrowness of the entrance required ships to warp in against the prevailing westerlies.

7. Admiral Sir Erasmus Gower spotted Quilliam's potential on *Lion*'s voyage to China and in 1795 secured his transfer to *Triumph* as master's mate. He almost certainly had a hand in Quilliam's subsequent moves to *Chapman*, *Ethalion* and *Amazon* and, having been Commodore-Governor of Newfoundland in 1804–06, may also have influenced his secondment there in 1813.

8. Captain Edward Riou. Shelley's miniature shows Riou as he would have been when Quilliam joined *Amazon* in March 1800. A strict disciplinarian and a master ship handler, Riou provided the model for Quilliam's command of his own frigates, *Alexandria* and *Crescent*.

9. Vice-Admiral Horatio Nelson. Beechey's head and shoulders sketch for the full-length portrait in St Andrew's Hall, Norwich, was made in 1801 and shows Nelson as he would have been when Quilliam first met him on *Amazon* at Copenhagen. Nelson recognised the talent of 'Gwiliam 1st in the Amazon in which my flag was long hoisted' when he needed a new first lieutenant for *Victory* in the Mediterranean in August 1803.

10. Admiral Sir James de Saumarez. Himself a past master of the art of frigate warfare, Saumarez soon recognised Quilliam as a safe pair of hands to which he could entrust increasing responsibility among the shoals and dangerously political waters of the Baltic.

11. The Battle of Groix or Bridport's Action, 12 June 1795. In the first of Quilliam's four fleet actions, this somewhat crude watercolour by an unknown artist, 'British School', almost certainly shows Bridport's flagship *Royal George* firing on *Tigre*, which Quilliam's ship *Prince George* later took in tow. The ship on fire is *Formidable*, which, like *Tigre* and a third French ship, *Alexandre*, was forced to strike.

12. The Battle of Camperdown, 11 October 1797. Thomas Whitcombe shows Duncan's flagship *Venerable* engaging the Dutch flagship *Vrijhead* to port at the moment that, as Quilliam's ship *Triumph*'s log recorded, 'the Vrijhead's three masts went over the side'. In the right foreground is the Dutch *Hercules*, which *Triumph*, with Quilliam then an acting lieutenant, took in tow and brought back to Yarmouth.

13. The Battle of Copenhagen, 2 April 1801. Nicholas Pocock's detailed depiction of the action shows the British fleet once it had come to anchor with *Elephant*, Nelson's flagship, left of centre flying his blue vice-admiral's flag at the fore, and Rear-Admiral Graves' *Defiance*, three ships ahead and the furthest right of the two-deck 74s, flying his rear-admiral's flag, the cross of St George, at the mizzen. Immediately ahead of *Defiance* is *Amazon* with the other two frigates, *Blanche* and *Alcmene*, in turn ahead of her. Opposing the three frigates at the extreme right are the redoubts of the formidable Trekroner or Three Crowns battery.

14. The Battle of Trafalgar, 21 October 1805. Rather than providing an exact depiction of one particular incident or moment in time, Turner's image is an impressionistic conflation of different aspects of the battle. Thus *Victory* is still flying Nelson's 'England expects …' signal rather than his final 'Engage the enemy more closely', which remained flying throughout the battle. The painting depicts the moment when, according to Quilliam's log, 'at 1.30 the *Redoubtable* having struck her Colors we ceased firing our Starboard guns'. Turner, however, shows *Redoubtable* on *Victory*'s larboard or port side with *Téméraire* just coming into view on the left, although she had in fact already collided with *Redoubtable*'s starboard side. Beyond *Victory* is the mighty *Santissima Trinidad* and beyond her the stern of Villeneuve's flagship, *Bucentaure*.

15. George Murray, Lord Bishop of Sodor and Mann. Murray was the nephew of the Duke of Atholl, Manorial Lord of the Isle of Man, who increased existing local resentment by appointing him to the Bishopric at the age of only thirty. His various actions, particularly over tythes, further exacerbated relations with the House of Keys and its leading members, including Quilliam and his friends George Quayle and John Christian Curwen, and eventually led to both his and his uncle's effective expulsion from the Island. Murray was subsequently translated to the see of Rochester.

16. The Quilliam window in St Columba's church, Arbory. Commissioned by the Quilliam Group and with generous support from the Trustees of Manx National Heritage, the window is the work of local artist Colleen Corlett and was dedicated in 2015.

4

War

When the medicines and other supplies arrived, they brought with them momentous news. Not only had revolutionary France executed her king but she had declared war on Great Britain. The Ambassador had also heard the news in Pekin and immediately decided to return home. He sent a letter to Gower at Chu-San, telling him to wait for the Pekin party, but it hadn't arrived before *Lion* left. Nor had a second, sent to Canton, before she left for Japan.[1]

The declaration of war gave Gower authority to press English seamen and he took two out of a Genoese ship and another nineteen 'out of a brig and schooner wearing Hamburgh colours'. Then, on 2 November the lookouts spotted a ship under French colours. *Lion* slipped her cable and gave chase, firing two shots at her before she escaped into Macao. Frustrated, *Lion* returned to recover her anchor and, following a number of false starts imposed by the weather, finally got to sea. Heading up the Straits of Formosa, they encountered extreme gales and by 15 November were back at Macao with the fore and main topmasts both sprung. They were still repairing the damage five days later when they 'fired an 18 pounder shotted and brought to a brig under American colours'.[2] Known as *Emilla* and actually from the Île de France, by an extraordinary coincidence she was the very ship the seal hunters on St Paul had been waiting for. Gower sent her into Macao under a prize crew, leaving the seal hunters marooned until they were rescued by an English merchantman two years later.

When *Clarence* arrived from Canton two weeks later, she brought instructions from Lord Macartney to bring *Lion* up the river and two days before Christmas she moored at Wampoo, 10 miles short of Canton itself. Lying there they also found *Jackall* and *Hindostan*. The Ambassador's baggage came on board together with thirteen chests containing presents from the Emperor for the ships' companies. These were divided on New Year's Eve with officers and men each receiving the same-sized parcel containing 'five pieces, two of them course yellow gause & the other three of course linen, the whole worth about 30 shillings'. Thirty shillings (£1.50) was five weeks wages for Quilliam, or more than £130 in modern-day purchasing power. Meanwhile, Gower put *Lion* on a war footing as he 'exercised great guns and small arms'.

A week later the Ambassador and his retinue embarked and *Lion* dropped back down river to Macao. Here Macartney received despatches from Batavia reporting the arrival of a French squadron that had already taken a British Indiaman, while a larger force was expected soon. Clearly *Lion*'s duty lay in protecting the fifteen ships of that year's China fleet, valued with their cargoes at some £3 million at a time when the UK's entire Gross National Product (GNP) was just £200 million. They would take at least another month to assemble, however, and, in the meantime, messages were sent to other major ports inviting homeward-bound vessels of friendly nations to join the convoy.

While the Ambassador's party waited ashore, *Lion*'s ship's company prepared for the passage home, a process interrupted on 15 February when the purser paid prize money for the unfortunate *Emilla* and her cargo. Of the total of 5,372 Spanish silver dollars or 'pieces of eight', Gower received $2,014.5, while the 247 seamen, marines and boys shared $1,343. Quilliam's share as an able seaman would have been some $5.44 or £1.15, almost a month's pay and worth about £105 in modern purchasing terms.

A week later, the Ambassador's party re-embarked but it took another two weeks to assemble the convoy, which eventually comprised thirteen British East Indiamen, together with a Portuguese ship from Macao, a Spaniard from Manila and a homeward-bound American. Finally, on Monday, 17 March 1794, Gower 'at 6 made the signal and weighed ... Made sail and stood to sea'. After a little under nine months in China, Quilliam and *Lion* were on their way home.

From the outset Gower took the enemy threat seriously. Although *Lion* packed the heaviest punch, all the Indiamen were heavily armed and he expected them to form part of the protection of the convoy as a whole. The first leg took them 1,700 miles back to the Sunda Strait, the gateway to the Indian Ocean. En route they were shadowed by small pirate vessels hoping to pick off stragglers and cleared for action when strange sails were spotted. Happily, the ships responded to the private signal and proved to be three armed Indiamen from Bengal, which stayed with them as far as the Straits where they and *Jackall* parted company for Calcutta.

Having replenished their water at Anger Point at the northern end of the Straits, *Lion* and her convoy headed out into the Indian Ocean with St Helena their next port of call, 6,500 miles away. There followed weeks of what blue water sailors called 'flying fish weather' but as they approached the coast of Africa they were hit by a violent thunderstorm. One of the Indiamen was struck and lost her mizzen topmast and topgallant mast and the captain and officers eating their dinner below were stunned and received shocks and burns. That was only the overture. On 29 May they ran into a severe gale, which blew for four days. When it began to moderate on what proved to be the 'Glorious First of June',[3] Gower had only five of his charges still in sight and one of those, *Hindostan,* had sprung her foremast. They had, however, been carried round the Cape of Good Hope, or the 'Cape of Storms',[4] into the Atlantic.

Over the next few days all but three of the missing Indiamen re-joined but on 18 June, as they approached St Helena, two men-of-war were spotted astern. Again Gower cleared for action, shortening sail to put himself between the convoy and the strangers, who were eventually identified as HM Ships *Sampson* and *Argo*, a 64-gun battleship and a 44-gun frigate sent out from England to escort the convoy. Later the same day, they anchored at St Helena where, over the next two days, the remaining stragglers re-joined. The Ambassador's party took up residence ashore while twenty of *Lion*'s men were sent to sick quarters. Thirteen days later they were on their way again with the carpenters 'fixing shot lockers around the hatchways' while the gunner and his mates 'filled powder and completed the whole to fifteen rounds', precautions against a possible encounter with the enemy as they approached home waters.

Shortly after crossing the equator, the preparations looked to be justified as the two leading Indiamen reported seven sail in the north-east. This time they didn't respond to the private signal and Gower ordered the convoy to leeward while the men-of-war formed a line ahead to confront what appeared to be 'five of the strange ships coming down in line of battle abreast'. *Lion* beat to quarters and, as the opposing forces closed, a fog bank intervened. When it cleared, the 'enemy' were right on top of them but, before a shot had been fired, they were identified as 'a convoy for China and India 1 month from England', The failure to respond to the private signal was explained when one of the escort provided the latest signal codes.

Gower continually 'exercised the people at the great guns' and 'the marines at small arms' as they headed north but there were no further encounters before, on 4 September, they 'saw Scilly bearing NEbN 5 or 6 leagues' and that night were 'passed by a large number of ships supposed to be the English fleet under the command of Lord Howe'.[5] Next morning off Bolt Head, *Argo* parted company, taking the convoy up Channel, and *Lion* headed for Spithead where, 711 days after she had left, she anchored on Sunday, 7 September 1794.

With the Ambassador and his party disembarked and no fewer than sixty sick men sent to the hospital,[6] *Lion* was ordered to Chatham and on Saturday, 4 October, with all her armament and munitions already removed, she moved up to Chatham harbour. A week later Gower made his last entry in *Lion*'s log: 'At 6 the men all disembarked on board the Prince George.' Among them was John Quilliam, now a career ocean-going seafarer with a rich reservoir of hands-on experience that he would refine and exploit over the next twenty-two years of war. *Lion*'s voyage to China had transformed him into a man-of-war's man, Britain's most important resource in her hour of need, and secured him the support of one of the Royal Navy's senior captains.[7]

5

Quartermaster's Mate

John Quilliam would spend little more than a year in HMS *Prince George* and, during his first six months on board, she moved just 10½ miles down the Medway to the Nore, the fleet anchorage in the Thames Estuary. Launched at Chatham in 1772, she was a 98-gun, three-deck battleship[1] and, when Quilliam and the rest of *Lion*'s ship's company joined her on Monday, 13 October 1794,[2] was lying, without guns or ballast, in Gillingham Reach, a couple of miles down the river from the dockyard, accompanied by a number of hulks holding French prisoners of war.

Quilliam's new captain was thirty-nine-year-old James Gambier, an evangelical Christian who had distinguished himself at the Glorious First of June when his ship, *Defence,* had been the first of Lord Howe's fleet to break the French line. That may be why he was able to obtain such prime seamen for his new command. Of the 205 men who joined from *Lion,* only five were rated at less than able seaman. Their task over the next few months was to transform *Prince George* from a hollow shell into one of the most powerful weapons of the age.

By mid-December all the signs were that she was ready to move down river but when the pilot came on board on 3 January 1795 there was too little wind to proceed. She didn't actually move for another two months as snow fell in huge quantities and the river froze over in the coldest single month between 1659 and the present day.[3] The log was still recording frequent snow showers in the first week of March as final preparations were at last made for departure and this time there was no delay. On the morning of Thursday, 5 March a pilot came on board and, at 11am, *Prince George* 'slipp'd the bridles and made sail'.[4] An hour and a half later she moored at Blackstakes, upriver from Sheerness. There she received her guns from the gun wharf and her powder and shot from the magazine at Upnor Castle higher up the river. She also received a new

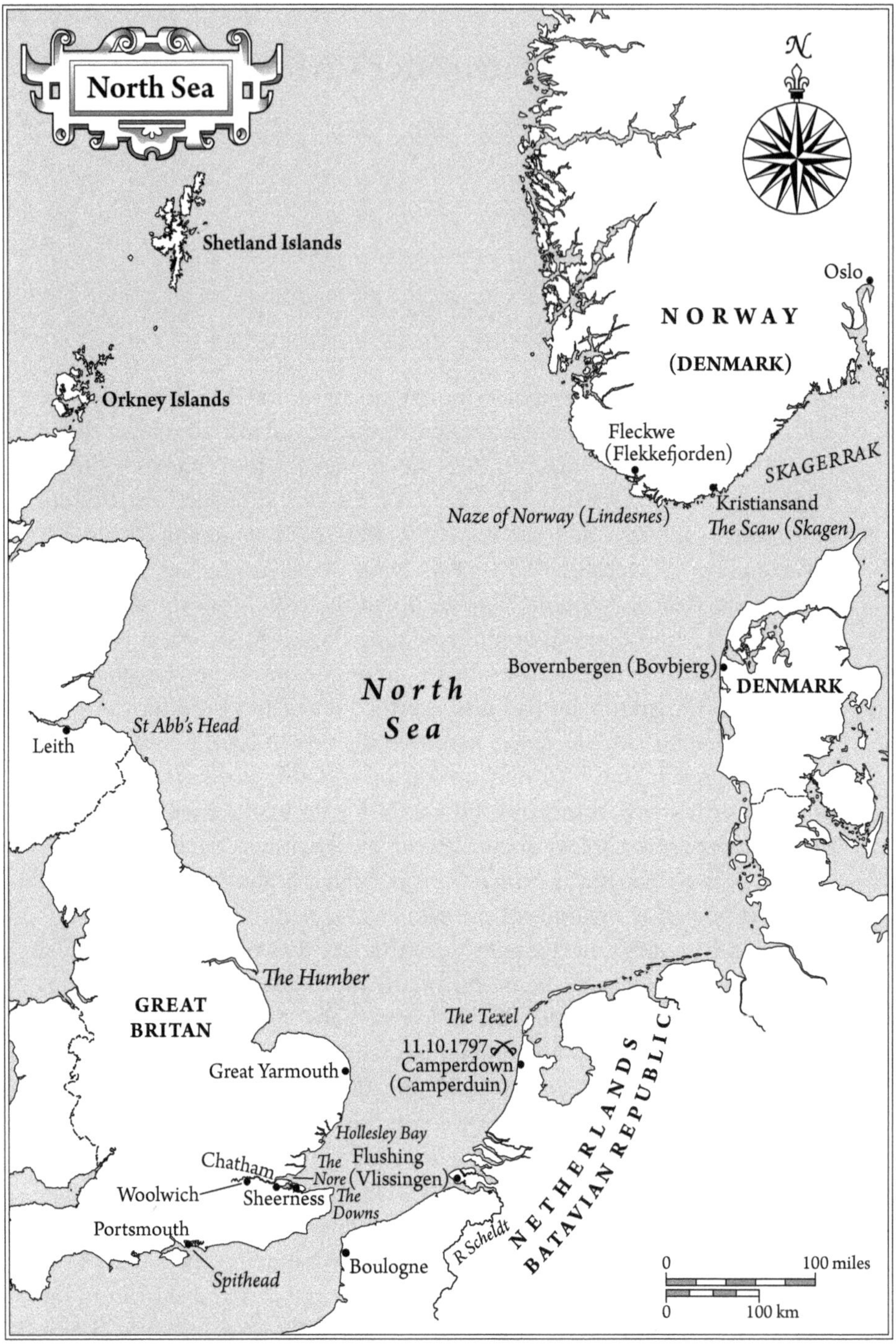
North Sea
Shetland Islands
Orkney Islands
NORWAY
(DENMARK)
Oslo
Fleckwe
(Flekkefjorden)
SKAGERRAK
Kristiansand
Naze of Norway (Lindesnes)
The Scaw (Skagen)
Bovernbergen (Bovbjerg)
DENMARK
North Sea
St Abb's Head
Leith
The Humber
GREAT BRITAN
The Texel
11.10.1797
Camperdown
(Camperduin)
Great Yarmouth
Hollesley Bay
Chatham
The Nore
Flushing
(Vlissingen)
Woolwich
Sheerness
The Downs
Portsmouth
Spithead
Boulogne
R Scheldt
NETHERLANDS
BATAVIAN REPUBLIC
0
100 miles
0
100 km

captain. Gambier's name had reached the top of the post-captains' list and, anticipating his imminent promotion to Rear Admiral of the White, he had been appointed a Lord of the Admiralty. His legacy to *Prince George* was another evangelical officer, his protégé, Lieutenant Francis Austen, brother of the then unknown novelist Jane Austen.

Quilliam's next captain was a forty-four-year-old baronet, Sir John Orde, a veteran of the American War and more recently Governor of Dominica. Under his command, on 15 April *Prince George* unmoored and two and a half hours later anchored at the Nore, where she received a series of drafts of men that brought her close to her full complement.[5] She also gained a new quartermaster's mate in the form of John Quilliam, who was promoted on 30 April.[6]

Quartermaster's mate was a petty officer as distinct from a warrant or standing officer rate, being entirely in the gift and at the discretion of the captain. Along with quartermasters, quartermaster's mates were part of the navigation department headed by the master but ranked below and reporting to master's mates. Their precise duties are unclear, but most authorities seem to agree that the primary responsibility of the quartermaster team was helming the ship, a task critical to her sailing performance and overall fighting ability. A little over a week after he took up his new duties, *Prince George* left the Nore and on the afternoon of Wednesday, 13 May arrived at Spithead, joining the Channel Fleet under the command of Lord Howe, the victor at the Glorious First of June. With Howe in poor health, the command at sea devolved on Lord Bridport, who was in the unenviable position of having responsibility without ultimate power.[7]

Before she put to sea again, *Prince George* underwent another change of captain as Sir John Orde was also promoted to Rear Admiral of the White. His successor, Quilliam's fourth captain in three years, was William Edge,[8] who had served with great distinction as a lieutenant under Bridport's brother, Lord Hood, when the British had withdrawn from Toulon two years earlier. Still only a commander, he would only be made post-captain after he had commanded *Prince George* in a major engagement.

Four days after Edge's appointment, Bridport hoisted his flag on *Royal George* and on Friday, 12 June 1795 made the signal to weigh. His fleet comprised no fewer than fourteen battleships together with five frigates and various smaller craft. Bridport's mission was to cover a fifty-strong convoy of transports, escorted by Commodore Sir John Borlase Warren's squadron,[9] which was to land 2,500 French émigré troops in Quiberon

Bay on the south coast of Brittany. If the French fleet in Brest attempted to intervene, Bridport was to drive it off or, better still, bring it to action.

By 17 June Bridport's fleet, together with Warren's squadron and convoy, was working its way down from Ushant and, next day, was some 15 miles WNW of the Pointe du Raz, often described as 'France's Land's End'. Shortly afterwards, Warren and his charges parted company for Quiberon Bay while the main fleet stood off to cover the landing. Early on the morning of the 22nd, *Prince George* 'saw the French fleet to the Eas'd' and, in the afternoon, counted '23 sail of French ships in sight' and 'beat to quarters and cleared ship for action'.[10] This wasn't the first time Quilliam had been on a ship clearing for action, but to beat to quarters with the enemy clearly identified was another matter. However, Admiral Villaret de Joyeuse, realising he was outnumbered, made all sail for Brest and Bridport ordered a general chase.

With the wind dropping, it wasn't until dawn the following morning that the leading British ships got within range, with the Isle de Groix, which was to give its name to what followed, just 5 miles to the north-east of the main body of the French fleet. Descriptions of the action vary but *Prince George*'s log describes her coming up with the enemy's rearguard only half an hour after it began and remaining engaged for two hours until Bridport, concerned at the proximity of a lee shore, broke off the action. By that point three French battleships, *Alexandre*, *Formidable* and *Tigre*, had struck their colours while the remainder escaped into Lorient. *Prince George* suffered no casualties and the only obvious damages were shot holes in the sails and a burning fore studding sail that had been thrown overboard. It was a different matter on *Tigre*, which lost 130 killed and many more wounded. *Prince George* took her in tow and sent her carpenters over to make temporary repairs while eighty prisoners were removed. Although Bridport came in for much criticism, the action was regarded at home as a victory and he, along with his subordinates, received the thanks of Parliament. Rather less usefully for Quilliam, for whom this was the first of his four fleet actions, veterans of the battle were awarded the Naval General Service Medal with the clasp '23rd June 1795,' but not until 1847, eighteen years after he died.

Prince George parted company with the fleet in mid-August and, pausing only to take possession of an American ship 'loaded with flour and bound for Nante', was at anchor in Cawsand Bay at the entrance to Plymouth Sound by the end of the month. There she underwent emergency repairs to what may have been damage below the water line incurred on 23 June and prize money was paid for the American ship, just four days after she had been taken into Plymouth. Urgent repairs completed, she was under way again on 8 September and on the morning of the 10th was towed into Spithead by her boats in a flat calm. While intense work began on her masts and rigging, on 14 September she underwent another change of command as Captain Edge handed over to Captain James Bowen.

Why Edge was superseded is not clear, but he doesn't seem to have been sacked. However, he never went to sea again and it has been suggested his experiences at Toulon caused a breakdown. Bowen had a most unusual career. Master of one of his father's merchantmen at the age of twenty-five, he transferred to the Navy, again as master, and fought at the Battle of the Dogger Bank in 1781. He was master of Lord Howe's flagship, *Queen Charlotte*, at the Glorious First of June, earning a commission, and was immediately made first lieutenant. Retaining the position under Bridport, after the Battle of Groix he was promoted commander and, in short order, on 2 September, post-captain.[11] It cannot have escaped Quilliam's attention that his new captain was a former merchant ship sailor. Bowen's career, like Quilliam's, reflected the meritocratic nature of the wartime Navy. The best men were promoted and rewarded, both for their deeds and to encourage others.

Prince George had been selected by Rear Admiral Christian[12] as his flagship for an expedition to attack the French and Dutch colonies in the West Indies. Christian had served with Bowen before and almost certainly requested his transfer from Bridport's flagship. Two days after Bowen read himself in as captain.[13] Christian hoisted his flag in *Prince George*, but two months of steadily deteriorating weather elapsed before his squadron, transports and troops were ready to leave. Departure so late in the season proved disastrous for the expedition but fortuitous for Quilliam. When *Prince George* and the largest troop convoy ever to have left England finally sailed, he wasn't with her.

In the event *Prince George* didn't go to the West Indies either. Two days out, off Portland Bill, the convoy was hit by a violent storm; several transports foundered and *Prince George* lost her rudder. After limping back to Spithead, the damage was deemed so severe that Christian transferred his flag, Captain Bowen and most of the ship's company to another ship, HMS *Glory*. Another attempt in December met a similar fate in the second of what became known as 'Christian's Gales' and the admiral shifted his flag and his flag captain again, this time to HMS *Thunderer*. The expedition finally got away in March 1796 but, once in the West Indies, its luck changed and the islands of St Lucia, St Vincent and Grenada were captured.[14]

6

Master's Mate

While Admiral Christian was trying to assemble his huge West Indies convoy, John Quilliam was settling into both a new ship and a new role. The ship was HMS *Triumph*, a 74-gun battleship,[1] the role, that of master's mate, to which he was appointed when he joined her on Friday, 6 November.[2] *Triumph*'s captain was none other than Sir Erasmus Gower and it seems almost certain that he directed Quilliam's move and promotion. Promotion to master's mate, a role effectively interchangeable with that of midshipman, finally put Quilliam on the path to becoming a commissioned officer.[3] *Triumph*'s three master's mates were permitted to walk the quarterdeck, mess in the gun room and berth with the warrant officers.

Under Gower's command, *Triumph* had distinguished herself in the celebrated action later known as 'Cornwallis's Retreat' in which, in the previous June, Vice Admiral Cornwallis's squadron of five battleships had for two days held off the entire French fleet before escaping. She had subsequently sustained irreparable damage to her main mast and bowsprit in a severe gale off the Ile de Groix.[4] Quilliam joined her just in time to assist in setting up the rigging for her new main mast and swaying up the topmast and topgallant masts. However, it was not until the beginning of February that she joined Vice Admiral Gardner's squadron tasked with escorting a 160-strong West Indies convoy on the first leg of its journey. After a succession of false starts they eventually got away on 21 February and by 2 March were 100 miles off the south-west tip of Portugal, where they parted company with the convoy and were joined by Lord Bridport.

Their new assignment was to watch for any sign of the French Toulon fleet escaping into the Atlantic. The real challenge, however, again proved to be the weather. The squadron was hit by a succession of gales, *Triumph* again suffering severe damage to her rigging, including a sprung main mast. Quilliam's talents and experience would have been at a premium;

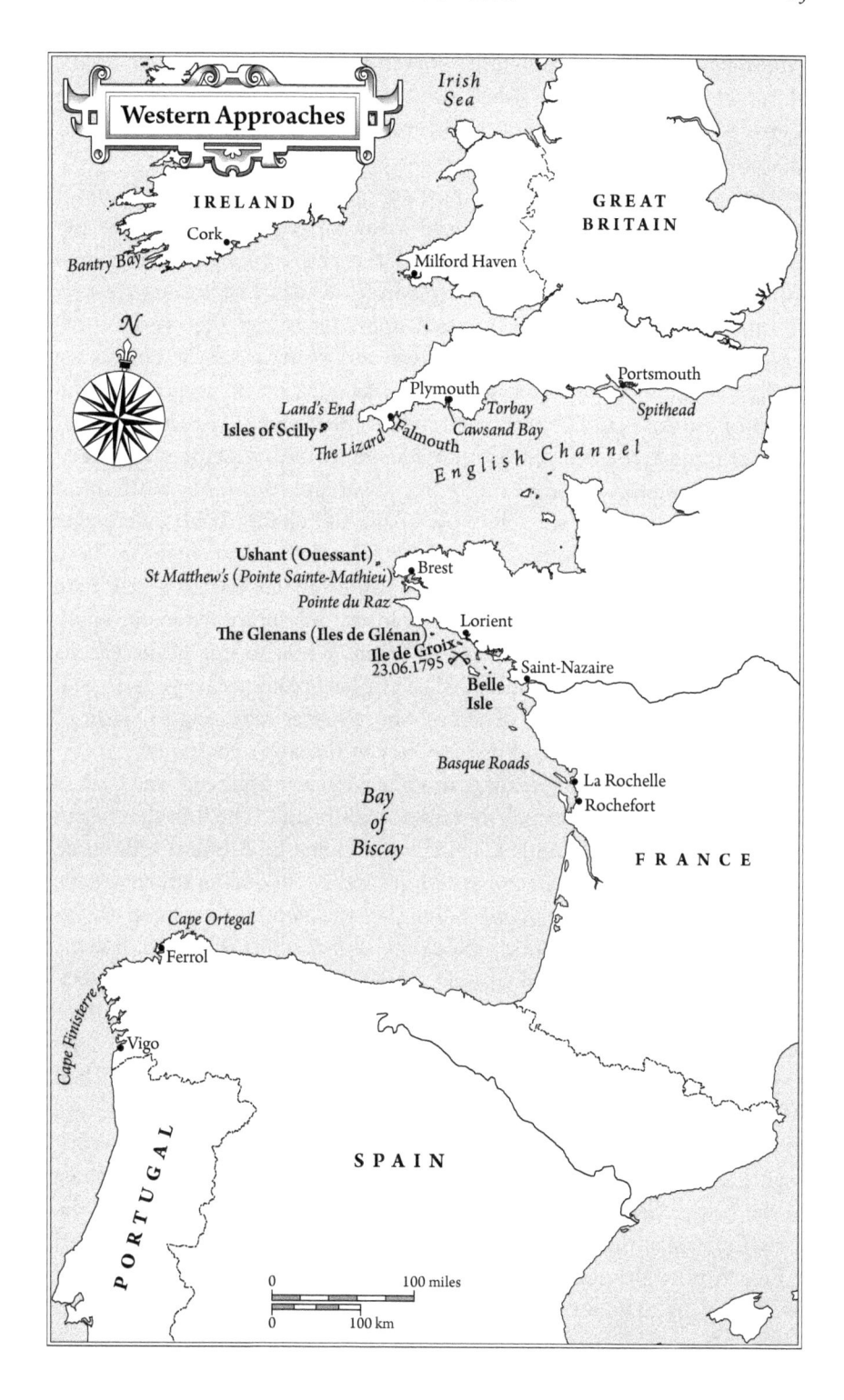

Western Approaches

Irish Sea

IRELAND

Cork
Bantry Bay

GREAT BRITAIN

Milford Haven

Portsmouth
Plymouth
Land's End   Torbay   Spithead
Isles of Scilly Falmouth Cawsand Bay
The Lizard

English Channel

Ushant (Ouessant)
St Matthew's (Pointe Sainte-Mathieu) Brest
Pointe du Raz
The Glenans (Iles de Glénan) Lorient
Ile de Groix Saint-Nazaire
23.06.1795
Belle Isle

Basque Roads La Rochelle
Rochefort

Bay of Biscay

FRANCE

Cape Ortegal
Ferrol

Cape Finisterre
Vigo

PORTUGAL   SPAIN

0   100 miles
0   100 km

Triumph was rerigged and fully operational within forty-eight hours. However, damage to the other ships in the squadron necessitated a return to port and by Sunday, 27 March they were once more at anchor at Spithead.

Artificers from the dockyard hurried on board the next day and a month later *Triumph* was once more ready for sea, having replaced her main mast and completely overhauled the entire rig. She now joined Admiral Lord Hugh Seymour's squadron, whose task was to escort another convoy through the western approaches and then resume the watch off the Iberian coast. Squadron and convoy left St Helens on 18 May and by the 30th the squadron was back on its cruising ground south of the Azores. They returned to Spithead in mid-August and, after another rapid turnaround, were at sea again by mid-September as part of a powerful squadron comprising *Formidable* and four other battleships, two frigates and a fire ship. By now Spain had changed sides, declaring war on the British empire. Admiral Sir John Jervis had therefore been forced to withdraw his outnumbered Mediterranean fleet to a new base in the Tagus,[5] so *Triumph* and her squadron only patrolled as far south as Cape Ortegal, the north-west tip of Spain. While no significant actions ensued, the tight blockade, intended to cripple Spain's treasury and naval power, yielded a succession of prizes. Shortly after returning to Spithead in November, *Triumph* 'paid prize money to the ship's company'.

Triumph's chance of spending another winter at Spithead was dashed by France's decision to launch an invasion of Ireland. The fleet that began leaving Brest on 15 December, again commanded by Admiral Villaret de Joyeuse, comprised seventeen battleships and twenty-seven other vessels, carrying some 18,000 troops.[6] Sailing in the depths of winter, things didn't go well from the outset. Not only was the fleet scattered, but the 74-gun *Séduisant* foundered with the loss of 700 of the 1,300 men aboard. One of the British frigates shadowing the fleet raced back to Falmouth to report and, by 3 January 1797, *Triumph* was one of fourteen sail of the line headed down Channel.[7] Part of the French fleet had already reached Bantry Bay on 21 December, but easterly gales prevented a landing and forced many of the ships to seek the safety of the open sea. Not a single French soldier set foot on Irish soil and, by the time *Triumph* and the rest of the British fleet entered the bay on 9 January, it was deserted. Of the forty-four ships that left Brest on 15 December, just thirty-one regained a French port although only seven, the largest a frigate, were captured by the British. The rest, including two ships of the line,[8] were wrecked or foundered. Several of Bridport's pursuing ships were also seriously damaged and unable to join the fleet when it next put to sea.

One of them was *Triumph*. Back at Spithead on 5 February, she did not get to sea again until 6 April, when she once more joined Lord Hugh Seymour's squadron. This time four ships of the line and a frigate were to escort an East Indies convoy until it was well south of Madeira and then lie in wait for that year's Spanish treasure shipment from the Americas.[9] As a result, *Triumph* was hundreds of miles away when, on 15 April, the seamen of *Royal George* 'ran up the shrouds and gave three cheers'[10] to signal the start of the Spithead Mutiny.

By the time the squadron returned empty handed to Spithead on 22 May, the mutiny was over. The mutineers' modest demands for improved wages, better treatment of the sick and provision for leave had been conceded and embodied in an Act of Parliament and a Royal Pardon granted. Consequently, implementation of the settlement on *Triumph* should have been a formality. Gower, however, had a rude awakening on the morning after their arrival when, having 'Read His Majesty's proclamation and other papers relating to the late mutinous proceedings' to the ship's company, 'they tossed out of the ship Lieut Lowe, Mr Giles Mate, Mr Paten Mid, Mr Jones the Boatswain …'. Numerous attempts were made by Gower and Lord Hugh Seymour to persuade the men to return to their duty, but it was not until 4 June that order was finally re-established and the officers' and petty officers' authority restored. By then Gower had departed to command a force assembled to deal with the much more serious mutiny at the Nore, which had also infected Admiral Duncan's North Sea fleet confronting the Dutch.[11]

7

Camperdown

Triumph's new captain was forty-four-year-old William Essington. His previous command had been the 64-gun battleship HMS *Sceptre*, in which, in June 1795, he had captured no fewer than eight Dutch East Indiamen off St Helena. His immediate task was to get *Triumph* ready to reinforce the increasingly precarious situation in the North Sea, where the powerful Dutch fleet under Vice Admiral Jan de Winter was threatening to leave the Texel[1] with 14,000 troops and mount another invasion of Ireland.[2]

De Winter had two obstacles to overcome, one the prevailing westerly winds, the other Admiral Adam Duncan's North Sea fleet. However, unbeknownst to the Dutch, when Duncan signalled his fifteen ships of the line to leave Great Yarmouth on 29 May 1797, only one followed his flagship, *Venerable*; the remainder turned south to join the mutineers at the Nore.[3] Arriving off the Texel the next day, Duncan found conditions perfect for the Dutch to put to sea: he had just two battleships and a frigate to confront sixteen sail of the line. As the Admiralty rushed reinforcements from Spithead, Duncan kept his battleships close inshore while the frigate *Circe,* further out to sea, sent signals to a phantom fleet over the horizon. Convinced that the entire British fleet was just out of sight, de Winter stayed in the anchorage. By the time *Triumph* arrived on 15 June, the immediate crisis was over.[4] Not only had the wind changed, making exit from the Texel much more difficult, but Duncan's force now numbered nine sail of the line as well as several frigates and a brig.

Duncan reimposed the blockade and by the middle of August de Winter had been forced to abandon the invasion project. As a result, Duncan's priority changed from keeping the Dutch in their anchorage to luring them to sea and destroying them. He therefore withdrew the fleet offshore, leaving the frigates to watch whether de Winter would take the bait. It wasn't until the British had returned to Yarmouth for supplies at the end of September that he finally did so.

The fleet had been at anchor in Yarmouth roads for a week when an armed lugger came in sight flying the signal for an enemy. By noon the entire fleet was under way and at ten o'clock on the morning of 11 October *Triumph*'s log recorded that she 'saw 21 sail bearing SSW on larbd tack'. De Winter had formed a line of battle some 9 miles off the Dutch coast not far from the village of Camperduin or, to the British, Camperdown.

With the enemy close to the shore and in shallow water, Duncan had neither time nor space to form a line of battle. Instead he attacked in two divisions, *Venerable* leading the larboard division, the starboard division led by Vice Admiral Onslow in *Monarch*. Close astern of *Venerable* was *Triumph*, giving Quilliam a front-row seat. The log recorded how at '10 mins to 1 Adml Onslow began to fire on the centre of the enemy & engaged the Dutch vice adml' and at '10 mins past 1 we began to engage with 2 ships of the enemy'. *Triumph* passed through a gap in the Dutch line and engaged the battleship *Wassenaar* but then found herself at the centre of a cluster of enemy ships, her log recording how she 'Back'd & fill'd occasionally frequently engaging with 5 ships of the enemy at once. ½ past 2 wheel shot away'. With the entire larboard division in some difficulty, it was Onslow's division, which had already overwhelmed the Dutch rearguard, that delivered the coup de grace. First on the scene was William Bligh's *Director*, closely followed by *Powerful* and *Russell*. Minutes later, *Triumph*'s log recorded the capitulation of the Dutch flagship as 'at 20 past 3 the Vrijhead's three masts went over the side'. Duncan had achieved the most complete victory by a British fleet over an enemy of equal strength up to that time. Sixteen British ships had confronted fifteen Dutchmen, taking nine of them without loss.[5]

With the battle won, both the British fleet and its prizes were in a precarious position just 5 miles off a lee shore. *Triumph* had suffered heavy damage, with thirty-one killed and seventy-five wounded, including the captain, two lieutenants and the master. A third lieutenant had been sent to take charge of a prize. Essington, however, had two master's mates within months of taking the examination for lieutenant. He immediately made both Edward Greensword and John Quilliam acting lieutenants and set them to work. There was plenty to do. The log recorded: 'Found 3½ feet of water in the hold. Masts & yards much sprung. 3 guns disabled & 7 carriages, most of the lower rigging cut to pieces.'

Work went on throughout the night and the following days, and it was not until the morning of Monday, 16 October that *Triumph* and her Dutch prize *Hercules* finally anchored back in Yarmouth roads. Yarmouth had no facilities to handle ships of the line so, after further repairs, *Triumph* left for Spithead nine days later. In the meantime, the lieutenant who had taken charge of *Hercules* had returned, ending Quilliam's twelve days as an acting lieutenant.

Triumph spent the remainder of 1797 and the whole of January 1798 in dry dock, her ship's company accommodated in the hulk *Fortitude*. Quilliam may have been among the seamen who, according to *The London Gazette*, attended the procession and service of thanksgiving for the victory at St Paul's Cathedral on 23 December, an event that revived the spirits of a badly wounded Horatio Nelson.[6] By early February the ship was out of the dock, re-joining Bridport's Channel Fleet on 26 March. In the meantime, a first instalment of prize money was paid, based on an initial estimate of the value of the Camperdown prizes. However, it was not until some years later that a final settlement totalling £150,000 was made; Quilliam's share would have been around £35, over £3,000 in modern values.[7]

Back at sea, *Triumph* re-joined the blockade off Brest where, on the night of Sunday, 22 April, she 'heard the report of several guns & saw the flashes for upwards of an hour in the east quarter'. What they had witnessed, albeit from a distance, was a celebrated, bloody single ship action in which the British battleship *Mars* defeated the brand-new French 74-gun *Hercule*. *Triumph* was back in Torbay by the middle of May but when, at the end of the month, she once more weighed and made sail, Quilliam was not with her. Instead, on 6 June, having completed six years at sea and three as either midshipman or mate, he presented himself for examination before the Navy Board. That he successfully negotiated the ordeal is certain, although his actual passing certificate has been lost. It was therefore as a 'Passed Midshipman' that he re-joined *Triumph* off Ushant. She made another visit to Cawsand Bay at the end of August before returning to the blockade, but these were Quilliam's last days as a master's mate in *Triumph*. On 9 September he transferred to Bridport's flagship *Royal George* 'On promotion'[8] and five days later joined the 98-gun battleship *Neptune* in Cawsand Bay, Plymouth.[9]

It seems almost certain the transfer had been instigated by *Neptune*'s captain, Quilliam's earlier patron, Sir Erasmus Gower, last seen setting out to quell the mutiny at the Nore in the newly commissioned *Neptune*.

Although the mutiny had collapsed before Gower's arrival, he had retained the command and joined the Channel Fleet. The key question is why Gower became Quilliam's patron? He almost certainly had a link to Quilliam's original Manx benefactor, John Crane, but he must have seen something in the young man while on *Lion* that marked him out as command material. Moreover, while himself a Welshman, he did have an indirect Manx connection, having in 1775 served as first lieutenant of HMS *Levant* under Captain the Hon George Murray. Murray's nephew was John Murray, 4th Duke of Atholl and manorial Lord of Mann; on 4 June 1775 Atholl had visited *Levant* and received a fifteen-gun salute.[10]

Quilliam was entered on *Neptune*'s books as 'Acting Lieutenant', but stayed for only twenty days, all of them in Cawsand Bay. Her muster book lists him as Discharged on the grounds of 'Promotion' on 5 October,[11] the day before he received his commission to join HMS *Chapman* as a lieutenant. *Chapman*'s captain, Robert Keen, had written to the Admiralty four days before, requesting a replacement for his newly departed first lieutenant.[12] He must have been gratified to get such a prompt response, but it seems likely he had Sir Erasmus Gower, shortly to be promoted rear admiral, to thank as much as their Lordships.

8

Lieutenant Quilliam

HMS *Chapman*, a 24-gun sloop with a complement of 121 men and boys, was 'at single anchor in Plym'th Sound' when Quilliam joined her on 11 October 1798,[1] and shortly afterwards 'weigh'd & made sail' with a small convoy. By the morning of the 13th, having added to the convoy at Falmouth, she was working her way south-west towards the Lizard. As the afternoon wore on, the weather deteriorated and Captain Keen was forced to progressively reduce sail and eventually became separated from the convoy. With no clear idea of his position, by midnight the situation had become critical as, in pitch dark and what was now a full gale, breakers were sighted ahead.

Keen now faced the sailing ship mariner's ultimate nightmare as he tacked ship but 'found she would not clear land on either tack'. As he recorded in the log, he 'For the safety of the ship & our lives let go the small bower & veer'd to a cable ... & brought her up in 13 fms in Garrons Bay. Nare Pt EbS 1½ miles.'[2] They lay just yards off the beach for almost twenty-four hours until the following night, when the wind veered and moderated sufficiently for Keen to make sail. Even then he was 'obliged to cut for the safety of the ship & our lives', abandoning the small bower anchor. Twelve hours later they were once more at anchor in Carrick Roads, with Keen writing to the Admiralty to explain why he was back in Falmouth while the convoy was somewhere west of the Lizard.[3]

Four days later *Chapman* slipped her cable to chase a ship that failed to answer the private signal, but she soon had to return once more to the anchorage. She was still there at the beginning of November when Lieutenant Handfield was appointed to the frigate *Proselyte* and Quilliam stepped up to replace him as first lieutenant. Quilliam's career was moving rapidly; the war ensured a constant demand for good officers.

Chapman eventually left Carrick Roads for Plymouth on 15 November in company with *La Bellone,* a French frigate captured the previous month at the Battle of Tory Island off the coast of Donegal.[4] Also at anchor in Plymouth Sound when she arrived was the frigate *Ethalion,* one of the victors of that battle. Her presence had a direct bearing on Quilliam's next move, as almost certainly did Sir Erasmus Gower. Once she had discharged her prisoners, *Chapman* moved up into the Catwater[5] but it was not until 18 December that she next made sail out of Plymouth Sound. Calling once more at Carrick Roads, she took two brigs under convoy and this time had no difficulty rounding the Lizard. By the evening of 20 December she was 'working up Milford Haven' where Quilliam's last passage in her finished early next morning.[6]

Quilliam's commission as *Ethalion*'s third lieutenant was dated 14 December 1798 but he didn't make his first appearance until the 29th.[7] The 38-gun Artois-class frigate with a design complement of 270 had been launched in March 1797.[8] Her captain, George Countess, was in his early 50s and had commanded two other frigates before taking command in July 1797.[9] The vacancy that Quilliam filled had been created by the promotion of her first lieutenant to commander following the Tory Island action. Quilliam's skills were in demand because, at the time he joined her, *Ethalion* had already spent six weeks in Hamoaze repairing storm and battle damage and another four would pass before she was back at sea. In company with HMS *Anson,* a 44-gun frigate placed under Countess's orders, she left Plymouth on 28 January 1799 and by the following day was riding out a westerly gale off Ushant.[10] Too good an officer for the humdrum world of small coastal convoys, Quilliam had moved on to the front line of the naval war, the blockade of Brest, where large frigates kept watch on the main French fleet, the fleet that had twice attempted to invade Ireland. It was a station that wore out ships and men at an alarming rate, but it was too important to abandon.

The frigates were also cruising to counter the French privateer threat and secure Britain's trade. A week later, 90 miles south-west of Belle Isle, they chased and brought to *La Boulonnoise,* a 14-gun, ninety-man privateer from Dunkirk. The capture was especially satisfying since, as the British revenue cutter *Swan,* she had been captured by the French two years earlier in an action that had cost the life of her commander. She was soon on her way back to Plymouth under a prize crew while the frigates resumed their patrol. After a further series of strong gales, during which they rescued four men from a Spanish sloop shortly before it sank, on 15 February, 60 miles south-west of La Roche Bonne, they detained an American brig with false papers. After intense questioning the master admitted that he was bound for France; Countess ordered *Anson* to escort her into the nearest English port.

Meanwhile *Ethalion,* by then 100 miles south-west of the Belle Isle, on the afternoon of 6 March chased two ships, of which the further was seen to 'hoist French colours and haul them down soon after'. The nearer ship proved to be the English frigate *Naiad*, while the Frenchman was the 18-gun, ninety-eight-man privateer *Heureux Hazard*. Although she had struck to *Naiad*, *Ethalion* would share in the eventual prize money. Hardly was *Naiad* out of sight the following morning when *Ethalion* chased another Frenchman. It was late afternoon before she hauled down her colours and *Ethalion* hove to and took possession. This latest capture proved to be *La Indefatigable* from Nantes of 18 guns and 120 men. Having taken off her crew as prisoners, Countess sent Quilliam with '3 petty officers and 30 men on board to work the ship'.[11]

Ethalion kept company with the prize for a week but then left it far behind as she chased another privateer. Quilliam made his own way back to Plymouth, to be reunited with *Ethalion* when she arrived on 7 April. Secured below were four Irishmen, found among the crew of *La Indefatigable* and detained separately on suspicion of being 'Traytors'. Their ultimate fate would be out of Countess's hands because the same day 'Capn Countess left the Ethalion & Capt Young superceded him'.[12]

9

Spanish Gold

Aged thirty-seven, James Young came from a naval family and had been a post-captain since 1795. *Ethalion* was his third frigate[1] but, before he could take her to sea, she needed serious attention including replacement of her mainmast, work that was very familiar to her dockyard-raised third lieutenant. A month of frantic activity saw her back in the Sound on 3 May and four days later putting to sea as part of Rear Admiral Hawkins-Whitshed's squadron, which comprised his 100-gun flagship *Queen Charlotte,* four other battleships and two more frigates.[2]

The escape from Brest on 25 April of Vice Admiral Bruix with twenty-five sail of the line had made sailing urgent. Bruix had headed south and, evading Lord Keith's blockading squadron off Cadiz, passed through the Straits of Gibraltar on 5 May and made for Toulon.[3] From there he threatened to undo the huge strategic gain of Nelson's annihilation of the French at Aboukir Bay[4] in August 1798, including the British seizure of the key fleet anchorage at Port Mahon, Minorca. Earl St Vincent, commander-in-chief in the Mediterranean, immediately recalled Keith and by 20 May had a fleet of twenty-three battleships in Port Mahon, but the Spanish fleet in Cadiz, taking advantage of Keith's absence, sailed through the Straits to the Mediterranean base at Cartagena.[5] With such large forces stalking each other in the comparatively confined waters of the Western Mediterranean, a major battle seemed inevitable and the Admiralty's response had been to reinforce St Vincent with Admiral Hawkins-Whitshed's squadron.

Twelve days after leaving Plymouth, the squadron hove to off Gibraltar and, without even pausing to take on water, headed into the Mediterranean. Two days later, halfway to Minorca, they met the frigates *Caroline* and *Terpsichore* bringing new orders for the admiral. *Ethalion* was detached to cover possible French or Spanish moves against Minorca, while the remainder of the squadron hastened to join St Vincent. By the time she made the briefest of calls at Mahon for water on 8 June, St Vincent's worsening health had forced him to return to Gibraltar and Lord Keith had taken the fleet east towards Genoa in search of the French. Resuming the patrol, *Ethalion* began seizing Spanish shipping. On 10 June off Dragonera[6] her boats took possession of '5 small Spanish vessels laden with corn and sheep' and, hours later, two brigs 'loaded with sheep & corn from Barcelona to Majorca'. Two days later she 'Brought a small settee alongside and took out her cargo of bread, pease and pork' and the next morning, 'took possession of a Spanish brig'. However, commerce raiding came to an abrupt halt a few days later when 'the Marine arms chest on the quarter deck blew up'. Six marines were badly burnt and Young immediately headed back to Mahon to transfer them to the hospital.

Nevertheless, they were soon back harrying Spanish trade and scouting for the fleet. On 22 June they took another 'settee from Barcelona to Majorca' and two days later 'a small tartan ... being a Spaniard from Barcelona to Majorca'. Then, on the 27th, they chased and fired several shots at two other settees, but this time the quarry 'got close in with the land in Xebea Bay', about 40 miles south of Valencia. Young now turned south down the coast and, on 29 June, 'observed 10 sail of French line of battle ships lying in Carthagena Road'. Lord Keith, back from his fruitless search off Genoa, had no idea that Bruix had left Toulon and linked up with the Spanish. In fact, though Young could not know it, the ships he had seen were only a rearguard, Bruix having left for the Straits on 24 July.[7]

Young's duty was clear. Wasting not a moment, *Ethalion* 'haul'd our wind and stood off' to join Lord Keith at Mahon. Progress was frustratingly slow, however, and it was not until 10 July that the fleet, now numbering thirty-one sail of the line along with their accompanying frigates, was under way back to the Straits. When they arrived at Gibraltar on 29 July, they were greeted with the news that the combined fleet of fifty sail, including forty battleships, had passed through a full three weeks earlier.[8] Hours later the fleet was back at sea, heading into the Atlantic in pursuit. Quilliam had been in the Mediterranean for barely two months and would not return for another four years.

It didn't take long for Keith to establish that the combined fleet was not in Cadiz but, though he didn't yet know it, he was just a week behind and closing. Twelve days later and 80 miles west of Ushant, he ordered *Ethalion* and two ex-French 74s, *Impétueux* and *Pompée*, to look into Brest. They confirmed the presence of forty French and Spanish battleships, which had arrived only the previous day.[9] Though relieved that the combined fleet was not loose in the western approaches, Keith had failed by just one day to bring it to battle.

Ten days later *Ethalion* arrived back in Plymouth, having sailed some 5,000 miles and spent only two days at anchor since leaving three and a half months earlier. She stayed less than three weeks, repairing wear and tear and replenishing water and stores, before sailing on 13 September to re-join Lord Bridport and the fleet off Brest. Days later she was sent south and on the 25th fell in with another frigate, the 32-gun *Triton*, 10 miles north-east of Cape Ortegal.[10] The two frigates worked closely together over the next three weeks, patrolling the north-west coast of Spain and keeping watch for any Spanish ships that might have slipped out of Brest. On the afternoon of 16 October, however, *Ethalion* was on her own when, as Young reported in his subsequent letter to Lord Bridport, 'We discovered three large Sail on the Weather Bow, evidently Men of War, steering S. E. with all Sails set.' When the sternmost of the three made the private signal, he realised that the other two were enemy frigates and 'made all possible sail in Chace'. By daylight, the British frigate, now revealed as *Naiad*, had been joined by another, *Alcmene*. William Pierrepoint, *Naiad*'s captain and the senior officer, ordered *Ethalion* to pass the nearer enemy ship, which she did, firing upon her as she went. Then, at 11.30, she came up with the leader and after 'a well-directed Fire of Two Broadsides from the Ethalion, and a running Fight of an Hour, exchanging Bow and Stern Chaces ... I had the Pleasure of seeing her haul down Spanish Colours to His Majesty's Ship under my Command.'[11]

She proved to be no ordinary prize. The 36-gun *Thetis* was homeward-bound from Vera Cruz in Mexico with a cargo of 'One Million Four Hundred and Eleven Thousand Five Hundred and Twenty-six Dollars, and a Quantity of Cocoa'. Young finished his letter by commending his first lieutenant, Lieutenant Pym, for 'the able Assistance I received from him on the Quarter-Deck' and 'Lieutenant Jauncey and Quilliam, for their great Attention to the guns on the Main-Deck'.

Five days later *Ethalion* shepherded her prize into Plymouth Sound. However, because the chase had taken the other frigates out of sight, it was not until twenty-four hours later that the full scale of their achievement became apparent when *Naiad*, *Alcmene* and *Triton* brought in the other Spaniard, *Santa Brigida*. She, as Pierrepoint related in his own despatch, proved to be, like *Thetis,* 'of immense Value, having on board One Million Four Hundred Thousand Dollars, independent of a Cargo of equal Estimation'.[12]

The arrival of the two prizes was a sensation. The silver and gold totalled not less than 2,785,290 dollars, worth £626,691 or some £51 million in 2018 purchasing power, and weighing about 85 tons. Simply unloading it took the rest of the month, with a huge procession of soldiers, sailors and marching bands accompanying the sixty-three artillery wagons required to convey 'the treasures to the dungeons of the citadel of Plymouth'.[13] Later in the month the bullion was transferred by wagon to London for safe keeping at the Bank of England, where it made a critical contribution to national liquidity. The Spanish dollars were reissued with George III's head stamped symbolically on the neck of Carlos IV to make them legal tender, 'the head of a Fool on the neck of an Ass', as a contemporary wit had it.

10

Shipwreck

Service in frigates on blockade was the supreme test of officers and men and especially of captains and first lieutenants. Only the most able, confident and resourceful could meet the challenge and Quilliam's early career was rich in the frigate experience a patron would advise.

Ethalion returned to sea under her third captain in less than a year, James Young having been superseded by John Clarke Searle. Made post-captain in 1796, he had most recently been captain of Sir Hugh Christian's flagship, *Tremendous*.[1] No log has survived covering the last few weeks of Quilliam's time on *Ethalion* but we know from the logs of other ships that by 15 December 1799 she was three leagues south-west of Ushant in company with two other frigates, *Fisgard* and *Clyde*, both commanded by experienced and able captains, and the sloop *Sylph*.[2] That same day the squadron 'had looked into the outer road of Brest, and then appeared ready for sea near fifty sail of all descriptions'.[3]

The combined French and Spanish fleet had been blockaded in Brest ever since the previous August and the frigates' task was to cut off any seaborne supplies and watch out for any sign that they were ready to move. This was no easy assignment. Small coasters hugged the shore, while to 'look into Brest' a frigate had to get close enough to see into the road and the inner harbour. The approach lies up a progressively narrowing passage between, on the north side, the Pointe de Sainte Mathieu, to the English simply St Matthews, and on the south the Pointe de Toulinguet. Further out, on the north-side islands, shoals and rocks stretch out eventually to Ushant, while to the south are more shoals and rocks known as the Chaussèe de Sein or, to the English, the Saints.

By 18 December *Fisgard, Ethalion* and *Sylph* had parted company with *Clyde* and had been 'driven off the coast by a hard gale of wind'.[4] When the weather had moderated, it was vital that they get back to

Brest since it was in just these conditions that the French would be most likely to break out. *Fisgard*'s Thomas Byam Martin, the senior of the two captains, signalled Searle to separate so that 'by one ship standing to the northward and the other to the southward ... one of us should regain the station'.[5]

What happened next would illustrate the risks inherent in the close inshore work on which depended Britain's command of the sea and hence her ability to defend her trade and counter the threat of invasion. By 4pm on Christmas Eve, *Ethalion* was a few miles to the south-west of St Matthews but, with little daylight left, Searle decided to continue 'standing off and on, off St Matthews, with an intention of beating to windward in the morning, to reconnoitre the position of the enemy's fleet'. Despite having only St Matthews' light to guide them, both Searle and the pilot were confident that by keeping it in sight, they would keep clear of the southern edge of the channel.[6] Quilliam took over the watch from the second lieutenant, Henry Jauncey, at midnight and at 1.30am the pilot asked him to wear and head southward away from the light as 'there was room to stand on 'till daylight if there was no more wind'.

A little more than an hour and a half later, when 'the ship had not gone more than two miles from the time of her being wore', Quilliam, now in sole charge, went forward to check the lookouts. He'd hardly taken a step when one of them sang out that he could see rocks ahead. Quilliam rushed forward and saw the rocks 'not a cable length ahead upon the weather bow'. Hardly able to believe his eyes, he 'sent for the captain & pilot' while doing 'everything in my power to wear the ship as quick as possible. In wearing I saw a rock close under the lee bow. I ordered the helm starboard; haul'd down the head sails and ordered an anchor to be let go, but ... the ship struck.'

Despite the ship's hopeless situation, all the officers and men fought desperately to save her, but it was less than an hour before she began to break up. By 4am, Searle later recalled, she 'knocked away the stern post' and he 'Made signals of distress to the Sylph'. In fact, *Sylph* wasn't the only friendly ship nearby, daylight also revealing *Danae*, a 20-gun post-ship, and the cutter *Nimrod*.[7] Searle 'sent away the idlers, and first division of seamen' and by 11am had 'got all the people out of the ship'. He then ordered the first lieutenant to 'set fire to her remains' and a master's mate to 'cut away her lower masts.' Finally, 'after I had seen all the commissioned officers and master into the remaining boat, I was then under the painful necessity of abandoning her'.

Astonishingly, not a single man had been lost or even injured and the whole ship's company was transferred to *Fisgard* next day. Rumours of the disaster had already reached Plymouth when she arrived on 4 January 1800, another cutter, *Swift*, having already reported finding 'between the Saints and Penmarks ... several pieces of floating wreck; one piece of a gun carriage marked Ethalion ... and a writing desk'.[8]

Just six days later, on 10 January, a court martial assembled on board the Plymouth guard ship *Cambridge* 'to enquire into the cause and circumstances of the loss of His Majesty's late ship Ethalion, and to try Captain John Clarke Searle, the officers and company of the said ship for their conduct on that occasion'. Sitting with Admiral Cuthbert Collingwood were twelve captains, one of them Searle's predecessor but one, George Countess. It must have been a considerable ordeal for Quilliam who, as officer of the watch when the accident occurred, was the first witness. Searle, however, mounted a spirited defence, arguing that 'the shortness of the days at this season of the year makes it utterly impossible for any ship to reconnoitre the enemy's fleet in Brest, unless she keeps off St. Matthew's during the night' and calling in support his two fellow captains, Cunningham of *Clyde* and *Fisgard*'s Martin. The proceedings were soon over and the court, made up of captains who could well imagine themselves in a similar situation, wasted little time in reaching the conclusion that 'the conduct of the Captain, officers and ship's company on this occasion was highly praiseworthy' and 'doth therefore acquit Captain John Clarke Searle, his officers and ship's company'.[9]

If that was a relief for Captain Searle, for the majority of his late ship's company the really good news came four days later when the prize money for *Thetis* and *Santa Brigida* was paid. At £652,000, the total sum was one of the largest ever paid out for a single event. Captains Gore, Digby, Pierrepoint and Young each received some £41,000[10, 11] or £2.7 million in modern purchasing power while, at the other end of the scale, each seaman received about £180, sufficient, as one historian put it, to 'set himself up with a cosy pub'.[12, 13] Not all husbanded their windfall so carefully, however. Sailors were reported walking the streets of Portsmouth with 'bank notes stuck in their hats, buying watches for the fun of frying them' while in Plymouth 'a seaman of the Ethalion ... drank so much liquor, that he fell, fractured his skull, and died instantly'.[14]

As a lieutenant, Quilliam's personal share was £5,090[15] or some £340,000 in modern purchasing power. Put simply, the twenty-eight-year-old who, fourteen years earlier, had joined the Royal Dockyard as a ship keeper, was seriously rich. However, the events of Christmas Day had taken their toll and he wrote almost immediately to the Admiralty explaining that 'from the late fatigues of Service which I have experienced as Third Lieutenant of His Majesty's Ship Ethalion I feel myself much indisposed' and requesting that he be 'indulged with three weeks leave of absence from my duty'.[16]

In fact, it was not until 14 March that he joined his next ship and there is some reason for believing that he spent the intervening eight weeks returning to the Isle of Man for the first time since he joined *Lion* eight years earlier, and quite possibly since he started in the dockyard in 1785. What is certain is that by April 1800 he had already invested part of his prize money in two properties on the Island, immediately adjacent to his birthplace at Ballakelly.[17] It may be that he made further financial arrangements at that time because, over the next few months, his father invested substantial funds as mortgages that he later 'bought over'. It is significant that, when Quilliam, like so many contemporary naval officers, invested the fruits of success in a domestic economic base, he chose to do so on the Island. While he served in the British Navy, he remained first and foremost a Manxman. Meanwhile, with his affairs in order and his health restored, he was ready to join HMS *Amazon*, riding at her moorings at Spithead.

11

HMS *Amazon*

Amazon, one of only two ships in her eponymous class, was, like *Ethalion*, a 38-gun frigate.[1] These large and highly regarded fleet and cruising warships were prime appointments for any captain or lieutenant. When Quilliam joined her in March 1800, she was less than a year old. With a design complement of 284, she was armed with twenty-eight 18pdr cannon on her upper deck, two 9pdrs and twelve 32pdr carronades on her quarterdeck and two 9pdrs and another two 32pdr carronades on the foc'sle. In command since her commissioning had been Captain Edward Riou.

Ten years older than Quilliam, Riou had gone as a midshipman on Cook's last voyage to the South Seas and served as a lieutenant in the West Indies during the American War. He achieved some fame when, in 1789, *Guardian*, which he commanded, struck an iceberg twelve days out from the Cape of Good Hope while carrying stores and convicts to Botany Bay.[2] Riou allowed the 260 of those on board who wished to take to the boats to do so, while he and sixty others, after 1,200 miles and nine weeks and with the decks awash, beached the ship back at the Cape. Of those who had left her, just fifteen survived.[3] Made post-captain in 1791, Riou's most recent command had been the 40-gun *Beaulieu*, from which he had been invalided, only recovering his health in time to take over *Amazon*.[4]

Riou was a complex character with strong religious beliefs, on the one hand compassionate enough to solicit pardons for the convicts who stayed with him on *Guardian*,[5] on the other 'a strict disciplinarian with a fanatical regard for cleanliness'.[6] At a time when, in theory, the maximum number of lashes allowed without a court martial was twelve, in the twelve months after Quilliam joined *Amazon*, thirty-six lashes were administered on no fewer than nine occasions and twenty-four a further fourteen times.

Riou certainly believed in working his ships, officers and men hard. That may be why in the first eleven months of the commission he got through no less than six lieutenants and by the end of March 1800 had none at all. Nevertheless, of the three who took up their appointments within days of each other in April 1800, one remained until promoted more than a year later, a second for a full two years and Quilliam until the ship was paid off in August 1802. Riou may have been a hard taskmaster but he'd already shown the ship's company that he was brave, skilful and, perhaps most important to them, lucky.

In fact, *Amazon* does not seem to have been the Admiralty's first choice for Quilliam after the loss of *Ethalion*. A surviving unsigned memo reveals that his original commission was to *Neptune,* the ship on which he had served briefly before joining *Chapman* in 1798.[7] Since *Neptune* was Sir Erasmus Gower's last command before his promotion to rear admiral,[8] it is not too fanciful to see his invisible hand at work on Quilliam's behalf once more. However, Quilliam was already a frigate officer and a good one, too good to be wasted in a line of battle ship at this stage of the war, while Riou, an officer of great promise, needed a good frigate lieutenant.

Unusually, *Amazon*'s muster book gives each of the new lieutenants' seniority and reveals that Riou appointed them in that order: Joseph Ore Masefield as first lieutenant, Quilliam as second and David Johnston as third.[9] *Amazon* was then lying at Spithead repairing damage suffered returning from Ireland the previous month; it was a further six weeks before she was ordered to sea. In the meantime, Riou 'exercised people at reefing topsails' and developed their gunnery, being granted 'leave to exercise and fire at a mark' and recording in detail how much powder his 32pdr carronades required as they heated up with repeated firing.[10]

Riou's immediate role was the defence of trade, taking charge of the escort for a large West Indies convoy. In addition to *Amazon*, the escort would comprise two other frigates, two gun brigs, a sloop and a cutter. They finally got away with '121 trading merchant vessels in company' on 26 April 1800 and, having been forced by a shift in the wind to shelter in Torbay for five days, by 19 May were off Madeira. That escort duty was no formality was indicated by Riou's subsequent report that 'two french cruizers kept hovering about the fleet for two or three days which determined me to chace the largest entirely out of the fleet, and we should have taken her in two hours had we continued the chace with the risque of parting company with the fleet'.[11] Instead, after a classic convoy defence operation, an object lesson for Quilliam, he had to be content with the thought of possible prizes on the return journey.

On 26 May, with Funchal 500 miles astern, *Amazon* 'made signal that an opportunity offered for sending letters into port' and the following afternoon parted company with the convoy and the rest of the escort. More than two weeks elapsed before they saw another sail but on 25 June, 370 miles south-west of Cape Finisterre, a lookout reported 'a strange sail to windward coming down before the wind'. *Amazon* 'set all possible sail and chased' and three hours later was 'coming up with the chace, a brig which had hoisted a Danish flag at her main topgallant mast head'. That the Danish flag was a ruse seemed to be confirmed when 'at 1.00pm ... she bore up about 4 points and set studding sails'. Riou 'Beat to quarters and at about 2 o'clock began to fire at the chace'. By now the brig's captain and crew knew the game was up. Facing certain destruction from the frigate's overwhelming fire power, 'at about half past 2.00, our shot nearly reaching her, she hoisted French national colours and hauled them down again immediately and brought too'. She proved to be *La Julie,* 'a letter of marque belonging to Bordeaux from which place she sailed last Tuesday in company with a brig privateer bound on a cruise and two other letters of marque ... She had 8 guns part of which she had thrown overboard. Had 220 men and was 260 tons.'[12]

Realising that there was a real chance of a further success, Riou wasted no time in taking out the prisoners and sending a prize crew on board before he 'stood to the Eastward for the night, for the better chance of falling in with the consorts of our prize'. His luck was in. Although dawn revealed an entirely empty horizon, the lookouts 'at 4.00pm saw a strange sail on the lee bow'. *Amazon* immediately 'made sail and chaced' and, after just three hours, had 'gained upon the chace and coming up very fast and being within gun shot we fired the chace guns at her till we came very near when she hoisted English colours union downwards[13] and hauled them down again'. This latest success turned out to be the British merchantman *Amelia,* bound from Savannah to London with cotton, rice and deer hides. She had been taken a week earlier by *Minerve,* another French privateer from Bordeaux. Again Riou 'Took the prisoners out of her and sent an officer and a party of seamen to navigate her'. Such recaptures were a vital element of trade defence, reducing losses and hence insurance rates while detaining prime enemy seamen for the duration. With her speed limited by the prizes, it was almost two weeks later that *Amazon* brought them into Plymouth Sound.[14]

Increasing tension with Russia and the Baltic states, prompted in particular by Britain's assertion of her right to search all neutral ships, coupled with signs that France, under newly self-appointed First Consul Napoleon Bonaparte, was planning an invasion of Britain, shifted the naval spotlight to the North Sea. Riou, a rising star, was ordered to the area of maximum danger. In early August *Amazon* joined three other frigates, *Pomone*, *Prevoyante* and *Terpsichore*, and the lugger *Nile* off Ostend. By 9 August they were at anchor in the 'Denloo[15] Passage' at the outer end of the River Scheldt, the obvious starting point for an invasion. 'From the mast head three French frigates were seen lying at anchor as well as the new Dutch 64-gun ship that has been recently launched.' They spent the rest of August and the first half of September patrolling the Dutch and Belgian coasts while Riou continued to train *Amazon*'s gunnery teams.

When *Pomone* parted company on 15 September, Riou took command of the squadron, 'at sunset standing in to examine the ships at Flushing; found them as before'. However, he was soon reminded just how inhospitable the North Sea could be as the squadron was driven off the coast by strong gales and squalls. By daylight on 21 September *Amazon* had 'no land in sight nor one of the squadron' and was 50 miles north-west of the Texel. Making their way southward again two days later, they 'saw the yards or boom of some small vessel close under the lee bow floating ... the remains of the yards and masts and rigging of some small sloop or cutter rigged vessel foundered at the spot'.

By 22 December 1800 *Amazon* was at anchor in Yarmouth roads but in the interim the strategic situation had taken a further turn for the worse. Austria's defeat at Hohenlinden left Britain the only state at war with France. This strengthened Tsar Paul's determination to end her claimed right to stop and search neutrals, creating a 'League of Armed Neutrality' linking Denmark-Norway, Prussia, Sweden and Russia. The League's implicit threat to deny Britain access to the Baltic and its vital naval stores was interpreted in London as not so much a declaration of neutrality as an act of war.[16] Submitting to the Tsar's demands would cripple the Royal Navy and lose the war, so a fleet was to be quickly assembled to uphold the belligerent right of search. Newly arrived at Yarmouth were *Pomone* and three battleships, *Raisonable*, *Ardent* and *Polyphemus*. Experienced observers might have noted that the shallower draft 64s were eminently suited to operating in the Baltic's restricted and shoal waters. The focus was moving inexorably north, allegedly prompting Riou to go ashore to make arrangements for the Danish members of his crew not to have to fire on their fellow countrymen.[17]

In command at Yarmouth was Vice Admiral Archibald Dickson, who had led a naval diplomatic mission to Copenhagen the previous August and now had the task of assembling a larger fleet for a rather less diplomatic return visit. By the middle of January 1801, Admiral Sir Hyde Parker had been appointed commander-in-chief, while Vice Admiral Lord Nelson was named second-in-command.[18] Parker's role was to talk; Nelson's to fight if talks failed.

Amazon remained at Yarmouth until the end of January, caulkers working on her decks while the ship's company set up the rigging and stowed the holds. Riou, maintaining his professional focus, 'exercised great guns and small arms and fired at a mark' as well as firing two royal salutes, the one on New Year's Day 'to celebrate the union with Ireland'.[19] Then, on 26 January, she headed back to the Texel.

As the build-up continued at Yarmouth, Britain swept the North Sea clear of Danish merchantmen. *Amazon* soon had 'several sail in sight' as smaller British men-of-war hunted down the Danes while *Amazon* herself on 31 January 'fired two shot and brought to a Danish brig from Norway bound to London. Detained her and sent an Officer and 10 men to take charge.' Hours later a 'Danish barque from Norway to Ireland' received the same treatment, as did 'a Danish brig from Norway to Ostend'. By 7 February she was at anchor in the Humber, having sent the Danish detainees into Hull, while Riou 'exercised great guns and fired shot at a mark' in four live fire exercises in just ten days. Tuned to concert pitch, on the morning of 19 February they 'made sail out of the Humber' and twenty-four hours later 'came to in Yarmouth Roads'.

By then the squadron assembled by Dickson, newly promoted to full admiral, only lacked its commander-in-chief and his deputy. *Amazon* replenished her stores 'to complete to 5 months' and on the morning of 4 March was ordered to sea to patrol off the anchorage. Two days later a lookout reported 'a sail in the SW quarter supposed to be a ship of war' that failed to answer the private signal. *Amazon* 'Cleared for quarters and stood towards her', only to discover that she was 'His Majesty's ship *St George* with Vice Admiral Nelson's flag aboard'. That same afternoon the two ships again 'moored in Yarmouth roads'.[20]

Nelson, acutely aware that the extended build-up at Yarmouth had given the Danes ample warning of British intentions, was outraged to discover that his superior's startlingly young new wife was organising a ball for the following Friday, a full six days hence.[21] He immediately wrote to two friends, newly appointed to the Admiralty, his old boss Earl St Vincent and Sir Thomas Troubridge. To the former he hinted that 'Our friend here is a little nervous about dark nights and fields of ice',[22] while asking the latter to 'Consider how nice it must be laying in bed with a young wife, compared with a damned cold raw wind'.[23] The effect was instant. Lady Parker's ball was cancelled and on the morning of 12 March *Amazon* 'At 7 made all sail ... in company with the fleet under the command of Admiral Sir Hyde Parker'. Rather more mundanely, 'At 8 fell overboard John McNally seaman; hove to and sent the boats and saved him.'

The entire fleet of fifty-three sail, including fifteen line-of-battle ships, now headed up the North Sea with *Amazon* scouting ahead. By 19 March they were at anchor off the Scaw, the northernmost point of the Jutland peninsular, and the following morning *Amazon*, on a classic frigate scouting and intelligence gathering mission, 'made sail ahead of the fleet' down the Kattegat. Later the same day she anchored off The Koll, the headland on the Swedish shore marking the entrance to the Sound or Øresund, the narrow passage into the Baltic between the island of Zealand and Copenhagen itself to the west and the Swedish mainland to the east. Three days later the fleet joined her.

While the British lay at anchor and the Danes worked on their defences, Hyde Parker tried to make up his mind what to do next. Should he attempt the passage of the Sound, risking bombardment from both shores, or take the longer but less exposed route through the Great Belt to the west of Zealand? Should he even attack Copenhagen at all or, as Nelson had originally suggested, bypass it and directly confront the Russians? His Captain of the Fleet, the Baltic expert William Domett, favoured the Great Belt, his Flag Captain, Robert Otway, the Sound. Nelson didn't mind which way they went as long as they did something. With time slipping away, however, his preference now was for an immediate descent on Copenhagen by the shortest possible route.[24]

For *Amazon*, the first indication that Nelson had won the argument came on 27 March when 'at daylight Vice Admiral Lord Nelson shifted his flag from the St George to the Elephant', the move to the shallower-draft 74 clearly indicating that Copenhagen was the objective. However, it was not until the morning of 30 March that *Amazon* 'weigh'd with the fleet' and 'at 6 bore up in line of battle and enter'd the Sound'. With the commander of Kronborg Castle having already made clear his intention of denying the British safe passage, all now depended on his Swedish opposite number at Helsingborg. It soon became clear Swedish commitment to the League was lukewarm: the fleet hugged the Swedish shore, well out of range of the Danish artillery, without provoking any response at all from the Swedes. Half an hour later they had 'passed Cronenberg Castle which commenced a heavy fire upon the fleet but without the least effect' and by midday the fleet was 'anchored off Copenhagen with the town bearing SWbS about 5 miles'.[25] Act One of the drama had been something of an anticlimax; the remaining acts would be anything but.

12

Copenhagen

Standing at the widest part of the Sound, Copenhagen was a walled city surrounding an inner harbour in which lay the entire Danish seagoing navy. In front of the ramparts extended drying mudflats, beyond which, across the half-mile-wide King's or, to the English, Gasper Channel, lay the huge Middle Ground Shoal. The normal approach to the city from the north was via the King's Deep to the north-west of the Middle Ground, while ships heading for the Baltic would pass to the east through the Outer Deep, bounded on its eastern side by the Saltholm flats.

While the British fleet lay at anchor, *Amazon*'s log recorded that, shortly after midday, 'came on board Vice Admiral Lord Nelson'.[1] With the ship's company at battle stations, she then 'fill'd and stood near the inner roads of Copenhagen to reconnoitre the enemy's force'. It was no accident that *Amazon* had been chosen for this tactical reconnaissance. Nelson recognised Riou's expertise and always put his trust in such men.

Having 'at 1.30 anchored in 7 fms', *Amazon* remained under the enemy guns for more than four hours as 'the enemy fired a number of shot at us, but without effect'. Finally, she 'at 5.15 weighed and made sail to windward' and two hours later anchored back with the fleet. By then Nelson had gained a detailed picture of the Danish defences, and worked out how to unlock them.

The Danes had taken full advantage of the time they'd been granted. The linchpin of their defences, the massive Trekroner or Three Crowns battery, mounted sixty-eight guns on mudflats south of the inner harbour entrance. Two ships of the line, a large frigate and two gun brigs were moored in the entrance itself, with a line of twelve floating batteries stretching southwards.[2] Before the seagoing fleet or the city could be attacked, these batteries had to be suppressed so that bomb ships could anchor and lob their shells into the inner harbour. However, Nelson had spotted that, while the Trekroner battery barred access via the King's Deep, the much weaker battery covering the southern entrance to the Gasper Channel provided little threat to ships approaching from the south. A fleet taking that route could in theory silence each of the floating batteries in turn before bringing all its firepower to bear on the Trekroner battery. Now he had to persuade Hyde Parker to let him have the ten battleships he needed to do the job.

Next morning both he and Hyde Parker were aboard when *Amazon* 'at 6 weigh'd and stood in again to reconnoitre the enemy'. By early afternoon Nelson had convinced his chief that the plan could work and Hyde Parker had promised him twelve rather than the ten battleships he had asked for. The following day Nelson put his faith in Riou's pilotage skills as *Amazon*, with some of the smaller vessels, surveyed and buoyed the channel: later the same afternoon she 'led the Van division under the command of Vice Admiral Lord Nelson, thro' the Outer Deep; at 6 anchor'd off the Gasper channel in 7 fathoms … The enemy threw 3 shells which fell between the ships of the fleet.'

Nelson's plan, when the wind allowed, was for the battleships to advance up the Gasper Channel in line ahead, each anchoring opposite its designated opponent, the remainder passing outside to anchor ahead.[3] Meanwhile, Hyde Parker would remain at the original fleet anchorage with the two 98-gun three deckers, *London* and *St George,* and the remaining 74s and 64s. As soon as the action began, they would start to work their way down to the northern entrance to the Gasper Channel to engage the Trekroner battery and the ships at the harbour entrance.[4]

In a battle at sea, the frigates kept well clear, but in the restricted waters of the Gasper Channel not only was this not possible, but their extra fire power would prove invaluable. Nelson gave 'the Gallant & good Capt. Rieu' command of the three frigates, together with the other smaller craft, with instructions to 'assist in the attack of the ships at the harbour's mouth' and 'perform such service as he is directed by Lord Nelson'.[5]

Thursday, 2 April 1801 dawned 'moderate and cloudy' with the wind set fair for the passage up the Gasper Channel. In *Elephant* Nelson was joined by all the captains, including Riou, for a final meeting[6] and 'at 10 the signal was made to weigh in succession and engage the enemy closely; the fleet weighed in succession and ran up the Gasper channel in line of battle.' Half an hour after the leading ships had got under way, *Amazon* herself 'weigh'd and hove too' and then 'bore up and pass'd the enemy's line of floating batteries, firing on them when opportunity offer'd'. Quilliam, as second lieutenant, would almost certainly have been in charge of a section of the larboard or port-side guns, controlling their fire as they came to bear on each of the enemy batteries in turn.

Unfortunately, no sooner had the division started to get under way than *Agamemnon*, whose orders were to anchor opposite the very first ship in the Danish line, ran aground and took no further part in the action.[7] As a result, when *Amazon* approached the Danish line, the battleship she was following, *Polyphemus*, pulled across and anchored in *Agamemnon*'s place and Riou closed up on the next ship in the column, Rear Admiral Graves' *Defiance*. With two other battleships aground, their places filled each time by the next ship in the line, the consequence for the three frigates only became apparent as they reached the top of the line and 'at 10 mins past 11 let go our anchor by the stern right ahead of the Defiance Rear Adml Graves and commenced our fire upon the enemy'. By filling the vacant positions at the end of the British line, *Amazon*, *Blanche* and *Alcmene* were looking straight down the barrels not only of 64 guns on a pair of Danish battleships but also of more than 80 guns on the Trekroner and associated batteries, many firing red hot shot. The three frigates kept up the unequal contest for an astonishing hour and a half before, at 'about 40 minutes past 12 the *Alcmene* made the signal 39, cut the cable and stood off. She was soon followed by the *Blanche*'.[8]

Signal 39, the message to discontinue the action, could be seen 'flying on board the London', placing Riou in a dilemma. Not only was his natural instinct to remain where he was, but obeying the order would involve making a sharp turn to starboard and giving every one of the Danish guns the opportunity to pour in shot, which would smash through *Amazon* from stern to stem. With *Elephant* completely obscured by smoke and no sign of Rear Admiral Graves repeating the signal on *Defiance*, Riou decided to stay put. So did Nelson, famously making a joke of his blind eye. However, when Graves repeated Parker's signal thirty-five minutes later, Riou had no option and, with the comment 'What will Nelson think of us?,'[9] 'cut the cable and stood off'. Moments later, with the cry, 'Come, then, my boys, let us all die together!,'[10] 'at 1.18 Captn Riou was kill'd by a shot from the enemy.'[11] Riou had given Quilliam and his other officers a masterclass in leadership, skill, composure and resolve. It would not be wasted.

Some later accounts claim Quilliam took command and brought the ship out of the action. This is unlikely since there is no record of Masefield, the first lieutenant, being injured, although plenty of others had been:

'Number kill'd 14 of which 1 a marine and 13 seamen; wounded 23 of which 5 marines and 18 seamen.' What we do know is that she 'at 2.10 anchored in 7 fathms, Copenhagen town SW about 7 miles' and 'At 2.30 observ'd a Danish flag of truce going off to the Elephant when the fire ceased.'[12] Meanwhile, Quilliam, as soon as the ship turned away and his guns could no longer be brought to bear, was almost certainly drawing on all his experience to get the ship back into some kind of order. There was plenty to do: 'Damage – main & mizzen masts with the bowsprit wounded, one of the carronades dismounted, a number of the lower shrouds and running rigging cut and shot away.'

The pressure to get the ship ready for action again was intense. While Nelson negotiated under the flag of truce, he faced not only the threat posed by the still undamaged Danish seagoing fleet but also both the Swedish fleet, rumoured to be at sea, and, somewhere over the horizon, potentially the Russians.[13] All night and into the following morning, *Amazon*'s crew were 'employed refitting the damages, the flag of truce flying on board the London', pausing only while they 'committed the body of Capn Riou to the deep with the usual ceremony'.

According to legend, that morning also saw the first encounter between Quilliam and Nelson when the latter 'came on board and enquired who was in charge ... a voice, that of Quilliam, ascended from the main deck, "I am" and on the further question "How are you getting on below?" the answer to the unknown inquisitor was "middlin". This greatly amused Nelson who so appreciated Quilliam's coolness that he took an early opportunity of getting him on his own ship the 'Victory' of which he was appointed First Lieutenant.'[14] There are so many aspects of this story that are either wrong or are extremely unlikely that it is tempting to dismiss it entirely. First, it is based on a repeated incorrect assertion that 'All Quilliam's superior officers were killed, so that he was left in command'; second it is alleged to have taken place at a time when Nelson is known to have been ashore negotiating an extension of the ceasefire; and third it records the incident as Quilliam's first encounter with the admiral, when that had almost certainly taken place five days earlier. However, the implication that 'middlin' was a favourite expression of Quilliam's is plausible; it is still used widely on the Isle of Man and his usage of it might well have been reinforced during his time in the dockyard, where it was used officially, for example in the term 'a middling repair'. That he on more than one occasion over the next four years responded to a Nelsonian enquiry with 'middlin' thus seems more than likely.

For Quilliam, however, the most significant development came the following morning when 'came on board Sam'l Sutton Esq and took command of the ship'.[15] Sam Sutton had commanded *Alcmene*, anchored alongside *Amazon* off the Trekroner battery on 2 April. He had served in the West Indies in the American War and was made post-captain in 1797. Prior to joining *Alcmene* less than three weeks before she sailed for Copenhagen, he had been flag captain to two admirals, Sir Richard Onslow in *Monarch* and Sir Charles Cotton in *Prince*.[16] Though a couple of years older than his predecessor, he seems to have been cut from the same cloth, imposing firm discipline while gaining the respect and even the affection of officers and foremast hands alike. He would provide a second model for Quilliam in succession to Riou.

Despite the heavy damage sustained in the battle, by six that evening and little more than forty-eight hours since *Amazon* stood off from the Three Crowns, she 'at sunset made the signal that the ship was again ready for service'. Nevertheless, four days later she still had 'carpenters repairing the shot holes' and, more than a week after that, 'making a new Mizen T Gt mast'.

Nelson meanwhile had been able to agree a fourteen-week armistice, the suspension of Denmark's membership of the League of Armed Neutrality and freedom for the British fleet to obtain supplies and water, the agreement being confirmed when 'the flag of truce was hauled down on board the Admiral'. With the Danes thus neutralised, Hyde Parker could move against the Russians but before he could do so he received the news that the Tsar had been assassinated. The fleet was therefore back at anchor in Kioge Bay south of Copenhagen on 25 April when *Amazon*'s first lieutenant, Joseph Masefield, received his promotion to commander. Quilliam's elevation to first lieutenant did not follow immediately and it was not until completion of the muster table for July and August 1801 that he signed as first lieutenant, with Lieutenant Johnston moving up to number two and George Walpole joining the ship as third lieutenant.[17]

While Quilliam supervised *Amazon*'s carpenters fitting 'a 74-gun ship's topmast for a new mizzen', dispatches arrived from England bringing Hyde Parker's recall and Nelson's appointment as his replacement.[18] The effect was dramatic. The next morning *Amazon* 'weighed per signal as did the fleet'. Having informed the Swedes that he would take immediate action against any Swedish fleet he might encounter, Nelson left a third of his force off the Swedish base at Karlskrona and hurried to confront the Russian fleet at Reval (modern-day Tallinn) in the Gulf of Finland.

However, Hyde Parker's prevarication had allowed the Russian fleet time to retreat to its main base in the massive fortress of Krondstadt. Nevertheless, Nelson's presence with eleven battleships proved effective. Days later the Russians and the Swedes raised the embargo on British ships in their ports; the Baltic crisis was effectively over.[19]

On the morning of 20 June, *Amazon,* by then cruising north of Zealand, 'saw a brig to leeward which proved to be the Kite with Vice Adml Lord Nelson on board'. With the mission complete, Nelson was on his way home, leaving orders to chart the Great Belt, charts Quilliam would have need of a decade later. *Amazon* and the rest of the fleet had to wait another month before their recall to face an even greater crisis. France and Austria had signed the Treaty of Luneville on 9 February, bringing the European war to an end and allowing Napoleon to focus on Britain, concentrating his armies around the Channel ports for an invasion. By the time *Amazon* anchored at the Nore on 9 August, Nelson had been put in charge of coastal defence from Sussex to Suffolk and, with a vast assemblage of smaller shallow-draft craft, ordered to disrupt or destroy any invasion craft crossing the Channel.[20]

With frigates at a premium, *Amazon,* still bearing the scars from Copenhagen, was hastily refitted at Sheerness dockyard. Two weeks after arriving, new main and mizzen masts had been fitted and the ship had joined Nelson off Ostend. That she was ready for sea in such a short time was due in no small part to her newly confirmed first lieutenant and his deep understanding of dockyard practice, acquired in those early years at Portsmouth and once again turned to advantage.

The previous three weeks had been among the most challenging of Nelson's career. His attack on Boulogne had been repulsed with heavy losses, although it had exposed the futility of the French threat from that quarter. Instead the focus had shifted to the primary invasion hub at Flushing on the Scheldt, with a view to a further attack, although in Nelson's view there was 'some doubt whether if I was to order a boat expedition it would be obey'd'.[21, 22] In the event, by 27 August *Amazon* was back at the Downs and the following day 'Vice Adm'l Lord Viscount Nelson shifted his flag from the Medusa on board this ship',[23] *Medusa* having suffered heavy casualties in the earlier attack.

In what was almost certainly the most important period thus far in Quilliam's career, *Amazon* remained Nelson's flagship for the next eight weeks. It is doubtful if the admiral spent much time on board; both the Hamiltons and his brother William and family stayed at the Three

Kings Hotel in Deal for some of the time, during which he was finalising the purchase of Merton Place, the country property south of London where he planned to retire with Lady Hamilton.[24] Nevertheless, as first lieutenant, Quilliam would have had frequent contact with him in the frigate's relatively confined quarters.

By early September peace negotiations were well advanced, the invasion threat had diminished and Nelson had ordered 'all the River Barges & sailing vessels lately hired serving under my command to return to the Nore immediately'. Despite a preliminary armistice, the Treaty of London,[25] being made public at the beginning of October, *Amazon* and Nelson remained in the Downs for the best part of two months, making just two brief excursions, the second something of a farewell visit to the forces off Dungeness. The time was marred by the death of Nelson's protégé, Captain Edward Parker, from wounds received at the second attack on Boulogne. On Monday, 28 September, *Amazon* 'hoisted the colours half-mast and fired half minute guns' during the funeral at St George's church, Deal, where the memorial paid for by Nelson can still be seen. Finally, on 22 October, the day appointed for all hostilities to cease and the blockade to be lifted, Nelson handed over the command to Captain Sutton's namesake, Commodore Evelyn Sutton, and struck his flag the following morning.[26]

While Nelson headed for Merton, where he established a curious ménage à trois with the Hamiltons, *Amazon* remained 'thumping in the Downs'[27] from November 1801 right through until June 1802, at times carrying Commodore Sutton's pendant, at others Admiral Lutwidge's[28] flag and, for a month, both. By the end of April she was one of the few men-of-war left in the anchorage. However it was not until 7 June that Captain Sutton was ordered to 'cruize for the purpose of preventing the illegal Practice of running Brandy and other goods, as well as the exportation of wool' with another frigate, two sloops and two gun boats under his command.[29] The war was over but smuggling threatened the national revenues required to refill the war chest for the widely anticipated resumption of hostilities.

Amazon pursued her campaign against smugglers up and down the Essex and Suffolk coast for the next two months but by 1 August she was back 'moored at the Nore' and on the 3rd came to anchor at Greenhithe. Next day 'Came on board the Commissioner to pay the ship off.' Although many ships were being laid up, she was to receive a brief refit and be put back in commission. Sutton and his officers, in contrast to the many already on half pay, had been reappointed. However, Quilliam had been at sea almost continuously for over ten years. Peacetime revenue cruising was a tedious business that held few attractions after sailing to China, three major battles, a serious shipwreck and a rich haul of prizes. On 4 August 1802 Sutton forwarded his request for the 'Lords Commissioners of the Admiralty to put me on the half pay list and not to inforce my taking up the Commission their Lordships have been pleased to sign.' The dusty response that 'their Lordships will not be disposed to give Lieut. Quilliam any employment in future until every Lieut. desirous of employment has been provided for' didn't change his mind.[30] Further activity with his property investments suggests that, within days, he was on his way home to the Isle of Man. Aware of his own value, and with fresh patrons to replace Erasmus Gower, he could expect an early recall if war should come.

Captain Sutton was not far behind in making his own application to go on the half pay list but had to wait until the middle of November before he got his wish.[31] By then the treaty signed in Amiens the previous March was already beginning to unravel and it would be less than five months before Sutton and Quilliam were reunited on the quarterdeck of a man-of-war. This time, however, it would be the 100-gun battleship, HMS *Victory*.

13

Mediterranean

By early 1803, less than a year after the final Treaty of Amiens was signed, relations with France had deteriorated to such an extent that the British government shelved plans to reduce the size of the army and accelerated recruitment for the Navy. Then, on 22 March, in a move designed in part to deter Bonaparte, Nelson was named commander-in-chief in the Mediterranean, although the appointment was not officially confirmed until 6 May.[1] In the meantime, Nelson began to make preparations, writing to Captain George Murray, who had led the fleet into action at Copenhagen and whom he hoped to appoint as his Captain of the Fleet or chief of staff, that 'Sam. Sutton is to fit out the Victory for us, which I am very glad of, as she will be well fitted.'[2]

Along with Murray and Sutton, the third key officer Nelson intended to take to the Mediterranean was Thomas Masterman Hardy, most recently his flag captain in the Baltic. However, of the three only Sutton was immediately available in early April, Murray and Hardy both being at Portsmouth, respectively commanding the 74-gun battleship *Spartiate* and the 32-gun frigate *Amphion*. Sutton would therefore 'fit out the Victory for us' at Chatham, where she had just completed a major refurbishment, changing places with Hardy once he had brought her round to Portsmouth or *Victory* and *Amphion* had reached the Mediterranean.

Because *Victory* had been out of commission for more than five years, Nelson was able to select her other officers in consultation with Murray, Hardy and Sutton. Among the ten lieutenants he named as having been appointed in a letter he wrote on 10 April was 'Gwiliam 1st of the Amazon in which my flag was long hoisted',[3] although it seems likely that Quilliam had Sam Sutton as much as Nelson himself to thank for the appointment. Sutton, who would be doing the work, valued Quilliam's ability around an unfinished or damaged ship. Nevertheless Nelson, a master of detail with a keen appreciation of superior talent, had his own reasons for following Sutton's advice.

Quilliam's appointment to *Victory* was dated 4 April 1803.[4] However, he must have already been aware of it and in England before that because, as her muster book records, he and Lieutenants Pettit, Lackey, Bligh and Yule joined the ship on the Medway at Chatham on 9 April.[5] Pettit, the most senior on Nelson's list, assumed the position of first lieutenant and the first entry in Quilliam's own log recorded that, the same afternoon, 'At 1pm Lieut R Pettit put the ship in commission.'[6]

Victory was lying alongside the sheer hulk in the River Medway and, with no masts, no guns and little ballast, riding some 10 or 12ft higher in the water than normal.[7] Next morning the first 170 of her full complement of over 800 men came on board and, assisted by 'artificers from the dockyard ... got the lower masts in'. The following day Captain Sutton arrived and 'took the Command of His Majesty's Ship Victory'.[8] Over the next fortnight she was transformed from a floating hulk into a fully rigged man-of-war that, on the morning of 23 April 1803, 'cast off the moorings & made sail ... down the Medway'. An hour and a half later she 'came too with the best bower at Long Reach'.[9]

By now Nelson's list of lieutenants was almost complete and Captain Sutton allotted each his position and responsibilities. We know from the opening page of the muster table begun on 'the First Day of June 1803', that for the earlier period having been lost, that the eight lieutenants initially held their positions in strict order of seniority. As a result, after Pettit, the second lieutenant was Pasco, the third Yule and the fourth King. Quilliam, far from being the first lieutenant at this stage of the commission, is clearly designated on the June muster as fifth lieutenant, with the remaining three, Lackey, Layman and Bligh, respectively sixth, seventh and eighth.[10]

With Long Reach conveniently positioned halfway between the magazine at Upnor Castle and the gun wharf at Sheerness, *Victory* spent three weeks taking in provisions, water and other stores, as well as her guns, shot and powder. She also received drafts of men, although she 'cast off from the moorings & made sail down the Medway' on the afternoon of 14 May still well short of her full complement. Heaving to at the Nore while she 'discharged the Pilot & took in another for the Downes', by the afternoon of 16 May she had 'anchored wt the best bower at Spithead'.

Two days later, on the afternoon of Wednesday, 18 May, the day on which Britain formally declared war, *Victory* 'at 3.30 hoisted the Right Honble Ld Vct Nelson's flag at the fore and saluted with 17 guns which was answered with 13 guns from the Endymion'. Surprisingly, even at this late stage, it was still not certain that Nelson was to have *Victory*, despite him having sent his furniture and stores on board. Rather he had orders to offer her to Admiral Cornwallis, who had sailed from Cawsand Bay the previous day to blockade Brest. Nelson hoped Cornwallis would have no need of her.[11]

On Thursday morning, as Quilliam recorded, 'joined the ship Capt Geo Murray as Capt of the Fleet and Lieut Pearce as signals officer' and on the afternoon of Friday May 20th 1803 in 'Mod^{re} breezes w$^{t.}$ Rain' *Victory* 'at 2 unmoored ship at 4 weighed & made sail ye Amphion in co'. She would not see Spithead again for more than two years.

By the following Sunday afternoon, *Victory*, *Amphion* and a second frigate, *Sirius*, were a few miles off Ushant looking out for the fleet. However, having failed to locate Cornwallis by the Monday afternoon, Nelson decided to head south in *Amphion* without delay and leave Sutton to continue the search. That evening Quilliam's log recorded that *Victory* 'Shortd sail & hove too. At 7.40 out boats the Admiral shifted his flag to the Amphion. At 11 lost sight of the Admiral.'

In the event, and despite taking a French brig, 'the Tresconnel from Porte au Prince to Nantes', it took Sutton just a day and a half to find Cornwallis and on the morning of Wednesday, 25 May, *Victory* 'Joined the fleet Adm'l Cornwallis's flag on board the Dreadnought Capt went on board the Aml.' As Nelson had expected – he and Cornwallis had been friends for more than twenty years – two hours later Sutton returned to *Victory* which 'made sail parted the fleet'.

Victory headed out into Biscay and, with the uncertainties resolved, Sutton set about welding the ship's company into an efficient fighting unit as, on successive mornings, they 'exercised great guns & small arms'. The passage to Gibraltar proved remarkably profitable. Days after leaving the fleet, *Victory* took possession of 'the French Brig La Blonde from Cape Francois[12] to Bordeaux' and the next day overhauled and forced to strike 'the French National frigate Ambuscade'. This was a particularly satisfying encounter since the 32-gun frigate had been captured from the British in 1798 by the smaller French corvette *Bayonnaise*. Even then Sutton's luck had not run out. Two days later, on the morning of Monday, 30 May, *Victory* 'took possession of the French schooner L'Amicable Agatha from Martinique to Bordeaux with coffee and sugar'.

In contrast to *Amphion*, which reached Malta in just twenty-six days, *Victory* encountered head winds throughout the entire passage. Having stayed three days at Gibraltar 'receiving on board various provisions, stores from the dockyard & water', she 'came too with the best bower anchor in Villett'[13] on Friday, 8 July, almost three weeks after Nelson had left. Having spent two days 'employed watering & bringing on board Wine', she set off in pursuit and on Saturday, 30 July, some 30 miles south west of Cape Sicie,[14] 'At 6am saw the fleet bearing NW. At Noon joined Lord Nelson.'[15]

That was Samuel Sutton's last log entry as captain of the *Victory*. Quilliam's log records how, that afternoon, she 'Hoisted Vice Adml Lord Nelson's Flag & joined Capt G Murray Capt of the Fleet & Capt TM Hardy superceded Capt Sutton as Capt of the Victory & Capt Sutton to HMS Amphion. HM Ships Donegal, Renown, Belleisle, Gibraltar, Monmouth, Active, Amphion & Phoebe in company.[16] Emp'd getting on board Lord Nelson's baggage from the *Amphion*.'

Although his command covered the entire Mediterranean, Nelson's primary focus was Toulon, where the French commander-in-chief Vice Admiral La Touche-Tréville had seven battleships ready for sea, two under repair and another five building.[17] However, unlike Cornwallis, whose objective was to keep the French bottled up in Brest, Nelson's aim was to lure the French out and destroy them. Again unlike Cornwallis, he had no base within easy reach. Gibraltar lacked a secure anchorage, while Malta was so far distant that '… when I am forced to send a Ship there, I never see her under two months'.[18] The fleet would have to be maintained, refitted, watered and provisioned at sea until the French made their move.

For Quilliam, however, the most significant development came on Monday, 1 August 1803 when 'left the ship Lieut Robert Pettit being appointed to command of HM Sloop Termagent'. Pettit's departure left Pasco the senior lieutenant but Nelson appointed Quilliam as *Victory*'s new first lieutenant, although he was only fourth in seniority behind Pasco, Yule and King. Despite repeated protestations by Pasco to the contrary over the succeeding decades, it is clear that Nelson had no intention of appointing anyone else to the post. Writing to the Admiralty more than two years later, Hardy explained that, after Quilliam and Yule, 'Lieutenant Williams, King, Pasco and Bligh have served under Lord Nelson's flag from his first hoisting it in the year 1803 and I never was informed by him which of those deserving officers stood first on his list of promotion.'[19]

Nelson had his own ideas about promotion, based on his personal knowledge of the individual. He appointed Quilliam because he knew him well and because he valued his capabilities and experience. As Hardy made clear, there is no truth to the assertion, first made in Marshall's *Royal Naval Biography*, that all of the other lieutenants were 'before Mr. Quilliam on his Lordship's list of promotion'[20] or that he owed his appointment to 'Nelson's custom to delegate executive duties to the "most junior"' among the lieutenants.[21] Not only is there no evidence of that being his custom, but Quilliam was not the most junior. Hardy's letter also undermines any suggestion that Quilliam's elevation was connected with or dependent on Pasco's becoming Nelson's signals officer. That appointment occurred twelve days after Pettit's departure when Lieutenant Pearce, the then holder of the post, was discharged 'on promotion to command Halcyon brig sloop'.[22]

Quilliam was now the fourth most important man in *Victory* after Nelson, Murray and Hardy. As first lieutenant, he was responsible for every aspect of the efficient running of the ship and would have taken command if Hardy had become ill or been wounded or killed. Indeed, when Murray left the ship in August 1805 and Nelson chose not to appoint another Captain of the Fleet, Hardy took over much of that role, leaving Quilliam fulfilling many of the duties of captain. Nelson wanted a quiet, well-run and well-maintained ship, which Hardy and Quilliam delivered. However, the only direct impression that can be gained of Quilliam as first lieutenant is in his role as the ship's chief disciplinarian. From the punishment records, the fairest thing one can say is that, while he was strict, perhaps even by the standards of the time, he reserved the harshest penalties for offences that would endanger the ship or the crew. Thus he regarded persistent drunkenness as more serious than, for example, insolence or striking a boatswain's mate.[23]

With intelligence reports confirming large numbers of troops awaiting embarkation in Toulon, Nelson expected the French to put to sea sooner rather than later. Despite the approach of winter, therefore, he kept the fleet at sea, ready to intercept them. By mid-October they had experienced almost a month of gales, squalls and heavy rain, ideal conditions for the French to slip out of Toulon unobserved. Nelson feared they would either break out into the Atlantic, or descend on Italy or Egypt. On 15 October it seemed as if that nightmare had come true. He received a report that a ship 'had seen, a few days before, twelve Sail of Ships of War off Minorca. It was in the dusk, and he did not know which way they were steering.' Nelson and the fleet immediately set off in pursuit and 'We were as far as Minorca, when the alarm proved false,' fresh reports confirming the enemy were still tied up in Toulon.[24]

17. St Runius church, Marown, where John Quilliam was christened on 29 September 1771 and where many of the family are buried. The porch is distinctive in being made up of twin staircases leading to a doorway, now blocked, which led to the West Gallery.

18. The warrant for Quilliam's examination for lieutenant, issued by the Admiralty office on 2 June 1798 and signed by the Secretary to the Board of the Admiralty, Evan Nepean. Quilliam was examined on 6 June by three captains who initialled the warrant.

19. HMS *Amazon* pursuing an unnamed French vessel. Nicholas Pocock's animated drawing captures the essence of why frigates were the apogee of a naval officer's ambitions. If, as has been suggested, the Frenchman is the 40-gun *Belle Poule*, then the event depicted is part of Sir John Borlase Warren's action off La Palma in the Canaries on 13 March 1806, four years after Quilliam left *Amazon*, when both the frigate and the French 74 *Marengo* were captured.

20. John Pasco as a rear-admiral. Pasco outlived Quilliam by twenty-four years, bearing to the end his grudge for only being promoted to commander after Trafalgar while Quilliam was made post-captain. He was eventually promoted post-captain in 1811 and in 1846 commanded *Victory* at Portsmouth. He was promoted rear-admiral in 1847 and vice-admiral in 1854.

21. Quilliam's uniform, recently cleaned and conserved and now displayed in the Manx Museum's 'Mann at War' gallery. Bloodstains and apparent battle damage discovered during conservation indicate that this may be the uniform coat worn at Trafalgar, although the two epaulettes of a captain of more than three years' standing suggest that it continued to be used long afterwards.

22. Lieutenant Governor Cornelius Smelt. Smelt was Lieutenant Governor of the Isle of Man from 1805 until his death in 1832. He twice selected Quilliam to serve as a member of the House of Keys and it was to Smelt that Quilliam wrote in December 1809 to resign his seat 'As I intend to quit this Island for some considerable time' on his appointment to command the frigate *Alexandria*.

23. Vice-Admiral Sir Richard Gordon Keats. Keats probably recommended Quilliam to Sir James de Saumarez as a safe pair of hands for the demanding Baltic theatre and subsequently asked for him when appointed commander-in-chief and governor in Newfoundland.

24. Captain Peter Heywood. Quilliam may have been a fellow student of Heywood's at Peter Fannin's School of Navigation in Douglas and their paths crossed again when the pardoned *Bounty* mutineer was a member of the court at Quilliam's trial in 1814.

25. Quilliam's plot, presented as part of his defence at his court martial, showing the relative positions of *Crescent* at extreme right and at extreme left the unknown stranger sighted hull down on 28 November 1813.

26. Balcony House on The Parade, Castletown, convenient for the House of Keys, was one of two establishments maintained by the Quilliams, the other being the 'Estate House' a few miles away at Ballakeigan, where they were married. Both were owned by Margaret Quilliam before her marriage.

27. Quilliam's 'Memorandum of Service'. At the Admiralty's request, Quilliam submitted the record in September 1817 detailing his rank, ship, captain, admiral and station over the twenty-three years between May 1792 and September 1815.

28. George Quayle, banker, inventor and politician. In 1820 Quilliam promoted his scheme for steam propulsion to the Admiralty. They subsequently both became embroiled in the dispute with the Duke of Atholl.

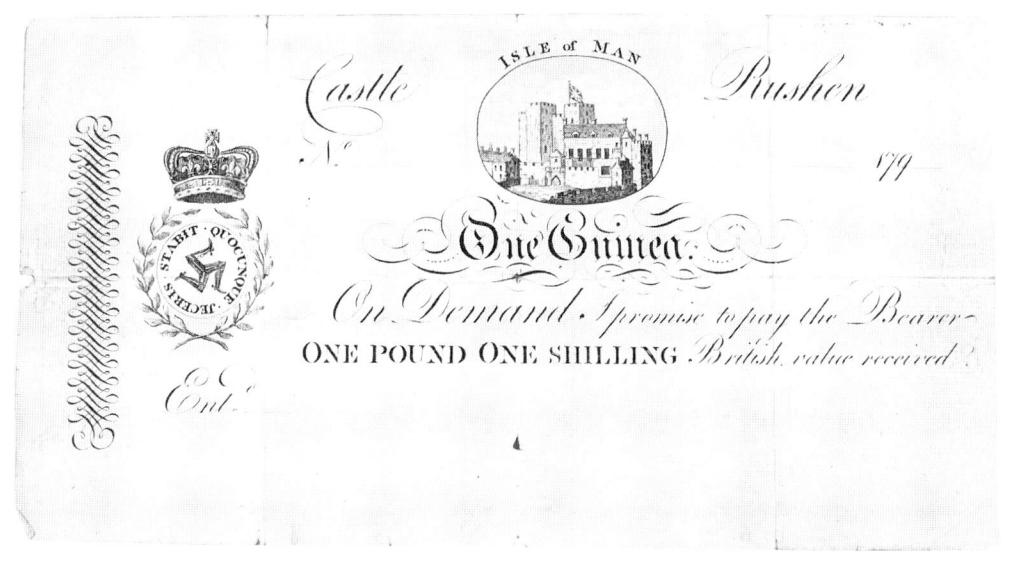

29. One guinea bank note issued by George Quayle's Isle of Man Bank. In 1817 Quilliam and others came to the bank's rescue and subsequently became trustee directors.

30. Castletown Lifeboat House, alongside Castle Rushen. Quilliam was appointed vice-chairman of the committee, which in 1826 commissioned architect Thomas Brine to design a boathouse and carriage for the Castletown lifeboat.

31. The memorial to her husband erected by Margaret Quilliam in St Columba's church, Arbory, in whose churchyard he is buried in the Stevenson family tomb. The draped urn above the inscription is decorated with an anchor and the stern of a man of war.

32. The Royal Navy's tribute to John Quilliam, the Q-class destroyer HMS *Quilliam* shown here under tow, was launched on Tyneside in 1941. In 1943 she was part of the escort to the troop convoy that carried joint author Andrew Bond's father to India.

Confirmation that frigates could maintain watch on Toulon in the worst weather persuaded Nelson he could risk taking the fleet further away in search of wood and water, fresh meat and vegetables. He needed a base sufficiently close to Toulon to keep in touch with the watching frigates and large enough to accommodate the whole fleet. A year before, Captain George Ryves of *Agincourt* had found and surveyed a superb anchorage in the Maddalena Islands off the north-east corner of Sardinia. Nelson decided to see if Agincourt Sound would serve as that base. By 30 October the six battleships were beating up the Straits of Bonifacio between Sardinia and Corsica, and on the afternoon of 1 November 'Shortened Sail and came too with the best Bower in ... Agincourt sound'. A delighted Nelson wrote the next day, telling Ryves it was 'absolutely one of the finest harbours I have ever seen'.[25]

Sardinia was then part of the independent and neutral kingdom of Tuscany and Nelson was able to arrange a supply of fresh provisions including live bullocks with the island's governor. The fleet stayed for eight days, the longest period *Victory* had been at anchor since she left Portsmouth five and a half months earlier. Yet, having replenished their water and obtained 'some refreshments for our crews',[26] the fleet was back on station a few miles off Toulon by the last week of November, having during the passage taken possession of a 'French schooner Le Renard' and a 'brig under convoy with French troops'.

The fleet returned to Agincourt Sound over Christmas, but by early January 1804 they were back on their winter station off Cape San Sebastian and, with the exception of a brief excursion to bring Algeria's ruler, the Dey, to heel, spent the first quarter of the year alternating between the Cape and the Maddalenas. When the fleet arrived back off Toulon on 9 April, the watching frigates informed Nelson that the entire French fleet had been at sea, but was safely back in port. Soon after their arrival, Quilliam recorded that his former ship 'Amazon took possession of a French Mercht Brig between Cape Sepet[27] & Porquerolles Observed the batteries at Sepet firing at the Amazon & that 3 Frigates came out of Toulon & stood for the Amazon & her prize'. *Amazon* was now commanded by another of Nelson's protégés, William Parker, one of the greatest of all frigate captains. Nelson signalled the battleship *Donegal* & the frigate *Active* to go to her support but Quilliam 'Observed 4 more of the enemy's ships coming out of Toulon round Sepet. The prizes standing off the land for the Squadron. At 6.30 the Enemy's ships tacked and stood in for Toulon.'

This encouraged Nelson to tempt the French out, splitting the fleet into inshore and offshore divisions and holding the latter out of sight from the mountains behind Toulon.[28] However, when the French had failed to react by the second week of May, he took the fleet, augmented when 'Joined HM Ship Leviathan with the Ætna, Thunder and Acheron bombs & their tenders',[29] the bombs designed to attack dockyards with heavy mortars, for a final visit to Agincourt Sound before the summer. Having 'Received 15 bullocks which makes the number rec'd 93 bullocks and 6 sheep at Magdalena Island' and 'Completed watr'g hav'g on board 315 tons', *Victory* 'weighed and made sail' out of the anchorage on 18 May,[30] the day on which Bonaparte was granted the title 'Emperor of the French'.

Back off Toulon, they found the French in a more active frame of mind. Nelson had sent Rear Admiral Campbell ahead with *Amazon* and two former French battleships, *Canopus* and *Donegal*. He found that La Touche-Tréville had shifted his flag to the newly commissioned 80-gun *Bucentaure*, bringing his total force to eight sail of the line. As Campbell's ships approached, they came under attack from a number of French gunboats and were threatened by five battleships and three frigates that emerged from the harbour. Seriously outnumbered, Campbell prudently stood offshore. Soon after, the French gave up the chase and headed back to Toulon.

Three days later, Nelson decided to take a closer look himself and brought *Victory* in company with the battleships *Excellent* and *Leviathan* inshore, where they saw 'the enemy's ships standing out to the eastward along the shore consisting of 4 ships of the line, 3 frigates, 2 brigs with some gun Boats. At 7 the enemy ships Tacked and stood in for Sepet.' Next morning saw 'two of the enemy's ships under sail off Sepet' and that afternoon *Victory* 'made all sail in chase of a French ship of the Line' but to no avail.[31]

If that encounter had been inconsequential, what looked a much more serious confrontation began to develop two weeks later. Nelson had again divided his force, leading an inshore squadron of five ships of the line and two frigates himself. This time *Victory* was accompanied by three battleships, *Canopus*, *Belleisle* and *Donegal*, when, as Quilliam recorded, he 'At 5 observed the enemy's ships coming out of Toulon consisting of 8 sail of the line and 4 frigates standing towards us'. Despite being outnumbered two to one, Nelson at once formed line of battle but again the 'Enemys Fleet Tacked' and headed for the safety of Toulon. Nelson was outraged to learn, some weeks later, that La Touche-Tréville claimed the British had run away.[32]

This may well have been the occasion when *Victory*'s surgeon George Magrath complained that, when clearing the ship for action, 'the Cockpit had become the recipient of much of the moveable lumber ... I was compelled to appeal to his Lordship on the Quarter-Deck, who promptly sent for the First Lieutenant (Quillam) to whom he gave peremptory orders instantly to see the Cockpit in a proper state, accompanied with the significant remark, that 'he (Quillam) might be the first to require its accommodation'.[33] Quilliam's battle station on the quarterdeck was known in the American Navy as 'the slaughter-pen'.

For the remainder of June and July 1804 the British held station off Toulon as a succession of increasingly heavy gales belied conventional impressions of a peaceful Mediterranean. Nelson found shelter to unload the latest transports in the Gulf of Palma in southern Sardinia, but the fleet was back off Cape San Sebastian by 20 August, where they heard La Touche-Tréville had died on the 18th. Nelson wryly observed that, 'The French papers say he died in consequence of walking so often up to the signal-post upon Sepet, to watch us: I always pronounced that that would be his death.'[34]

Autumn came early to the Mediterranean in 1804 and by mid-September Nelson was complaining of two weeks of continuous gales. Anglo-Spanish relations were deteriorating almost as rapidly, shifting Nelson's focus from attempting to draw the French out of Toulon to preventing a potential junction between them and the five Spanish battleships lying at Cartagena. Cruising between Cape Sicie and Barcelona in mid-November, he heard, erroneously as it later turned out, that a British merchant ship had been fired on. He ordered his ships 'in falling in with any Spanish Ship or Vessel of War, or Merchantman belonging to the Subjects of his Catholic Majesty ... to capture, seize, burn, sink, or destroy them'.[35] Over the next four days Quilliam recorded seven merchantmen taken prize close to *Victory*, while many more fell to detached cruisers.

The fleet continued to scour the waters off the Spanish coast well into December, when Spain officially declared war, but by then attention was focussed back on Toulon, where Vice Admiral Pierre de Villeneuve had hoisted his flag in *Bucentaure*. Nelson was convinced that, if Villeneuve did put to sea, his objective would be either Italy, Sicily or, most likely, Egypt. In early January 1805 he headed once more for Agincourt Sound, where he could cover all possible routes to the east. It was there on the afternoon of 18 January that the frigates *Seahorse* and *Active* were spotted off the anchorage flying the signal for the enemy at sea.

14

The Chase

By the time the two captains had reported to Nelson, *Victory* and the other nine battleships had 'unmoored weighed and made sail out of Agincourt Sound' heading south.[1] Villeneuve had left Toulon on the afternoon of 17 January 1805 with eleven battleships, seven frigates and two brigs and, as the weather deteriorated into a full gale, the British frigates maintained contact until 2am on the morning of the 18th before heading for the Maddalenas.[2] Nelson concluded, 'From their position when last seen, and the course they were steering ... they could only be bound round the Southern end of Sardinia.'[3] If the French were heading down the west coast of Sardinia before turning east, he would bring the fleet down the east coast to confront them.

As the fleet fought its way south against severe gales, *Victory* 'made the general signal to "Prepare for Battle"'. However, it was a further four days before, close to Cape Carbonara, the south-eastern extremity of the island, Captain Boyle of *Seahorse,* who had been sent ahead, reported that he had been chased off by a French frigate before he could establish whether the French were in the nearby Gulf of Cagliari.

Were the French at that very moment invading Sardinia or had they slipped past on their way east towards 'Sicily, the Morea,[4] or Egypt'?[5] Having established that all was quiet in Sardinia, Nelson turned east. Sending *Seahorse* ahead to alert the British minister at Naples, they covered the 200 miles to Sicily in less than forty-eight hours and by midday on 31 January were 'Tacking thro' ye Pharos of Messina'[6] with the 'Light House on Messina Mole Head NbW'.

Once clear of the strait, they made rapid progress and by noon on 5 February *Victory* had the 'Extremes of the coast of Africa from W to SbE½Et, dist off shore 4 or 5 leagues'. Desperate for news, Nelson sent ahead to the British Pro-Consul at Alexandria, wryly observing that, 'If the French are arrived before me, you will, of course, not receive this letter.'[7] When, on the morning of 7 February, *Victory* had the 'Pharos of Alexandria SEbE¼E Dist 4⅓ Leagues', there was no sign of the enemy and no report that they had been anywhere near. Nelson turned the fleet around and headed back to the west.

It was not until the morning of 19 February, when Quilliam gave *Victory*'s position as some 15 miles north east of Gozo,[8] that Nelson finally received confirmation from Malta of 'the Enemy's fleet having put back to Toulon in a very crippled state'.[9] In fact, all but four of the French ships had returned to Toulon two days after they left, severely damaged by the gale that struck when *Seahorse* and *Active* had left them to report to Agincourt Sound. Nelson, by contrast, after weeks of similar weather and a voyage to Alexandria and back, could report that, 'The Fleet under my command is in excellent good health, and the ships ... have received no damage, and not a yard or mast sprung or crippled, or scarcely a sail split.'[10] The contrast highlighted the superiority of Nelson's well-maintained ships and his experienced sea officers. Villeneuve was perfectly aware of the inferiority of his own fleet.

The French had already had the best part of a month to repair their damage and there was an urgent need to get the fleet back on station. However, there followed nearly three weeks of what Nelson described as 'without exception, the very worst weather I have ever seen'[11] before he was able to report on 14 March that 'the Fleet under my command arrived off Toulon yesterday evening, and that ... their Fleet is all in the above harbour, apparently in perfect readiness to put to sea'.[12] Still convinced that they were bound for Egypt, he set a trap for Villeneuve by taking up his old station off Cape San Sebastian. Having stayed there long enough to establish his presence, and leaving *Leviathan* to maintain the illusion, he took the remainder back to the 'Gulph of Palma' in southern Sardinia for provisions and water. By convincing Villeneuve that he was still off Cape San Sebastian, he hoped to induce him to keep well to the east of the Balearics and ambush him south of Sardinia. The trap seemed about to be sprung when *Phoebe* re-joined 20 miles south-west of the island of Toro on the morning of 4 April and reported that the French were back at sea. Once again Quilliam recorded *Victory* 'clearing ship for Action'.

Villeneuve had actually put to sea on the evening of 29 March with eleven battleships, six frigates and two brigs carrying 3,500 troops. *Active* and *Phoebe* shadowed them until nightfall on the 31st, when *Phoebe* parted company to report, leaving *Active* to maintain contact.[13] Based

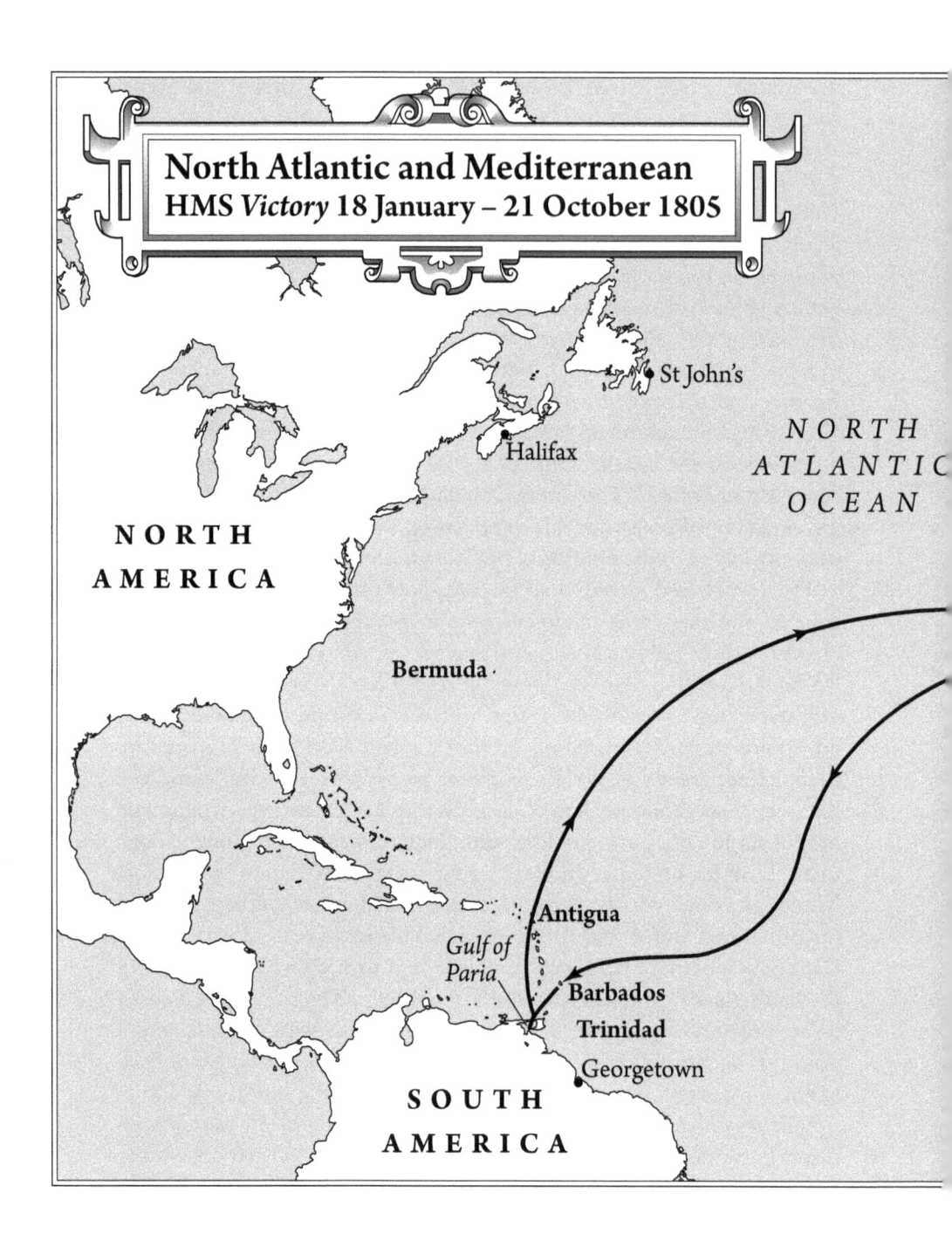

North Atlantic and Mediterranean
HMS *Victory* 18 January – 21 October 1805

NORTH AMERICA

St John's

Halifax

NORTH ATLANTIC OCEAN

Bermuda

Antigua
Gulf of Paria
Barbados
Trinidad
Georgetown

SOUTH AMERICA

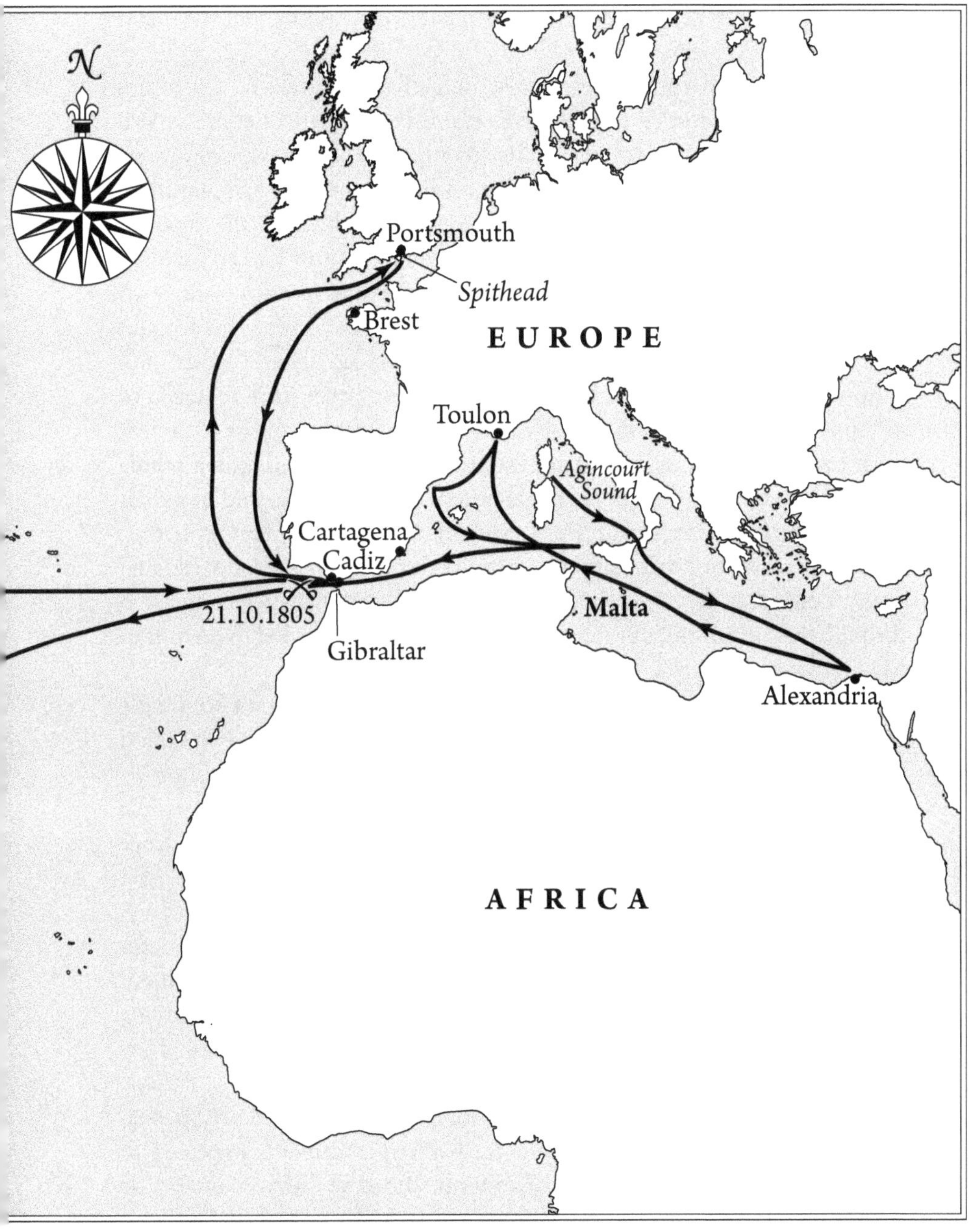

N
Portsmouth
Spithead
Brest
EUROPE
Toulon
Agincourt Sound
Cartagena
Cadiz
21.10.1805
Gibraltar
Malta
Alexandria
AFRICA

on *Phoebe*'s last sighting, Nelson believed it would be impossible for the French to get to the east without being detected by his fleet deployed across the narrow gap between the south coast of Sardinia and the north coast of Africa.

The plan began to unravel almost immediately, however, as within hours Quilliam recorded that 'Active rejoined', having lost contact with the enemy in the dark. In fact, Villeneuve had fallen for Nelson's ruse, planning to pass east of the Balearics until a Ragusan[14] merchantman warned him off. Instead he altered course and hugged the Spanish coast until he reached Cartagena.[15] Meanwhile, Nelson had to face the possibility that he might have gone round the north of Corsica or through the Straits of Bonifacio to fall upon Naples or Sicily. Sending his frigates off to alert possible destinations, he took the fleet slowly eastwards until 9 April, when he concluded that the French must either have returned to Toulon or 'are bound to the Westward' and the fleet began the long beat back towards Sardinia against the prevailing westerlies. It was a whole week before they were back off the southern tip of Sardinia and had their first reliable intelligence that 'the French Fleet (at least a Fleet) was seen on Sunday, 7th April, off Cape de Gatte, with the wind Easterly, steering to the westward'. By 18 April it was confirmed that Villeneuve had passed through the Straits and out into the Atlantic. Nelson decided to go 'out of Mediterranean after the French Fleet'.[16]

First, however, he had to reach the Straits. With the wind seemingly stuck in the west, it was not until shortly after noon on Monday, 6 May that *Victory* 'short'd sail & anchored in 45 fms … in Rossia Bay, Gibraltar'.[17] Shortly afterwards Donald Campbell, a Scots-born rear admiral in the Portuguese Navy, came on board with convincing circumstantial evidence that the combined French and Spanish fleet had indeed gone to the West Indies.[18] Nelson resolved to follow. Leaving Admiral Bickerton, his deputy, in charge of the Mediterranean, when an easterly breeze sprang up later that afternoon *Victory* and the rest of the fleet 'Weighed and made sail out of the Bay to the Westwd'. Legend has it that several officers, expecting a delay of at least twenty-four hours, had sent their laundry on shore. They would not to be reunited with it for another three months.

Villeneuve had left Cadiz on 9 April with twelve French and five Spanish battleships and seven frigates, with further reinforcements expected to follow. He was thus the best part of a month ahead and arrived in Fort de France in Martinique on 13 May, just two days after the British cleared Cape St Vincent.[19] Nelson, nevertheless, believed he could reach the West

Indies in time to prevent the French securing what he guessed was their primary objective, Jamaica. With just nine battleships and three frigates, he was outnumbered by almost two to one but anticipated improving the odds by adding the six battleships he expected to find at Barbados.

Life on board *Victory* rapidly settled down to the routine of an ocean passage, with Quilliam assiduously recording his variations of azimuth and amplitude almost daily. Equally frequently, *Victory* 'Exercised great guns' in preparation for the encounter expected to follow close on their arrival in the West Indies. In the meantime, Quilliam concentrated on ensuring that the ship was in the best possible state of repair with 'Caulkers caulking the lower and middle decks'. With the trade wind firmly established, Madeira was left to starboard on the 15th and the mid-point of the passage reached eight days later on the 23rd. By 1 June Barbados was just 400 miles distant when 'Amazon parted', sent ahead to warn of their imminent approach.

Nelson's first disappointment came on the morning of 4 June, when *Victory* 'anchord in 34 fms sand & stones in Carlisle Bay Barbadoes'. Instead of the six battleships he had expected, only the 74-gun *Northumberland* lay at anchor in the bay. There was worse to come. At that moment the combined French and Spanish fleet was at anchor less than two hundred miles away off Fort de France, Martinique.[20] Against his instinct, Nelson acted on a report from Brigadier General Brereton at St Lucia, less than a hundred miles south of Martinique, that he had seen the combined fleet off that island on 28 May steering south. 'There is not a doubt in any of the Admirals' or General's minds,' wrote Nelson that same morning, 'but that Tobago and Trinidada are the enemy's objects.'[21]

Next morning, having embarked 2,000 troops, the fleet 'Weighed & made sail to the Southwd'. Further intelligence suggested the enemy fleet was at anchor in the Gulf of Paria between Trinidad and the coast of Venezuela. As they approached the island on the morning of 4 June, Quilliam recorded that *Victory* 'Bent a Bo Cable to ye bower Anchor out of the gun room port' in preparation for engaging a fleet at anchor as at the Nile and Copenhagen. The anticlimax when, later that afternoon, the fleet squeezed through the Dragon's Mouth, the narrow channel separating Trinidad from the mainland, and found the Gulf of Paria entirely empty was total. A month later Nelson lamented, 'The name of General Brereton will not soon be forgot.'[22] His mood would not have been improved the following day when, as the fleet worked its way back through the Dragon's Mouth, he received despatches confirming that

Villeneuve had sailed from Martinique on 4 June. Fearing for Jamaica, he hurried north.

On 9 June Quilliam recorded *Victory* 'Hove too in Georges Bay Granada (sic)' where Nelson received reports 'proving all our former information false' and that on 6 June the enemy 'were under the Saints,[23] standing to the Northward'. By the time *Victory* approached Antigua on the morning of 12 June, he had learned that Villeneuve had landed his troops and stores at Guadeloupe and was on his way back to Europe. After Nelson landed his own troops at St John's, Antigua, the next morning the British fleet was also heading north, on the first stage of its passage back across the Atlantic. They had been in the West Indies just nine days.

On 17 June an American merchantmen reported seeing '22 Sail of Large Ships' some 400 miles south-east of Bermuda and Nelson concluded that 'we cannot be more than eighty leagues from them at this moment, and by carrying every sail, and using my utmost efforts, I shall hope to close with them before they get to either Cadiz or Toulon'. In case he didn't, he sent word ahead to Ferrol 'to the Admiral commanding off that Port, in order that he may be upon his guard against a surprise from a superior force'. Similarly, as the fleet approached the Azores, he sent his frigates ahead to ascertain whether 'the enemy have entered the Straits or are gone into Cadiz'. However, it was not until the morning of 19 July that *Victory* at '7.30 shortened sail & anchord in Rossia Bay Gibraltar' and Nelson 'went on shore for the first time since the 16th of June, 1803; and from having my foot out of the Victory, two years wanting 10 days'.[24]

With no sign of the enemy, the fleet took on fresh provisions and water at Mazrie Bay on the coast of Morocco before heading back through the Straits and turning north in search of Villeneuve. Plagued by adverse winds, they eventually joined the Channel fleet off Brest on the afternoon of 16 August when, as Quilliam recorded, 'Saluted Adml Cornwallis in HMS Ville de Paris with 15 guns which was returned with 11 Shortened sail & hove too.' Only then did Nelson learn that Villeneuve had fought an inconclusive action with Sir Robert Calder's reinforced Ferrol squadron, and taken his battered and travel-stained charges into Vigo.[25]

Nelson had no further reason to delay a return to England. Within hours *Victory* was under way again and on the morning of 18 August 'At 8.30 anchord at Spithead in 17 fms'. Desperate to get back to Emma, Nelson was frustrated when *Victory* was put in quarantine and it was the evening of the 19th before she finally 'At 9 Hauled down Lord Nelsons Flag'. With Hardy granted permission 'to go on shore for a short time ...

for the recovery of his health',[26] Quilliam was left in charge of the ship. Although the Admiralty appointed Captain John Conn as acting captain, there is no mention of him taking up the appointment before he left for Cadiz in temporary command of *Royal Sovereign*.

Victory had been at sea continuously for twenty-seven months and would, in normal circumstances, have gone into dry dock. Quilliam's log suggests that that was exactly what was intended. Within hours the ship's company was 'Empd getting guns out' and several days later 'sending Powder &c into the Hoyes'. All the indications were that she was not expected to be back at sea for some considerable time. Nor was Nelson. By the time he reached home he was doubtful whether there would be any need for him to return at all. However, within forty-eight hours all had changed as word reached the Admiralty that Villeneuve had left Ferrol. Nelson told Admiral Murray, 'Victory is ordered to sea; whether my flag goes out in her I have not heard.'[27]

Down at Spithead, *Victory* 'Rec'd the guns on board' and 'Compleated our water' and her ship's company was 'Employed fitting for sea.' On 1 September the frigate *Euryalus* arrived with the news that the combined fleet had put into Cadiz on 20 August.[28] Her captain, Henry Blackwood, taking a slight diversion from his route to London, called at Merton to be greeted by Nelson with the exclamation, 'I am sure you bring me news of the French and Spanish fleets, and I think I shall yet have to beat them.'[29] By 4 September he had been reappointed to a substantially extended Mediterranean command with *Victory*, previously earmarked to re-join the Channel Fleet, once more designated his flagship. Next day his baggage, personal effects and furniture were despatched to Portsmouth, where on 9 September *Victory* 'Rec'd sundry stores belonging to Adml. Lord Nelson' and, on Friday, 13 September, 'At Noon Weighed and made Sail to St Helens.' That just twenty-four days after returning to Spithead from more than two years and 15,000 miles at sea, a ship that had only a fortnight earlier had all her guns out, her rigging stripped and her topmasts struck down, dropped down to St Helens ready for departure is the ultimate demonstration of Quilliam's extraordinary ability to refit and repair ships. His fellow professionals valued that expertise far more than the lucky chance of finding and fighting an enemy.

While *Victory* lay at St Helens, Nelson enjoyed a last day with family and friends. That evening he 'At half-past ten drove from dear Merton ... to go to serve my King and country'[30] and next morning, Saturday, 14 September 1805, *Victory* 'at 11.30 hoisted the Flag of Admiral Lord Nelson'.

15

Quilliam's Trafalgar

At four o'clock on the morning of 15 September 1805, *Victory*, with only *Euryalus* in company, 'weighed and made sail to the SE'.[1] Ten days later, some 30 miles west of Lisbon, Nelson despatched Blackwood with letters to Sutton in *Amphion* lying off the Tagus and to Collingwood with the fleet off Cadiz urging them to 'not mention my near approach to Cadiz' and 'not to proclaim to the enemy every ship which may join the Fleet'.

By noon on 28 September *Victory* was 20 miles south-west of Cadiz and 'Saw the Enemy's fleet in Cadiz, amounting to thirty-five or thirty-six Sail of the Line'.[2] Later the same afternoon 'at 6 joined the Fleet off Cadiz under Admiral Collingwood'. Collingwood's priority had been to keep Villeneuve in port, dividing his twenty-six battleships into an inshore squadron of five under Admiral Louis with the remainder some 15 miles off shore. Nelson's objective was, once again, to lure the enemy out, withdrawing the inshore squadron and leaving frigates close inshore to keep watch while taking the battle fleet over the horizon. To maintain contact, he positioned his fastest battleships between the frigates and the fleet as signal relays; if Villeneuve showed the slightest sign of putting to sea he would know within minutes. At the same time, he prepared for a long watch, sending a few ships in turn to Gibraltar for water and provisions. First to go, protesting they would miss the battle, were Admiral Louis and six battleships.

In the event, it was Napoleon rather than Nelson who forced the Combined Fleet to sea. On the day Nelson arrived, Villeneuve received orders to use the 4,000 troops at Cadiz to seize Naples. Despite the order making a battle almost inevitable, when word reached him warning of his imminent dismissal, he decided to put to sea at the earliest opportunity.[3]

Quilliam's log for October 1805 presents an intriguing challenge. At first sight it appears to be missing a day, jumping from Monday,

14 October to Tuesday, 16 October and then regaining it by jumping back from Sunday, 21 October to Tuesday, 22 October. In fact, 21 October was a Monday, but correlation with Nelson's letters and diary indicates that the missing day is either Friday, 11 October or Saturday, 12 October, the former being the date designated by the Admiralty for the Royal Navy to switch from the day and date changing at noon to their changing at midnight. That would have meant the Navy's 11 October only lasting twelve hours or 12 October thirty-six hours and the 11th disappearing entirely, in effect what happened here. However, *Victory* and presumably the rest of the fleet, continued with the old convention at least until they reached Gibraltar at the end of the month, by which time such details probably seemed unimportant.[4]

The log for October 1805 that Quilliam signed off as his own is probably not in his own hand, which was common practice. It was almost certainly written up from the Master's Log, often following it verbatim, as does the Captain's Log. It seems likely that much of it was created at Gibraltar, when the new conventions were being adopted. Quilliam can hardly have been the only officer confused by the change when writing up the previous tumultuous month under the old convention and entries between 16 and 22 October have been amended in an unsuccessful attempt to account for the missing day. Despite these discrepancies, Hardy countersigned Quilliam's log as a true record.[5]

Quilliam's log entries for the three weeks after *Victory* arrived off Cadiz are uncharacteristically brief, although he continued assiduously to record wind direction, course, distance run, latitude, longitude and position at noon. As such they capture the combination of growing tension and mundane routine that characterised those twenty-one days. In 'Light breezes inclinable to calm', on only three days did the distance run exceed 20 miles and on the 18th it was a mere three. Moreover, on only one day did he record that they 'Saw the land, extremes from NEbE to NWbN'.

Quilliam's brevity can also be attributed in part to the continual stream of visitors including Admirals Collingwood, Calder and Northesk[6] and a succession of captains. With Hardy doing duty as both Captain of the Fleet and Flag Captain, Quilliam was for much of the time *de facto* captain as well as being on hand as each visitor arrived and departed. It was during this period that Nelson outlined to his visitors, few of whom had previously served under him, the battle plan set out in his famous Memorandum, a document that provided captains with ample opportunity to use their skill and initiative but concluded with some practical advice. 'In case signals cannot be seen or clearly understood, no captain can do very wrong if he places his ship alongside that of an enemy.'[7] This was the least that Nelson expected.

Despite the continuing absence of Admiral Louis, Nelson's force continued to increase as Quilliam recorded on 7 October that 'HM Ship Royal Sovereign joined from England' and on the 12th 'HMSs L'Aimable & Agamemnon joined from England'. Other newcomers included *Defiance, Leviathan, Belleisle* and *Africa*. While Collingwood shifted his flag to the newly recoppered 100-gun three-decker *Royal Sovereign*, the arrival of his former flag captain Sir Edward Berry in his old ship, the 64-gun *Agamemnon*, prompted Nelson to observe, 'Here comes that damned fool Berry. Now we shall have a battle.'[8]

That seemed increasingly likely. On 14 October, Nelson recorded in his diary, 'Enemy at the harbour's mouth.' Nevertheless, as late as the morning of 18 October Quilliam had nothing more noteworthy to add than 'at noon light airs the high Land of Cape St Mary's bore NbW 10 Leagues Fleet in company'. However, the peaceful atmosphere was deceptive. Nelson presciently noted in his diary: 'Fine weather, wind Easterly; the Combined Fleets cannot have finer weather to put to sea.'[9] Villeneuve thought so too. At sunset he and his Spanish colleague Gravina issued orders to sail the following morning.[10]

Saturday, 19 October dawned with 'Light airs', prompting Nelson to invite Collingwood to join him in *Victory*. It was not to be. By 7.30am the British frigates had spotted the first ships of the combined fleet in Cadiz getting under way. By 8am Blackwood could see as many as nineteen on the move and all but two of the remainder 'had their topsails to the masthead'.[11] With *Phoebe* firing off three-minute guns, the news was relayed to Nelson, who immediately 'Made the Signal for a "General Chase S.E"'.[12] to block Villeneuve's access to the Straits. By midday Quilliam had *Victory* steering 'S10E' with the wind 'ESE' and Cadiz 'S89E 17 Leagues'.

Meanwhile, with so many large, unwieldy ships crowding the entrance, the combined fleet was making heavy work of getting to sea. By noon when the tide turned only seven battleships and three frigates had got to sea: the remainder had been forced to anchor again.[13] Still under the impression that the entire enemy fleet was at sea, Nelson continued to chase to the south-east, Quilliam recording how *Victory* 'tried for soundings every two hours with 100fms of line'.

By the morning of the 20th the fleet was close to the mouth of the Straits and Nelson was sure the enemy could not have outrun him. He turned the fleet around and headed back north-west, keeping well off the coast and over the horizon. Further north, and closely observed by the British frigates, the remainder of the combined fleet finally got to sea, where Villeneuve was attempting to establish some kind of order, although, with the wind in the SSW, they were steering WNW on the larboard or port tack directly away from his objective.

From noon on Sunday, 20 October, Quilliam's log was back in step with events, albeit with the 21st still recorded as Sunday rather than Monday. Thus he records 'October 21st PM. (i.e. afternoon of 20 October) Light Breezes and squally with Rain at 2 taken aback came to the Wind on the Starboard tack.' The same shift in wind from SSW to west allowed Villeneuve to come about on a reciprocal course and head for the Straits. At the same time, *Victory* 'at 4 wore ship & up topgallant yards', bringing the opposing fleets on to parallel courses, the British heading NNW, the French and Spanish SSE, and the two converging at some 8 miles per hour. With sunset less than two hours away, Quilliam for the first time noted 'Lookout Ships making Signals of the enemy's positions'.

Rather than bring on a possibly inconclusive action that evening, Nelson was determined to achieve the 'annihilation that the Country wants'.[14] As darkness fell, he left Blackwood's frigates to maintain contact and pulled away to the south-west. Meanwhile Villeneuve, facing an imminent onslaught, ordered his disorganised fleet to form a single line of battle, clear for action and maintain its course SSE.[15] The first move in the Battle of Trafalgar came before dawn the following morning when Quilliam recorded 'At 4 wore ship' followed by the rest of the fleet and 'stood to the N.E' back towards the enemy. The die was cast.

As the eastern sky began to lighten, the fleet separated into the two columns required by Nelson's plan. Quilliam 'at 6 observed the enemy bearing EbS 10 or 11 miles' and, with the rest of the fleet, *Victory* 'bore up to the Eastwd. Out all Reefs topsails, set steering Sails[16] Royals, cleared for Quarters.' Preparing the ship for battle was Quilliam's primary responsibility. Within an hour, each of the gun decks was clear from stem to stern, shot in the garlands by the hatchways, guns loaded and run out, slow matches burning in their tubs. Quilliam would have reported to Hardy that the ship was ready for inspection, and accompanied Hardy and Nelson as they toured the lower decks.

Shortly before sunrise, the British fleet was spotted by lookouts on the French frigate *Hermione*. Fearing Nelson was attempting to cut him off from Cadiz, Villeneuve ordered the entire thirty-three-strong armada to wear and reverse course to the north.[17] Quilliam observed 'at 8 Light Breezes and cloudy Body of the Enemy's Fleet EbS 9 or 10 miles' while the last entry in Nelson's diary noted 'at seven the Enemy wearing in succession'.[18]

With *Victory* making between 2 and 3 knots there was ample time for final thoughts and belated requests. One of the most bizarre was contemplated by Lieutenant Pasco. Writing almost forty years later, Sir Nicholas Harris Nicolas, compiler and editor of Nelson's *Dispatches and Letters*, related Pasco's story that he went to Nelson's cabin intending to complain that he was 'very unfortunate, on so glorious an occasion, to be doing duty in an inferior station, instead of that to which his seniority entitled him'. However, finding Nelson on his knees, he '"could not at such moment, disturb his mind with any grievances of mine". Captain Pasco considers that but for this delicacy on his part, he should have been directed to assume his position as first lieutenant'.[19] Clearly Pasco had borne a grudge for four decades, despite the fact that Quilliam had held the post for more than two years and the impossibility of replacing the flagship's first lieutenant an hour before a major battle. There is no contemporary evidence to support his story.

At mid-morning Quilliam recorded, 'Still standing for the Enemy's Van the Royal Sovereign & her Line of Battle steering for the centre of the enemy's Line the enemy's Line extending about NNE & SSW.' Atkinson, the master, added in his version of the same entry, the enemy line 'consisting of 33 Sail of the Line 6 Frigates & 2 brigs.'[20] The British leeward column had the shorter distance to cover and was the first to come within range, *Royal Sovereign* leading the stately charge. Quilliam recorded the first exchanges in his last log entry for what he erroneously identified as Sunday, 21 October: 'at 11.40 the Royal Sovereign commenced firing on the Enemy, they having begun on her at 11.30.'

A mile or more to the north, *Victory* was still some 2 miles from impact. As the strip of water separating the two fleets narrowed, the northern half of the enemy line opened a sustained but as yet largely ineffective fire on *Victory* and the two other leading three-deckers, *Téméraire* and *Neptune*. Nelson, his task as a strategist almost completed, made three more signals before the battle began. First was the famous 'England expects ...', composed in Popham's 'talking telegraph'[21] code, Pasco as signal lieutenant having advised that he could transmit 'expects' in one hoist rather than having to spell out each individual letter of Nelson's preferred choice, 'confides'.[22] As the final hoist of the message came down, up went Admiralty code 63, 'Prepare to anchor after the close of day,' confirming Nelson's realisation that the long swell presaged an imminent storm. Finally, up went the flag that epitomised Nelson even more than 'England expects …', Admiralty code no 16, 'Engage the enemy more closely'; it would remain flying until shot away.[23]

Quilliam's first log entry for Tuesday, 22 October is a snapshot of *Victory* at noon: 'P.M. Light airs and cloudy, standing towards the Enemy's Van. all Sail sett.' At this stage George Westphal, a midshipman who had been sent with a report for Quilliam, places him on the quarterdeck close to Nelson.[24] Rather than meeting the enemy line at right angles, Quilliam and Atkinson both record that they 'at 4 minutes past 12 opened our fire on the enemy's Van in passing down their line'. Their narrative suggests that *Victory* wore on to the starboard tack, broadside on to the combined fleet, before finally 'at 12.20 in attempting to pass through their Line fell on board the 10th & 11th Ships when the Action became General'. Nelson had one last mission: to take out the enemy's commander-in-chief. He waited for Villeneuve to show his flag and then drove *Victory* under *Bucentaure*'s stern, firing a full 50-gun, double-shotted broadside through her stern galleries. With his ship unable to move, signal or fight, Villeneuve remained a helpless spectator as his fleet was annihilated in a series of single-ship actions.

From that point Quilliam's world shrank to *Victory* and her immediate surroundings as she delivered and received broadside after broadside on both sides. The next entries in both his and Atkinson's logs were made almost an hour later when at 'about 1.15 Admiral The Right Honble Lord Visct. Nelson K.B. &c and commander-in-chief was wounded in the Shoulder'. Later writers have not been slow to fill in the details of that hour and a half. William James, writing nearly twenty years later, has *Victory* under heavy fire throughout the latter stages of her approach until, 'Just as she had got within about 500 yards of the larboard beam of the Bucentaure … A shot also struck and knocked to pieces the wheel; and the ship was obliged to be steered in the gun room, the first-lieutenant (John Quilliam) and master (Thomas Atkinson) relieving each other at this duty.' Only then did *Victory* pass across the stern of *Bucentaure*, raking her with her full broadside, and, having 'put her helm hard aport … ran foul of the Redoutable'.[25] Thus Quilliam's actions had enabled Nelson to complete his tactical plan.

It is difficult to square this with Quilliam's and Atkinson's brief summary of events. Both say quite clearly that they 'fell on board the 10th & 11th Ships', by which they appear to mean *Bucentaure* and *Redoutable*,[26] implying a simultaneous collision of *Victory* with both French ships. However, by far the most interesting discrepancy between James's account and Quilliam's and Atkinson's logs is the total absence of any mention of the wheel being shot away, let alone steering her from the gun room. The incident is also reported quite differently in two other narratives, both of which pre-date James's version. *Victory*'s surgeon, William Beatty, in his *Authentic Narrative of the Death of Lord Nelson*, published just two years after the event, describes how, 'At twenty minutes past twelve, the tiller-ropes being shot away, Mr. ATKINSON, the Master, was ordered below to get the helm put to port; which being done, the Victory was soon run on board the Redoutable of seventy-four guns.' He makes no mention of the wheel itself being destroyed or of Quilliam being involved and he also goes on to relate how, as he was being carried below nearly an hour later, the wounded Nelson 'observed that the tiller-ropes were not yet replaced; and desired one of the Midshipmen stationed there to go upon the quarter-deck and ... request that new ones should be immediately rove'.[27]

Most significant, however, is Robert Southey's version in his *Life of Nelson*, first published in 1813, because Southey had the story of the battle from Quilliam himself. In a letter of November 1807 Southey described how Quilliam, 'a sailor of the old Blake & Dampier breed',[28] visited him and his brother Tom, a naval lieutenant, and 'told us more of Nelson than I can find room to write'.[29] Southey's account of the battle broadly agrees with Beatty but with one crucial difference. Like Beatty, he places the incident not on the approach but immediately after Hardy has informed Nelson that he cannot break through the line without running on board one or other of the enemy ships. He then relates how, 'The master was ordered to put the helm to port, and the VICTORY ran on board the REDOUTABLE, just as her tiller ropes were shot away.'[30] Thus there was no need for emergency steering, since *Victory* was already entangled with *Redoutable*.

James had queried both the logs and Beatty's account, the former on the grounds of 'the death early in the action of the two persons whose places (in succession) it was to take minutes'[31] and the latter not unreasonably because Beatty, by his own admission, was too busy in the cockpit to know what was happening elsewhere. While neither Quilliam's nor

Atkinson's logs record damage to the steering, there are other first-hand accounts that do, including that from 'R.J.' at Dover dated 16 December 1805 and published in *The Naval Chronicle*. Relating that he is 'just come from on board the Victory', he describes how 'a shot carried away four spokes from the wheel of the Victory, and never killed or wounded any of the men steering'.[32]

It is possible that *Victory*'s steering gear was damaged in two separate incidents, one rendering the wheel unusable, the other severing the tiller ropes, though whether either or both occurred during or after her contact with *Redoutable* is not clear. What is clear is that by the time she parted from *Redoutable,* aided, according to Beatty, by the helm being put to starboard, a jury steering system was operational.[33] Typically, the men heaving on the tackles below deck would have received their instructions via relayed shouted orders but recent research has revealed that *Victory* was fitted with voice tubes through which messages could be passed directly.[34] The two officers responsible both for rigging and operating the jury system would have been Quilliam and Atkinson, the one on deck, the other below. Thus Quilliam may indeed have had a hand, or at least a voice, in steering *Victory* at Trafalgar, though not quite as it has sometimes been depicted, most notably on his memorial tablet in Arbory church.

The fifteen minutes after Nelson fell saw the climax of *Victory*'s battle. Shortly after a French attempt to board had been repulsed, the British three-decker *Téméraire* collided with the *Redoutable*'s starboard bow and poured in a succession of raking broadsides that shattered the Frenchman's resistance. Quilliam recorded 'at 1.30 the Redoubtable having struck her Colors we ceased firing our Starboard guns but continued engaged with the Santissima Trinadada and some of the Enemy's Line on the Larboard side'.

The yawning gap between the two ships' upper decks prevented *Victory*'s boarders from crossing to *Redoutable* to take possession, giving us another glimpse of Quilliam. Beatty relates how, 'Several Seamen volunteered their services to Lieutenant QUILLIAM, to jump overboard, swim under the Redoubtable's bows, and endeavour to get up there; but Captain HARDY refused to permit this.'[35] Southey tells essentially the same story but without Hardy's involvement. Instead two midshipmen went across in a boat and took possession.

Victory then drifted away and Quilliam, 'Observed the Temeraire between the Redoubtable and another French Ship of the Line, both of which had struck.' He then summarised a further hour and a half of intense conflict, as *Victory* traded broadsides with the giant four-deck *Santissima Trinidad* and a succession of other enemy ships, in a single sentence: 'The Action continuing general until 3 o'clock when several of the enemy's ships around us had struck, observed the Royal Sovereign with the loss of her main and mizzen masts and several of the enemy ships around her dis-masted.' That suggests at least a pause in the drama, but it seemed that there might yet be worse to come as Quilliam recorded that he, 'At 3.30 observed 4 sail of the enemy's Van tack, and stand along our weather line to windward, fired our Larboard guns at those they would reach. At 3.40 made the signal, for our ships to keep their wind and engage the Enemy's Van coming along our weather line.'

The entire enemy van under Rear-Admiral Dumanoir had belatedly responded to Villeneuve's desperate pleas for support. However, the threat to *Victory* proved illusory. Numbering five rather than Quilliam's four two-deckers, they encountered two previously unengaged British 74s, *Minotaur* and *Spartiate,* which repeatedly raked Dumanoir's flagship *Formidable* and roughed up the others.[36] Quilliam recorded that 'at 4.15 the Spanish Rear Admiral to Windward struck to some of our ships which had Tacked after them, observed one of the Enemy's ships blow up and 14 Sail standing towards Cadiz and 3 standing to the Southward'.

Quilliam's next log entry, the most poignant in any of his logs, recorded how 'partial firing continued until 3.40 when a Victory having been reported to the Admiral Right Honble Lord Visct Nelson KB … and commander-in-chief, He died of his wounds.' Quilliam undoubtedly felt the loss deeply and personally. When transcribing Atkinson's log into his own, perhaps in a rush before his hurried departure from *Victory* ten days later, the handwriting becomes illegible in the middle of the customary recording of Nelson's honours and, unnoticed either by him, Hardy or seemingly any subsequent reader, the time of Nelson's death is recorded as '3.40' instead of the clear '4.30' in Atkinson's log, which agrees with the time given by Beatty.[37]

At this point there is another a glimpse of Quilliam on the quarterdeck, albeit one of dubious authenticity. The story is attributed to the Rev F W Stubbs, who related 'on what was locally held to be good authority … that when Nelson breathed his last someone hauled down the Admiral's flag. Quilliam, seeing this, hoisted it again.'[38] Interestingly, when Hardy suggested to Nelson more than two hours after he was wounded that, 'I suppose, my Lord, Admiral COLLINGWOOD will now take upon himself the direction of affairs,' the reply was immediate: 'Not while I live, I hope, HARDY!'[39] Quilliam knew his Nelson and his reaction to any premature attempt to haul down the flag would certainly have been as Stubbs described. Such a sign would only have disheartened the fleet.

Quilliam spent the half hour after Nelson's death in a preliminary assessment of the damage: 'at 5 the Mizen Mast fell about 10 feet above the Poop, the lower Masts, Yards & Bowsprit all crippled, rigging and Sails very much cut, the Ships around us very much crippled, Several of our Ships pursuing the Enemy to Leeward ... Saw Vice Admiral Collingwoods Flag Flying on board HMS Euryalus and some of our Ships taking Possession of the Prizes.'

Victory was in a desperate condition, wallowing in the Atlantic swell and hardly able to set a sail. With sunset less than an hour away, every unwounded man and many of those later classified as 'slightly wounded' were dragged into the fight to save the ship. Despite Nelson's earlier order to anchor, the seaman's natural instinct to put sea room between himself and a lee shore asserted itself: Quilliam recorded how *Victory* 'wore ship ... stood to the Southward under the remnants of Foresail and Maintopsail'.

Sunrise on the day after Trafalgar was at about 6.40am but it could have been as much as an hour earlier when Quilliam 'At Day Light saw our Fleet and Prizes 43 Sail'. Close by in *Euryalus*, Collingwood was grappling with his new responsibilities. His most immediate need was for a right-hand man whom he could trust. With his flag captain Edward Rotherham due to go home, he planned to replace him with his protégé, Richard Thomas, then commanding the bomb *Aetna* in the western approaches to Gibraltar. Knowing the esteem in which Nelson had held *Victory*'s first lieutenant, he appointed Quilliam 'Commander of His Majesty's Bomb the Aetna', the commission being given 'on board His Majesty's Ship the Euryalus off Cape Trafalgar, this 22nd day of October 1805'.[40]

Despite the admiral's instruction 'forthwith to go on board' *Aetna*, there was no way of doing so. Quilliam was fully occupied saving *Victory*. Work continued right through the next night with the 'watch empd woulding the lower masts' and later in the morning hands were 'Empd securing the Mast, Yards & rigging' while below decks he had 'Carpenters stopping the shot holes'.

The weather was now deteriorating but Hardy decided that, almost three full days after the battle, he could no longer delay a full assessment of the human toll. At 9am Quilliam 'Mustered the ship's company' and Atkinson recorded that they 'Found 54 killed and 79 wounded in the

Action' and listed every casualty by name and 'quality'. The killed ranged from Nelson to two 'Boys 3rd Class' while the wounded were subdivided into three categories: twenty-five 'Dangerously Wounded' including Pasco; twelve 'Badly Wounded' included George Bligh, the sixth lieutenant; and forty-two 'Slightly Wounded'. Nelson's tactics had worked. Only six British ships suffered serious losses. *Victory*'s 133 casualties were among the highest in the fleet, while her fifty-four killed was the highest by a significant margin, representing nearly 12 per cent of all British fatalities.[41]

While *Victory* counted her losses, Collingwood had decided that if the damaged British ships were to be saved, many of the prizes must be sacrificed. As a result, more of the relatively undamaged ships became available to assist and later that same morning 'Polyphemus took us in tow'. That was the cue for redoubled efforts to restore the ship's self-sufficiency while, after dark, those on deck saw the effect of Collingwood's earlier decision as they 'Observed a ship on Fire astern at 9.45 she blew up'.

The next thirty-six hours were the most harrowing of the entire campaign, as the wind consistently exceeded what would now be classified as Storm Force 10 and occasionally reached Violent Storm 11. Quilliam made just a single entry for the twelve hours from midnight to midday on the morning of 25 October: 'Strong gales and Squally'. Damage was inevitable. *Victory* at '5.10 carried away the Main Yard Split the Mainsail & Maintopsail all to pieces'. With darkness falling, the exhausted crew 'Cleared away the wreck'. Equally inevitably 'Polyphemus increased her distance supposing the hawser had parted'. Despite the fragile rig, there was no alternative: they 'bent a foresail and set the Mainstaysail'. Next morning revealed total devastation when Quilliam 'at Daylight saw the Royal Sovereign in the N.E. with Signal 314[42] flying' and 'Africa NNW with the signal of distress all her Masts being gone'.[43] *Victory* repeated 'the signal to Polyphemus with the Royal Sovereign's Pno', telling her to leave them and go to the three-decker's assistance.

In fact, the worst was over. Work was already in hand 'setting up the lower rigging & securing the Bowsprit' and later that afternoon Thomas Fremantle's 'Neptune took us in Tow'. Next day, 27 October, dawned 'Fresh breezes and cloudy' with the hands 'Employed clearing & refitting the ship', despite regular interruptions as shipmates who had 'departed this life of the wounds received on the 21st Inst' were 'committed to the deep with the usual ceremony'. With some semblance of normality restored, there was no alarm when, later that evening, *Victory* 'At 9.40 carried away the tow rope'. Next morning, when 'Neptune carried away her Fore Top Mast', *Victory* 'Made all sail' and 'rounded Cape Trafalgar' while 'Neptune anchored'.

By early afternoon, having shaken 'Out 1st Reef top Sails', *Victory* was 'Steering for Gibraltar' under her own canvas, Atkinson's and Quilliam's logs refuting subsequent reports that she was towed into the anchorage. Instead, shortly after sunset on 28 October and almost exactly a week after the last shots had been fired off Cape Trafalgar, she 'at 7 anchored in Rosia Bay Gibraltar in 25 fms ... Veered & moored with the whole cable'. Her very survival, let alone the fact that she had been able to complete the last stage of the journey unassisted, was a tribute to the extraordinary courage, determination and skill of her ship's company and, not least, of her first lieutenant.

Just five days later the ship's company was 'Employed clearing the Ship for Sea' when, on the afternoon of Saturday, 2 November, 'Anchored here H.M. Ships Royal Sovereign, Temeraire, Conqueror, Defence, Achille, Etna – & the Prize ships Ildelphonso and Swiftsure.' That was the last entry in Quilliam's log of *Victory*. When, on the evening of 4 November, as Atkinson recorded, she 'Made sail thro the Straights to the Westwd',[44] he wasn't with her. That same morning he had recorded his first entry in his 'Journal of the Proceedings of His Majesty's Bomb Aetna': 'AM at 9 Capt. Quilliam Superseded Capt. Thomas and took command of the Ship.'[45]

16

Captain Quilliam

Hardly had Captain Thomas disappeared over the side than *Aetna*[1] 'Weigh'd and made Sail to Westward',[2] reaching the fleet off Cadiz a matter of hours after *Victory* on the morning of 5 November. That afternoon the 'Captn went on board the Admiral' and next day, as *Victory* headed for Portsmouth, *Aetna* 'Parted Co with the Fleet' to take up her station off Cape Spartel.

For the next four months *Aetna* patrolled the western approaches to the Straits on a line between Cape Spartel and Cape Trafalgar, chasing, boarding and examining as many as three or four merchantmen a day, often in company with frigates including *Melpomene*, *Phoebe* or *Amphion*, but most frequently with the 24-gun post-ship *Eurydice*.[3] She was back in Gibraltar loading provisions and water from 19 November to 2 December before joining *Eurydice* off Cape Spartel to escort an inbound convoy into Gibraltar. Because 'HMS L'Aimable drove foul of us and carried away our Jib Boom and Spritsail yard', she was still there on 16 December 1805 when the change to a regular day was finally implemented. Thereafter Quilliam devoted a page of his log to each day at sea, dividing the hours AM from PM by the noon-day position.

That afternoon *Aetna* left to escort a convoy into the Mediterranean but, with the wind foul, was back in Gibraltar on the 19th and still there on Christmas Eve when Quilliam's promotion to captain was gazetted.[4] That news, however, did not reach him for another three months and he was still signing off the muster book as 'Commander' at the end of March 1806.[5]

Aetna spent the first three months of 1806 alternating between her station off Cape Spartel and Tangier, the Moroccan port where she could obtain fresh food and live cattle.[6] During the second visit she narrowly avoided disaster when, hit by a violent storm, the 'Ship parted both Cables let go the Sheet Anchor and brought up in 11 fms.' When she returned ten days later, Quilliam had the 'Boats sweeping [for] the Anchor' until they 'returned with the Best Bower and part of the Cable'.

Quilliam's last assignment with *Aetna* was to take a convoy through the Straights and into the Mediterranean, repeatedly having to 'Signal for ships astern to make more Sail'. Finally, on the afternoon of 27 March, she was 'beating into Gibraltar Bay'. Two days later Quilliam signed off his log. His successor, fresh from England, was the newly promoted Commander John Yule, formerly second lieutenant of *Victory*, who may well have brought confirmation of Quilliam's promotion.

Three days later, on the morning of Thursday, 3 April, the first entry in the Captain's Log of His Majesty's Ship *Ildefonso* recorded that, 'Captain J. Quilliam came and commissioned the Ship.'[7] *San Ildefonso* was one of only four prizes taken at Trafalgar to reach Gibraltar, of which three were now being readied to sail for England.[8] Quilliam was the ideal captain to prepare a badly damaged ship for the 1,150-mile voyage to Portsmouth. To assist him, he had a ship's company of just twelve[9] together with a workforce lent from other ships. The ship had been all but dismasted in the battle, but a jury rig was already in place. The first priority was 'Washing and cleaning the ship', removing the final traces of the thirty-four Spanish seamen who had died and 126 who had been wounded, 'whitewashing Ship' and 'stopping the shot holes'. Other hands were 'employed securing the upper Deck Guns and stricking Quarter deck & Forecastle Guns down in the Hold' while the lower deck gunports were sealed and caulked.

Aided by 140 men lent from *Dreadnought,* Quilliam had the ship ready in a little over three weeks, allowing *Ildefonso* to be 'warped out of the Mole'. Two days later, with forty-four invalid soldiers, sailors and marines, three women and five children on board, she 'Weighed & made Sail in co with the Britannia Dreadnought, Prizes and convoy'. Unfortunately, within an hour she had 'Carrd. Away the foretop Mast' but a replacement from *Dreadnought* was soon in place.

It took eight days for the convoy and escorts to clear Cape St Vincent and finally turn north. By then the battered *Ildefonso* had 'Carried away the Gaff', 'Carried away the Main topsail Yard' and needed 'a Spare Pump from the Dreadnought'. Moreover, there was still a very real chance of an encounter with Admiral Allemand's 'missing' Rochefort squadron.[10] That chance seemed to have become reality on the evening of 13 May when, about 100 miles south-west of Ushant, they 'saw Several guns fired' and 'observed a shot fired at the Dreadnought, beat to Quarters & cleared for Action'. A tense few minutes elapsed before, shortly after midnight, mistaken identities were resolved as 'Passed the convoy an English Squadron'. Five days later, leaving the 'Convoy going up Channel', the invalid ships and their invalid passengers arrived safely at Spithead.

With the invalids sent on shore, 'Surveyors from the Dock Yard came to Survey the ship' but it was another two weeks before, with most of her guns out and assisted by sixty men from the *Dreadnought,* Quilliam demonstrated his prowess as a ship-handler by sailing the shattered battleship up the harbour. This was one of the very rare occasions when Quilliam made an overt display of his seamanship. He did so at the spiritual home of the service and he expected to be noticed. Over the next ten days *Ildefonso* was stripped, derigged and had her masts out, and on Thursday, 19 June 1806 Quilliam made his last entry in the log – 'Discharged the Supernumeraries' – and signed it off.

How he spent the next eight weeks is not recorded although, while passing through London, he may have sat for the painter Benjamin West for inclusion in his painting of 'The Death of Nelson', completed that year. However, the 16 August 1806 edition of the *Manx Advertiser* reported the arrival the previous Tuesday of the packet *Duke of Athol,* among whose passengers 'were Captain Quilliam and Capt. Edward Clark; – the former, it is hardly necessary to say, was Lieutenant on board the Victory in the ever-memorable action off Trafalgar'.[11] He was back in London the following March, writing from his usual London address at 70 Great Russell Street,[12] evidently a hotel popular with naval officers, requesting their 'Lordships to give the usual directions for Paying such Persons as have wages due' for their time in *Ildefonso,*[13] but it would be another two years before the Royal Navy would require his talents.[14]

17

Flag Captain

Quilliam was now a man of some substance, actively managing his properties on the Isle of Man. On 26 October 1806 he assigned the mortgage on a house in Douglas to a John Cosnahan and was present to sign the document himself. He also renamed one of the two properties he had recently acquired at Ballacallin 'Merton', a tribute to his fallen chief.[1] Quilliam's place in Manx society was sealed by his election in September 1807 to the House of Keys, the lower house of Tynwald, the Isle of Man parliament.[2]

As a newly made, but relatively old, post-captain, Quilliam was something of an oddity on the Navy List. If he wished to return to sea, he needed friends in high places. Although his most notable patron had died at Trafalgar, he would have been known to many of the captains who served under Nelson up to that time and at least two of them, Stopford of *Spencer* and Keats of *Superb*, had recently achieved flag rank. Both would influence his later career, with Stopford, a former dynamic frigate captain, triggering his return to sea in June 1808.

Stopford's promotion to Rear Admiral of the Blue was confirmed on 21 April when he was ordered 'to hoist your flag on board HM Ship Spencer'.[3] That left *Spencer* without a captain when she was ordered to join the Channel Fleet under the newly ennobled Admiral Lord Gambier. However, Stopford had already selected his flag captain; on Sunday, 5 June 1808 *Spencer*'s Log recorded 'join'd the Ship Capt John Quilliam'.[4] Appointment as a flag captain under the watchful eye of an experienced admiral could be an apprenticeship for a newly promoted post-captain, but in this case Stopford went on leave as Quilliam joined, and did not re-join the ship for more than a month.

In the meantime, *Spencer* lay in Cawsand Bay outside Plymouth Sound undergoing minor repairs and maintenance before, on 21 June, leaving to join the blockade of Brest. On the same day, back in Douglas, Elizabeth Gelling swore in the Chapter Court that 'Captain John Quilliam ... is father of her illegitimate child'.[5] The matter went no further as, by the time Quilliam returned to the Island, the child had died and been buried at Old Kirk Braddan.[6] Elizabeth Gelling would make two further appearances in the records, with similar claims against other prominent men on the Island.

After weathering a severe summer gale off the Brittany coast that had 'The Ship plunging and the Bowsprit and Fore Mast working very much', *Spencer* joined the fleet on 26 June and over the next few days 'Made & shortend sail as Necessary to keep our Station' with the 'Admiral Manoeuvring the Fleet'. The skilled ship handling required was emphasised on 5 July when a topman fell overboard while bending on sail. Quilliam quickly backed ship, lowered a boat and recovered him.

Ushant has a justified reputation for summer fog and by the second week of July the fleet was feeling its way a few miles off the rocky coastline as 'the Admiral fired several fog guns'. The risk of collision was ever present and on the evening of the 10th *Spencer* 'at 6.30 ... hove all aback to prevent our getting on Board the Royal George'. Happily, three days later, the admiral ordered *Spencer* to distribute her surplus stores and water around the fleet and return to Plymouth. Back in Cawsand Bay the following evening she 'found riding here HM Ship Dreadnought with Rear Admiral Stopford's Flag' and the next day *Spencer* 'at 7.10 Hoisted Rear Adml Stopfords flag'.

While Quilliam was evidently not one of the Royal Navy's evangelical reformers, *Spencer*'s punishment returns suggest that he followed the same policy adopted on *Victory* under Hardy. Over this initial period he punished fourteen men, typically for drunkenness, disobedience and insolence, the last usually the consequence of the first. Quilliam's most immediate concern, however, was *Spencer*'s behaviour off the Brittany coast on her way out to join the fleet. This must have been a delicate issue to raise with Stopford, who had commanded her for the previous four years. Nevertheless, shortly afterwards Quilliam took remedial action as the hands 'struck the Mizen Top Mast' and 'shifted the Mizen Mast to alter the step'.[7]

Despite the speed with which the work was completed, it was another week before *Spencer* moved round to Torbay, where she 'found riding here the Channel fleet'. Although they stayed less than a day, Quilliam, showing the practical but compassionate side of his nature, found the time to write to the Admiralty requesting that one of the hands who had given himself up as a deserter from the Army 'to avail himself of the pardon offered ... in His Majesty's late Proclamation, And as the said Man is a good Seaman ... their Lordships will be pleased to allow him to remain on board the Spencer'.[8] With that, and having 'Received 12 bullocks & Hay for Do', *Spencer* put to sea and by the end of July was anchored off the Iles de Glénan, off the south coast of Brittany.[9]

Although French territory, the Royal Navy was at that time using the Glenan Islands, as it called them, as a forward base for frigates and smaller craft interdicting coastal shipping right down to the mouth of the Gironde, while ships of the line blockaded French forces in L'Orient, St Nazaire and Rochefort. When *Spencer* anchored off Penfret, the easternmost of the islands, she 'found riding here HMS Dragon', another 74-gun battleship, and was joined the following day by the 38-gun frigate *Statira* and two days later by two further battleships, *Saturn* and *Theseus*.

Treating the anchorage as a private fiefdom, *Spencer* sent parties ashore each day watering, fishing and even 'making a road from the well to the Beach to roll the casks on'. Having taken on supplies from a convoy of transports, she left the anchorage on 12 August 1808 and five days later, in company with two other battleships, two brigs and a schooner, reconnoitred the Basque Roads, the outer anchorage leading to the French base at Rochefort. Stopford would be back early the following year when his squadron was to play a significant part in the Battle of the Basque Roads. In the meantime, *Spencer* and the squadron worked their way back to the north, passing close to the Isle de Groix where Quilliam had seen his first action in *Prince George* thirteen years earlier before, on 22 August, anchoring once more at Penfret.

In her role as flagship, *Spencer* remained at Penfret for the next two months amid the continual comings and goings of the squadron, making just two brief excursions as far as Belle Isle. During the second, however, she 'struck on a Rock hove all aback finding her Clear fill'd on the Starb'd Tack'. Although there was no immediate mention of any damage, by the following morning, back at Penfret hands were 'Employed pumping, the ship making from 7 to 8 inches per hour'. Quilliam, perhaps drawing on past experience, adopted a temporary remedy widely used in the merchant service. Known as 'fothering', it involved 'thruming a sail to put under the Ships Bottom to prevent her Leaking' after which the hands 'got the Thrum'd Sail under the Ships Bottom and threw a Quantity of Ocham and dirt between it and the Bottom'.[10] Gratifyingly, they then 'Observed the ship make less water', although throughout their remaining time at the Glenans hands continued to be 'Employed pumping'.[11]

Spencer finally left Penfret on 29 October in company with *Statira*. Eight days later, after a stormy passage around Ushant, they anchored in Plymouth Sound and, the following morning, 'stood up the Harbour' and 'came too with the Best Bower in Hamoaze and took the Moorings in'. Though nobody as yet knew it, Quilliam would not go to sea again for more than a year and *Spencer* for more than five, although both were expected to be back in service within weeks.[12, 13] While the ship was being readied to go into dock, Quilliam wrote to the Admiralty, describing how *Spencer* was 'much inclined to stoop to her canvas'[14] and suggesting that 'a doubling of six inch plank upon her bottom might not in some measure remedy this important defect', the same to be 'carried into execution at the time the ship is in dock'.[15]

Stopford lent the suggestion his support, scrawling 'Approved Robert Stopford Rear Admiral' beside Quilliam's signature. In fact, the Admiralty opted for a different, and almost certainly cheaper, solution. Quilliam, however, had a further request that, since there were 'two spare ports upon the Main deck of His Majesty's Ship under my command ... two long 18 pounder Guns may be supplied to the Spencer to occupy the said ports'.[16] Again the request was endorsed by Stopford, but events soon rendered it irrelevant.

On 13 November 1808 Stopford left the *Spencer* for what proved to be the last time[17] and a week later, with her masts and bowsprit removed, Quilliam 'got the ship into Dock'. However, the damage incurred off Brittany proved more serious than anticipated and when she came out, Quilliam had already been advised that she was to be paid off.[18] Twelve days later 'Came on board the riggers to transport the Spencer further up the Harbour.'[19]

Shortly thereafter Quilliam was one of nine captains assembled on 19 December on the Plymouth guardship *Salvador del Mundo* under Rear Admirals Sutton and Stopford to try by court martial James Smith, master's mate of the sloop *Parthian*, who one week earlier had shot his captain in the back, killing him. The proceedings were described in detail by journalist Cyrus Redding, who was present. After the trial, during which Smith offered no defence and was condemned to death, both Redding and Quilliam were guests at Wembury House, some 5 miles outside Plymouth. Redding described how, on the Monday following, he accompanied Quilliam to the execution; Admiral Young, Commander in Chief at Plymouth, having ordered all the officers of the court to be present. Leaving early in order to reach Plymouth in time for the 8am execution and 'hurrying on at a rapid rate, both able to take long strides, for Quilliam, as well as myself, was above six feet high', they reached the River Plym, only to find the ferry on the other side. Quilliam was 'in a fit of great impatience ... for Admiral Young was a strict disciplinarian' but, despite 'having proceeded at a running pace', they were still a quarter of a mile short 'when the echo of a gun reverberated from the rocky heights. "He's at the yard arm," said Quilliam, posting still more rapidly' and 'reached the vessel twenty minutes after the sufferer had been suspended'.[20]

Quilliam nevertheless escaped censure from Admiral Young and it only remained for the ship's company to be reassigned before, on 11 January, *Spencer*'s commission came to an end as she 'at sunset haul'd down the Pendant'.[21] With that Quilliam re-joined the ranks of captains on half pay.

18

Frigate Captain

Almost a year after paying off *Spencer,* Quilliam wrote to the Governor of the Isle of Man from an address in Castletown to resign his membership of the House of Keys, 'as I intend to quit this Island for some considerable time'.[1] His letter had been triggered by his appointment to command the 32-gun frigate *Alexandria*.

Command of a frigate was the highest accolade for a post-captain in the last decade of the Napoleonic conflict, recognising exceptional seamanship and a capacity for independent operations. Modern analysis of how frigate captains were selected and operated provides a yardstick against which Quilliam's performance can be judged.[2] It leaves no doubt that, far from simply taking his turn, he earned the opportunity on merit. Moreover, the fact that barely a year later he was promoted into one of the Navy's newest and finest frigates confirms his outstanding ability.

Quilliam's opportunity came in early December 1809 when Captain Nathaniel Cochrane[3] wrote to the Admiralty 'requesting in consequence of bad health that another Captain may be appointed to the Alexandria.'[4] *Alexandria* had already been earmarked for Admiral Sir James Saumarez's Baltic Fleet, the most important naval formation of the day.[5] Charged with maintaining access to the Baltic states' vital timber, naval stores and grain, without which the Navy could not sail and Britain could not survive, Saumarez's genius had lain in keeping open the seaways despite French domination of the Continent, fending off powerful Danish gunboat flotillas that attacked convoys in the narrows, courting the Swedes who, despite declaring war, took no hostile measures and crippling the ramshackle Russian economy, which depended on British capital and British shipping.

Built of 'fir' or soft wood rather than oak, *Alexandria* was small for a frigate, but highly manoeuvrable, while her shallow draught was ideal for the restricted shoal waters of the Baltic. Such small frigates were typically the first commands of dashing young newly made post-captains, often in their mid or even early twenties. However, with immensely valuable and strategically critical convoys often numbering hundreds of merchantmen to protect, Saumarez needed proven experience, impeccable seamanship and the ability to command respect among legions of hard-bitten merchant skippers. Relatively junior on the Captain's List by seniority, but at thirty-eight more than a decade older than many of his peers, Quilliam was the epitome of a safe pair of hands. He had never served with Saumarez, himself a great frigate commander, but Rear Admiral Sir Richard Keats, who had known Quilliam since the Baltic Campaign of 1801, had just returned to England from the Baltic. It is likely Quilliam owed his new appointment to Keats.

Alexandria had just emerged from dock at Sheerness when, on 9 February 1810, 'at 11 came on board Captain John Quilliam to supersede Captain Cochrane'.[6] Quilliam was immediately immersed in the familiar routine of refit and preparation for sea. By the time *Alexandria* worked out to the Great Nore in the second week of February she had taken in her guns and shot,[7] 'shifted 11 tons of Iron Ballast from the fore to the after Hold' to adjust her trim to his satisfaction and had the 'Carpenters employed making the Gangways wider'. Widening the elevated walkways linking quarterdeck and forecastle to enhance the efficiency with which the ship could be worked became something of a Quilliam speciality. He may have learnt this lesson on *Amazon* under that notably proficient ship handler, Edward Riou.

Before leaving to escort a convoy to the Baltic, Quilliam had one more request to make of the Admiralty. The greatest threat to convoys and their escorts in the Baltic approaches arose when they were becalmed and became sitting ducks for the Danish rowing gunboats and their fearsome 32pdr cannon. The only effective counter was the warships' own boats, hence Quilliam's request 'to supply His Majesty's Ship Alexandria under my command with Two Twelve pounder Carronades for the use of her Boats,'[8] which received a satisfyingly prompt response.[9]

Alexandria's final departure was delayed by easterly gales but, on the morning of 28 March, she finally 'weigh'd and made sail Convoy in comp'y' and shortly after noon the following day 'came too with the best Bower in Yarmouth Roads in 9 fthms'. There she was joined by three 74-gun battleships, *Edgar*, *Orion* and *Saturn*, along with two sloops, *Ranger* and *Sheldrake*. Quilliam would have rarely left the quarterdeck

Baltic Sea

NORWAY (DENMARK)

SWEDEN

Stockho[lm]

SKAGERRAK

The Scaw (Skagen)

Gothenburg

Wingo (Vinga) Sound

KATTEGAT

The Koll (Kullen)

Anholt

Kronborg Castle

DENMARK

Hulm (Hjelm)

Matvick (Matvik) Karlskrona

Reefness (Røsnæs)

The Sound (Øresund)

Hano (Hanö)

Copenhagen (København)

02.04.1801

Trelleborg

Zealand (Sjælland)

Great Belt (Storebælt)

PRUS[SIA]

FINLAND

Åland I

Kronstadt
• St Petersburg

Gulf of Finland

• Reval (Tallinn)

Dager Ort (Kopu) peninsula

Gulf of Riga

RUSSIA

0 — 200 miles
0 — 200 km

as, battling severe gales, they shepherded the cumbersome timber ships across the North Sea and into the Skagerrak where, on the morning of 22 April, *Alexandria* 'came too with the best bower in Wingo[10] sound', the secure anchorage close to the Swedish port of Gothenburg from which the Baltic fleet controlled all shipping entering or leaving the Kattegat. Next day convoy and escort headed further into the Kattegat, passing the island of Anholt, which had been occupied by the British the previous year, and eventually anchoring off the island of Hulm[11] in the approaches to the Great Belt, the largest of the three passages into the Baltic. There they waited a full week for an opportunity to make a dash through the narrows without having to anchor. In the meantime, Quilliam exercised his boats with the guns, provoking a response as he 'observed 6 Danish gunboats off Reefness'[12] and in turn 'Got springs on the cable'.

When they finally got under way on the morning of 4 May, speed was of the essence and *Alexandria* soon 'repeated convoy signal for ships astern to make more sail with a Gun'. Once clear of the narrows, they parted company with the battleships and ten days later arrived off the Swedish naval base of Karlskrona, where the outward-bound convoy dispersed. *Alexandria* almost immediately 'hoisted convoy signal to the Southwestward' and moved down to the island of Hanö to wait for the homeward-bound convoy to assemble.

Hanö was the Baltic fleet's forward base and its main convoy assembly point. Quilliam immediately ordered 'Out boats sent them on shore for Wood and Water' and within twenty-four hours *Alexandria* was under way again with '124 sail of convoy in company'. By the end of May the battleships had re-joined off the southern entrance to the Great Belt, where a running skirmish developed with a flotilla of Danish gunboats and *Alexandria* 'Cleared for quarters' and 'Hauled up and fired several broadsides'. Once the gunboats had been left astern, Quilliam was ordered to escort the convoy, now grown to 145 merchantmen, out of the Great Belt and back to Britain with only the sloop *Sheldrake* in company.[13] *Alexandria* finally anchored at the Great Nore on the afternoon of 24 June, almost exactly three months after she had left.

While the frigate was docked and refitted at Sheerness, Quilliam identified further improvements, asking the Admiralty for the two 'short Six Pounders on the Forecastle' to be replaced by 'Two long Six Pounders for chace Guns', two of the 'short Six Pounders' on the quarterdeck to be swapped for 'Twenty Four Pound Carronades' and for 'Two of the longest Twelve Pounders for Chace Guns on the Main Deck as those at

Present on Board are so short that the concussion shakes her Stern'.[14] He also asked 'that oak planks may be put in the sides of the ship ... in the wake of the Scuttles in lieu of the Fir Plank'.[15] Clearly *Alexandria* needed a better armament to deal with the Danish threat.

Alexandria was out of the harbour and back at the Little Nore when, on 22 August, Quilliam was instructed 'to receive on board the ship you command Captain James Wilkes Maurice[16] whom we have appointed to Command the Island of Anholt together with the other Officers ... and putting to sea the moment wind and weather will permit proceed without loss of time to that Island and having landed the said officers ... make the best of your way to join HM Ships off Goutenbourgh'.[17] Four days later she 'received on board the Govr of Anholt with sevl officers for passage to Do' and, the same afternoon, 'Weighed and made sail'.

In contrast to her passage earlier in the year, only eight days elapsed before, on the morning of 4 September, she 'came too in 11 fms Anholt light house EbS' and shortly afterwards 'discharged Supernumeraries bound to Anholt'. Four days later she was back at Wingo Sound, where Quilliam was ordered to join the 36-gun frigate *Tribune* and two brigs, *Earnest* and *Urgent,* to patrol the entrance to the Sound, the easternmost of the three passages into the Baltic, which he had last visited in *Amazon* nine years earlier.

The patrol was maintained until the end of October, when *Alexandria* was recalled to Wingo Sound to accompany the last convoy of the season into the Baltic. Admiral Saumarez demonstrated his confidence by giving Quilliam command of the fifty-strong convoy and its escort including a second frigate, the 44-gun *Fisgard,* and the brigs *Cruizer* and *Wrangler.* With the days getting ever shorter, Quilliam took the bold decision to take the convoy through the narrowest section of the Great Belt during the hours of darkness and by 18 November *Alexandria* was again at anchor off Hanö. It was not until 4 December that the last homeward-bound convoy of the season, twenty-eight sail in all, was ready to leave, the escort this time consisting of *Alexandria,* the 32-gun frigate *Tartar* and the brigs *Reynard* and *Flame.* Nine days later, within the narrows they attracted the attention of '12 Gunboats off Knuds Head' and 'beat to Quartrs'. When the convoy was forced by the current to anchor, a gunboat got in among the merchantmen and Quilliam had to send *Reynard* to chase her off. Thereafter the gun boats kept their distance and, by 23 December, the convoy had cleared the narrows and was at the top of the Kattegat. Three days later *Reynard* parted company with a convoy bound for Leith while *Alexandria* and *Tartar* headed south with the remainder and, on 30 December, anchored in the Downs.

Quilliam had completed two full round trips to Hanö, on the second occasion taking overall responsibility for shepherding two immensely valuable and strategically important convoys through difficult and hostile waters. If that was something of a test then he had passed with flying colours and soon had his reward. On the afternoon of Thursday, 10 January, four days after *Alexandria* arrived back at the Little Nore, 'Came on board Captain Cathcart[18] to Super Cede Capt Quilliam'. Quilliam signed off the log at the bottom of that page and, while Cathcart 'read His Commission to the Ships Company', set off on the 30-mile journey up river to join his new command.

19

'A Very Fast Ship'[1]

Quilliam's appointment to command one of the Royal Navy's newest and most powerful frigates was a reflection of professional performance. With ever more ships coming into service, the Navy needed experienced, capable commanders and was not over-blessed with talent. The hapless John Surman Carden, appointed to the frigate *Macedonian*, a sister ship of Quilliam's new command, managed to lose first the support of his crew and then the ship itself through a combination of excessive brutality and rank incompetence.[2] By contrast Quilliam, who had impressed as *Alexandria*'s captain, was singled out for a larger command and greater responsibilities. Quilliam had acquired a new sponsor in Sir James Saumarez, himself a great seaman, because he was an exceptional captain.

Nevertheless, HMS *Crescent*, the Lively-class frigate launched at Woolwich on 11 December 1810, may not have been the Admiralty's first choice for his next command. Several authorities list him as actually being in command of the 36-gun frigate *Inconstant* between October and December 1810 while she was refitting in Portsmouth, although he was hundreds of miles away in the Baltic at the time.[3] Indeed, *Inconstant* is one of two other frigates pencilled in on Quilliam's record of service, the other being the 38-gun *Amelia*.[4] Be that as it may, an internal Admiralty memo, dated 29 December 1810 and now filed among his Captains' Letters at the National Archives at Kew, simply reads: 'Captain John Quilliam to have Commission for the Crescent.'[5]

That Quilliam himself knew that he was to have *Crescent* by the time *Alexandria* reached the Downs is clear since he wrote to the Admiralty from there on 3 January 1811 asking for his 'Commission for H.M. Ship Crescent to be forwarded to the Commissioners office at Sheerness.'[6] A week later he was writing from Sheerness, requesting that the Admiralty 'appoint Lieut Thos Crane … as first Lieutenant of His Majestys Ship

Crescent under my Command'.[7] Thomas Crane was not only a fellow Manxman and briefly a former shipmate but family, his brother having married Quilliam's sister Elizabeth during the peace of 1802–03. Unfortunately, Crane's tenure was short lived. Even before *Crescent* had completed her first deployment, he lost his big toe in action and was invalided home.[8]

The first entry in the 'Log-Book of the Proceedings On Board His Majesty's Ship Crescent ... Kept By Captain Quilliam'[9] was made on 11 January 1811, the day after he left the *Alexandria* and almost certainly the day he joined *Crescent*. While no doubt familiar with the Lively class, he would surely have been struck by the contrast with *Alexandria:* 27ft longer on the gun deck, more than 5ft wider in the beam and a design complement greater by seventy-five men. Most impressively, with twenty-eight 18pdrs and fourteen 32pdr carronades, she threw a total weight of shot more than 50 per cent heavier than the smaller frigate. Even for the former first lieutenant of a 100-gun first-rate battleship, *Crescent* was a seriously powerful weapon of war.[10]

Three days after Quilliam's arrival, *Crescent* 'Received ... 110 Men as part of Ships Company' and, after three weeks intensive work, on the morning of Thursday, 7 February, 'made sail down the river'. That first four-hour, 20-mile voyage brought her to Northfleet where, over the next month, the fitting out process was completed and an immense quantity of stores and provisions received and stowed away – only to be offloaded again when 'came alongside a lighter to take the Provisions in for the purpose of Chasing the Rats out of the Ship'. Quilliam made absolutely sure *Crescent* met his specific requirements, applying to the Admiralty for an 'After Bulk Head to be fitted in the cabin',[11] for materials 'for widening the Gangways to work the ship thereon'[12] and for 'two 32 pounder Carronades in lieu of two 9 pounders on the Forecastle (there being four) and the two remaining Guns to be long instead of short for chase Guns'.[13] She eventually left Northfleet on 3 March and two days later 'came to with the best Bower in 10 fms at the Great Nore'. HM Ship *Crescent* had joined the fleet.

Crescent lay at the Nore for the remainder of March, receiving three drafts of men to bring her close to her full complement. Crane allocated the ship's company, a mixture of experienced hands and raw landsmen, to their various watches, divisions and quarters. Then, with her provisions and water complete and the ship's company paid, on the morning of 31 March she 'weighed and made sail in company with Erebus and

Cruiser'.[14] Two days later, at anchor off Clacton, Quilliam took the opportunity to stamp his authority on the ship's company, imposing the full ritual of naval punishment on five offenders who received from thirty-six to just four lashes for offences ranging from drunkenness and insolence to disobedience of orders. The relative leniency towards some individuals suggests that Quilliam was prepared to match the punishment not only to the crime but to the individual. Within the conventions of the time, firm but fair seems to have been his approach, one that was respected by the majority of the ship's company.[15]

Once out into the North Sea, *Crescent* was soon showing just how well she sailed, the log recording how she repeatedly 'hove to for Erebus to close'. Six days after pausing briefly in Hollesley Bay[16] she reached her cruising ground, the 80 miles of open sea separating the Naze of Norway from the Bovernbergen headland on the west coast of Jutland, in effect the dividing line between the North Sea and the Skagerrak. *Crescent* was now attached to a squadron commanded by Captain Alexander Schomberg of the frigate *Loire*, who held the temporary rank of commodore, although, in his absence, command would devolve on Quilliam.[17] Comprising, in addition to the two frigates, a number of sloops and other smaller craft, its task was to stop and search all merchant shipping, much of it, despite Britain and Denmark having been at war for five years, Danish vessels carrying timber to Britain under licence. At the same time, as far as possible, it was to block all communication between Denmark and Norway, at this time parts of the same kingdom. Thus, on 11 April *Crescent* was 'in Chase of 5 enemy Brigs inside the Rocks' before they escaped into the nearby Norwegian port of Kristiansand.

Crescent's first patrol lasted seven weeks, during which she experienced the full spectrum of weather from calm with thick fog off the Naze to strong gales with snow off Bovernbergen three days later. Then, at the end of May, she was relieved by *Loire* and, having taken on water at Anholt, headed for Wingo Sound, where she 'found lying here' a total of seven battleships including Saumarez's flagship *Victory*. While *Crescent* received a huge quantity of provisions, James Crenon, a seaman, was sent 'on board the Anniball to be tried by a court martial for a Breach of the 2nd and 29 Articles of War'. Article 2 covered 'profane oaths, cursings, execrations, drunkenness, uncleanness, or other scandalous actions' while number 29 related to 'the unnatural and detestable sin of buggery and sodomy with man or beast' for which the penalty on conviction was death. When the prisoner returned the same afternoon, the log recorded 'article 29 not proved' but 'the 2nd Article in part proved for which he was sentenced to receive 300 lashes through the fleet'. Crenon had to wait several weeks before facing his terrifying punishment because *Crescent* was ordered to sea two days later.

Crescent's second patrol off the Naze followed a similar pattern to the first, albeit in more benign weather. As a result, Quilliam had the hands 'painting the ship inside' and, perhaps prompted by past experience on *Triumph* and *Victory*, the carpenters 'fitting the spare wheel on the main Deck'. Meanwhile, the ship's company was being welded into a disciplined unit, with a consequent marked reduction in punishment. Indeed, no seaman was punished during the entire patrol until it was cut short when Quilliam brought *Crescent* back to Wingo Sound for 'the Master & Carpenter of HM Ship Victory and the Carpenter of Cressy to survey the Mizon mast'. Next day sheer legs were rigged to lift the mast out 'for the Carpenters to fish' and, two days after that, the repaired mast was lifted back in and rigged. Unfortunately for James Crenon, it was a week before *Crescent* was ordered back to the Naze and, on 24 July, 'at 6 … came alongside the Boats of the Fleet to Attend the Punishment of James Crenon … at 10 returned the Boats with James Crenon having Recd 190 lashes being unable to receive more'.

Although *Crescent*'s third cruise off the Naze lasted more than two months, the most dramatic encounter occurred before she even reached her station. On the afternoon of 2 August, in company with the post-ship *Daphne* and two sloops, *Cruizer* and *Raleigh*, she sighted three enemy brigs and 'Made all possible sail Squad in co'. It is not difficult to imagine Quilliam pacing his darkened quarterdeck, seeking with 'Top Gt Sails & Studding sls' set to get every last fraction of a knot out of the frigate as the chase continued throughout the short northern night. By dawn *Crescent* had left 'Squadron Astern' and after another ninety minutes was close enough to fire 'three shot at the sternmost Brig'. Half an hour later 'one of the Brigs fired a shot' but that was as close as they got as the enemy hugged the shore and Quilliam was forced to tack. Two weeks later, by then in company with *Loire*, they again 'saw three strange brigs on the weather bow' and, answering the commodore's signal to chase, 'out Reefs and made all sail'. An hour later they 'lost sight of the chace' but four hours afterwards 'discovered two of the Enemy Brigs at Anchor under Fleckwe'.[18] Again, however, they were unable to close and 'at 6-45 wore within 2½ miles of the Rocks'. Ironically, they got their closest look at the enemy a month later when they 'Obsd a Danish Sloop with a Flag of

Truce' and, after heaving to, 'Received 14 Seamen 6 Marines 2 Pilots' and 'Sent away Danish Prisoners in exchange'.

Crescent was back at Wingo Sound in early October, where temporary repairs were made to the foremast. She remained there until mid-November when, despite the lateness of the season, she sailed as part of the escort for a large eastward-bound convoy commanded by Rear Admiral Manley Dixon in the battleship *Vigo*. By 23 November they had cleared the Great Belt when they were passed by a large homeward-bound convoy escorted by the battleships *St George, Defence* and *Cressy*. Unknowingly they were witnessing the first stages of a tragedy. A month later, both *St George* and *Defence* were wrecked on the coast of Jutland with the loss of over 1,300 lives.[19]

Quilliam was now entrusted with the gunboats and Ordnance store ships full of ammunition left behind at the behest of a Prussian officer at Colberg – modern-day Kołobrzeg – on the coast of Poland. Anticipating an early attack by the French ahead of Napoleon's invasion of Russia nine months later, the Prussians looked to the British for support and Saumarez, appreciating the value of potential allies in the region, was quick to offer help.[20] This command was the ultimate endorsement of Quilliam's judgement, seamanship and all-round reliability, from a master of war who, coincidentally, had commanded the previous HMS *Crescent*. Ordered to wait 'as long as possible' and be ready to co-operate with the Prussians ashore, Quilliam had the authority to decide for himself when it was time to get the ships out of the ice-bound inland sea. A month later, with the Prussians still undecided and recognising 'the great dangers and risks of the transports being exposed at this late season of the year in the Baltic', Saumarez ordered them home.

Quilliam and his charges joined the last Baltic convoy of the season, whose escort was commanded by Captain Charles Dashwood of the frigate *Pyramus*. If Quilliam, now just forty, was old for a frigate captain, Dashwood, at forty-six, was positively ancient, but had something of a dashing reputation,[21] which he proceeded to live up to, saving anything up to a week by taking the convoy through the Sound rather than the Great Belt. The plan almost came to grief when they were caught by a severe gale and forced to anchor for three days. Under way again on 27 December, *Crescent* 'fired several shot at a Privateer' and 'Observed Elsinore Castle fire several shot at the Squadn' with the 'Squadn firing and Several small privateers along the Danish shore'. Three hours later they were out into the open waters of the Kattegat.

During a stormy passage down the North Sea, *Crescent* lost contact with the convoy and, having 'carried away the Main Yard by the Main Braces', was forced to take shelter in Hollesley Bay. Nor was that the only damage. Quilliam subsequently had to request a new box of charts since that 'supplied to His Majesty's ship under my command has been very much Damaged by a Sea which stove in the stern sashes'.[22] After fabricating a new main yard out of 'a spare Top Gallant Yard Fore & Main and several small spar', she headed for the Thames and, on the morning of 12 January 1812 'Moored at the Nore'. After surviving the worst of the North Sea in winter, a week later at anchor in Sheerness harbour she carried away the figurehead and suffered other significant damage 'Occasioned by His Majestys Ship Helder[23] drifting athwart our hawse'. Quilliam's reaction and subsequent exchange of pleasantries with *Helder*'s Captain Serrell can only be imagined.

By the time she left the harbour two months later not only had *Crescent* received a new main yard and replacements for the fore and mizzen masts temporarily 'fished' in Wingo Sound, but she had also been modified to incorporate one of most important contemporary innovations in marine technology. Scottish naval officer and inventor Samuel Brown, with whom Quilliam became an enthusiastic collaborator, was so convinced of the superiority of his 'iron cable' over the massive hempen anchor cables then in use that he was prepared to provide and install them for trials at his own expense. In February the Admiralty wrote to the Navy Board advising them that 'Captain Quilliam of HM Ship Crescent is desirous of receiving an Iron Cable in that ship' and requesting 'one of the outer Hawse Holes of the side approved by Captain Quilliam to be fitted as proposed ... the Expenses to be charged against Capt Brown'.[24] Subsequently the log recorded 'Artificers fitting for chain cable' but it was not until the end of March when she was back at the Great Nore that she 'Received a Chain in lieu of a Cable One hundred and forty three fathoms long'. By then, however, what would prove to be, for Quilliam at least, an even more significant change had occurred when 'join'd the ship Lieutenant Thos. Bennett', her new first lieutenant.

Crescent left on her second deployment to the Baltic on 1 April 1812 in company with two brigs, *Bruizer* and *Earnest,* and ten days later arrived in Wingo Sound. Within twenty-four hours she had left again in company with Dashwood's *Pyramus* and the same evening 'Detained the Ebenezer Danish Galliott from Copenhagen to Christiansand with Brandy & Log Wood ... Took the Master & eight prisoners out of her & sent two Petty

Officers Four Seamen & Four Marines to take charge.' Four days later, having ridden out a gale that gave the new chain cable its first test, she was back at Wingo and 'Sent the Prize to the Prizes Harbour'.

Quilliam now had *Ethalion,* successor to the frigate in which he had been shipwrecked twelve years earlier, placed under his orders and was detached to 'keep in check the enemy's and armed vessels upon the coast of Norway and for the protection of the trade of His Majesty's subjects'.[25] The duty, in fact, closely mirrored the patrols of the previous year and for the next six weeks the two frigates and a number of smaller craft patrolled the Skagerrak between the northern tip of Denmark and the Norwegian coast. The spring and summer of 1812 proved exceptionally cold, *Crescent*'s log recording 'thick Foggy weather' alternating with 'Fresh Gales and cloudy Weather with Rain'. However, if the ship's company had been hoping for some respite when they returned to Wingo Sound at the beginning of June they were disappointed. Just four days after arriving, and fully provisioned and watered, they, 'Weighed & made sail in company with His Majesty's Ships Cressy, Bruiser and Baltic convoy.' Initially Quilliam came under the command of *Cressy*'s Captain Charles Pater but shortly after passing Anholt Rear Admiral Martin joined in the battleship *Aboukir* and took over command until the convoy had cleared the Great Belt. Shortly thereafter Pater bore up for Hano Bay, having placed 'the trade bound to the Russian ports in the Gulf of Finland under the charge of Captain Quilliam of the Crescent to see them as far as Dager Ort when he is to return to Hano Bay and put himself under the orders of Rear Admiral Morris, having also placed the trade bound for Libau and Riga under the charge of Captain Ross of the Ariel and Briseis'.[26] Dager Ort was at the entrance to the Gulf of Finland, in Russian waters, and the order once again reflected Saumarez's high opinion of Quilliam, giving him independent responsibility for a vast assembly of valuable merchant ships.

The mission took Quilliam deep into what had until recently been regarded as hostile waters and *Crescent* was shadowed by 'a frigate and a Brig under Russian colours' on the return journey to Hano. She stayed there just long enough to replenish her water before leaving in company with the battleship *Mars* to escort a homeward-bound convoy. The date was 24 June, the day on which, some 400 miles to the east, Napoleon's 680,000-strong Grande Armée, the largest army the world had ever seen, began to cross the River Niemen into Russian Poland.[27]

At the entrance to the Great Belt the escort was reinforced by two further battleships, two frigates and two gun brigs, and a firefight soon developed with 'Several gun Boats in shore' as Quilliam 'fixed the carronades in the Boats', 'Clear'd the ship for Action' and 'Beat to Quarters'. Once the convoy had arrived safely at the northern end of the Great Belt, Quilliam turned *Crescent* around and by 20 July was back in Hano Bay. By then the strategic situation had been transformed since, two days earlier in the Swedish town of Örebro, Russia and Sweden had signed separate peace treaties with Britain.[28]

Quilliam and *Crescent* were redeployed by Admiral Morris to patrol the entrance to the Sound in company with *Pyramus* and several sloops and brigs, basing themselves on the anchorage at Trelleborg. From there they were able to keep a close eye on the Danish gun boats in Corge Bay and, on 30 July, 'Running in shore under the jib ... Captured a small Danish schooner'. However, in the middle of August Quilliam was urgently recalled by the admiral. On the evening of 12 August, the wind failed when still 9 miles short and 'at Ten Fifteen the Captain shoved off in the Gig to go on Board the Vigo in Hano Bay'. Next morning 'At Five the Captain Returned'. What Quilliam had learned from his visit can only be surmised but *Crescent* spent the next ten days patrolling off Hano, paying particular attention to American merchantmen. It seems likely he had been given news of the American declaration of war on Great Britain of 18 June.

By the end of August *Crescent* was back at the southern entrance of the Great Belt as part of a squadron of three frigates and smaller craft that accompanied a succession of convoys through the narrows. In the last week of October at the upper end of the Great Belt, *Crescent* and the brig *Actaeon* were escorting the last inbound convoy of the season when Quilliam 'Observed a Privateer in Shore' and 'sent the Pinnace & Acteon's cutter in chase'. The boats came under fire from field artillery onshore as they closed with her but nevertheless later 'returned having run the Privateer on shore & hauled her Colours down'. She was subsequently hauled off using the frigate's ground tackle and joined *Crescent*.

Quilliam paid his last visit to Hano in the second week of November but this time, a sign of the changed international situation, *Crescent* spent five days moored in the nearby Swedish port of Matvick. Following the disasters of the previous winter, the fleet was to be withdrawn from the Baltic before the end of the year and by the last week in November *Crescent* was part of a squadron bringing up the rear as they traversed the Great Belt with 'several English and Russian ships of the line ahead'. Shortly afterwards, off Anholt, she 'took His Majesty's Ship Courageux in Tow She having lost her rudder' and on the last day of November frigate and battleship anchored in Wingo Sound.

Four days later *Crescent*, in company with the last of the squadron and a large convoy, 'Weigh'd and made all Sail per signal' and, once clear of the Skagerrak, made a fast passage down the North Sea. By 9 December she was off North Foreland but, instead of making for the Nore, two days later anchored at Spithead. She stayed just short of a week before continuing down Channel and, on the afternoon of 18 December, anchored in Plymouth Sound. Two days later, with her powder taken off, she moved up into Hamoaze and 'at One shortened Sail & lash'd the ship alongside of the Clara Hulk'.

Three seasons in the Baltic Fleet had demonstrated Quilliam's outstanding qualities as a cruiser commander. His handling of large convoys had made him a 'safe pair of hands' for the Fleet's core mission, while success in independent roles ensured his selection for the most demanding tasks. A decade older than his peers and a thorough seaman, Quilliam stood out from the crowd.

20

Newfoundland

The Admiralty decision to order *Crescent* to Plymouth had its origins on the other side of the Atlantic. Since the United States' declaration of war in June 1812, events had not transpired as either party had anticipated. The Americans had been disappointed that the Canadians had failed to throw off the yoke of British oppression, repulsing their attempted invasions, while the British, preoccupied by matters closer to home, had expected the war to fizzle out once the US government learned that the Orders in Council,[1] the ostensible *casus belli,* had been revoked before war had been declared.[2]

Matters did not improve when the tiny United States Navy proved it had real teeth and knew how to use them. In August off Halifax, Nova Scotia, the British 38-gun frigate *Guerriere* was overwhelmed by the 44-gun American super frigate *Constitution*. Two months later her sister ship *United States* took the 38-gun frigate *Macedonian* south of the Azores and at the end of December, while *Crescent* lay in Hamoaze waiting to go into dock, *Constitution* took and burned the 38-gun frigate *Java* off Brazil.[3]

The British government responded by appointing Admiral Sir John Borlase Warren commander-in-chief for the North American theatre, tasked with implementing the convoy system and imposing a tight blockade on the United States' Atlantic seaboard. Excluded from his command, however, was the sleepy backwater of Newfoundland, suddenly thrust into the limelight by its strategic position on the shipping lanes between Britain and Canada and the economic importance of its enormous seasonal cod fishery. Its security and well-being were entrusted to Vice Admiral Sir Richard Keats, in the dual role of commander-in-chief and governor.

To cover the vast area of sea 'At and about the Island of Newfoundland'[4] Keats was allocated just thirteen ships in addition to his flagship,

Newfoundland and Nova Scotia

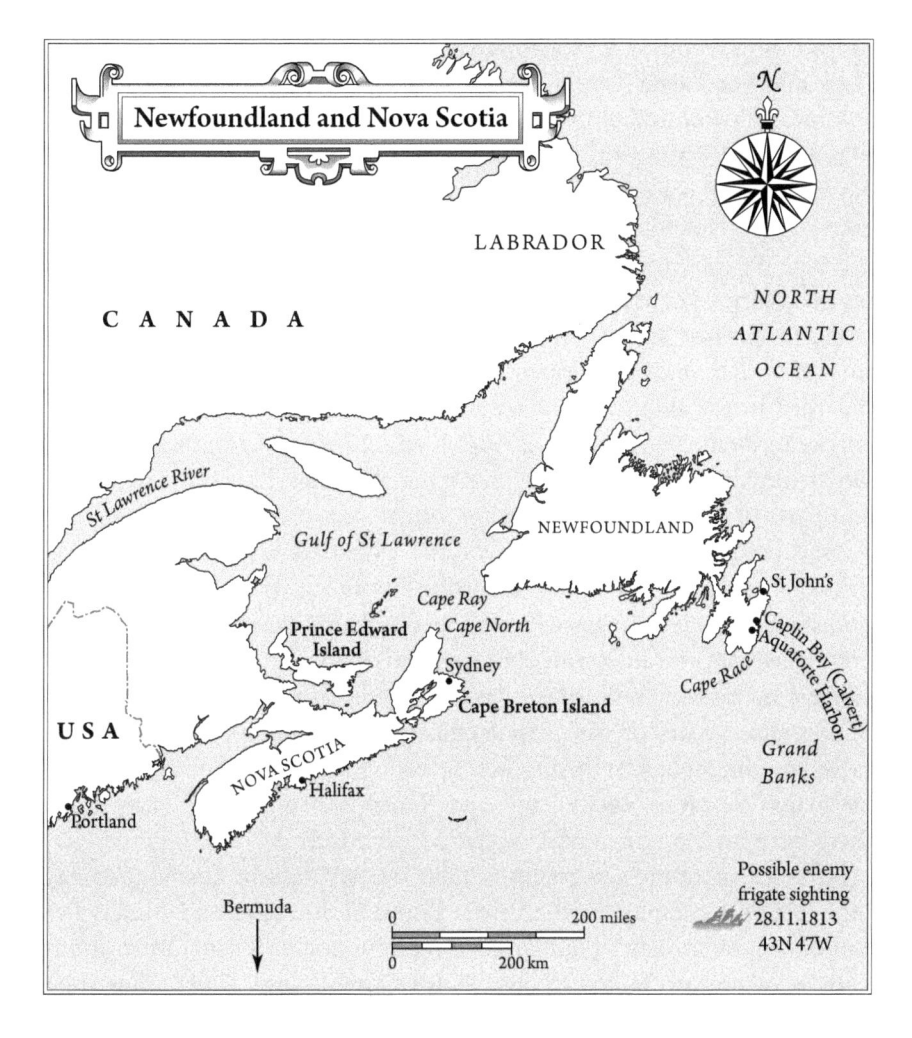

Possible enemy frigate sighting
28.11.1813
43N 47W

the famous old 74-gun battleship HMS *Bellerophon*. Only two were frigates, the remainder assorted post-ships, sloops and smaller craft, many of which would escort convoys back to England. Having most likely been responsible for Quilliam joining Sir James Saumarez's Baltic fleet in 1810, Keats may have approached the admiral to have *Crescent* and her captain seconded to his new command. Quilliam was almost certainly aware of this development even before he reached Plymouth, although the Admiralty only confirmed it a few days before *Crescent* left.[5] In the meantime, the ship had a comprehensive refit, including spending four days in dry dock 'on account of her leaky state',[6] while Quilliam had obtained an addition to her main armament in the form of 'four non recoil 32 Pr Carronades for the spare Ports on the Quarter Deck and Forecastle'.[7, 8]

Crescent's immediate destination on leaving Plymouth at the end of February 1813 was Cork, the assembly and final jumping off point for North Atlantic convoys. She remained there for over a month while her convoy for Newfoundland and Halifax assembled but Quilliam put the time to good use. Recognising that the American super frigates had revealed serious deficiencies in British gunnery, the Admiralty had earlier issued a circular to all commanders-in-chief requiring them not only to ensure that ships performed regular gun drills but that each drill be recorded in the ship's log.[9] It seems unlikely Quilliam needed any such encouragement, but between 2 March and 17 April *Crescent* 'Exercised Great Guns and Small Arms' on no fewer than eleven separate occasions and parts of the battery on a further four.[10]

One predictable consequence of the extended delay was increased drunkenness and attempted desertion, both dealt with in the first punishments meted out since leaving Spithead almost three months earlier. Nevertheless, *Crescent*'s crew showed a strikingly low turnover across the entire commission, reflecting a largely content ship's company. Typical of the latter years of the Napoleonic conflict, they were of decidedly mixed origin; alongside the English, Scots, Irish and Welsh were Africans, Germans, Swedes, Norwegians and Americans although, untypically, there were no Manxmen on *Crescent*'s lower deck.[11]

After a frustrating succession of false starts, *Crescent* finally got away on 17 April in company with the four sloops of the escort and 'Ninety five Sail of convoy in sight'. Quilliam had the commodore's usual frustrations with merchantmen failing to observe his signals but by 6 May they were approaching the Grand Banks south-east of Newfoundland, where the warm waters of the Gulf Stream meet the icy waters of the Labrador current. The resultant persistent fog made convoy discipline even more difficult and increased the danger of a privateer ambush. When one of the merchant skippers reported a strange sail in the convoy, Quilliam 'Beat to Quarters and Cleared Ship for Action' but to no avail.

Two days later, 30 miles south of Cape Race, the south-eastern extremity of Newfoundland, they 'saw the land ... and the Sea Coast covered with Ice'. After a brief exchange of messages and instructions, one sloop was detached with 'the convoy bound to St. Johns' while *Crescent* and the other sloops headed for Halifax with the remaining 'fourteen sail of convoy in Company'. It was a further week of fog interspersed with snow and gales before, entering Halifax harbour, *Crescent*'s jinx struck again as she 'got on Board of a Prize Brig' and 'Carried away our Jolly Boat and Ensign and Larboard Gallery'.

They stayed just a week, during which they replaced 'the greatest part of the Running Rigging' and 'Sent Lieut WA Thompson to the Hospital', he having only joined the ship in Cork ten weeks earlier. Leaving on the afternoon of 27 May with two brigs under convoy, by 3 June *Crescent* was 'surrounded with Ice Islands' as she approached St John's and, on the morning of the 4th, anchored at the entrance. The Narrows, the passage leading to the harbour, is less than 100m wide at its narrowest, impossible for a square-rigged ship to negotiate under sail with the wind in the west. Quilliam ordered, 'Out all Boats and ran the Stream Anchor out … and Warped the Ship up.' Once inside they found that *Bellerophon* had already arrived and 'saluted the Admiral with Seventeen Guns'.

Keats, sworn in as Governor on 1 June,[12] must have been relieved by Quilliam's arrival, having already reported to the Admiralty that 'vast quantities of ice on the coast had rendered the approach to Saint Johns' so difficult that very few vessels of either the Crescent's or Boreas's convoys had been able to get into Saint John's before my arrival on the coast'.[13] However, his most immediate problem was a growing number of American privateers, which were causing serious losses. These big schooners, typically 175 tons with a crew of sixty or seventy and from 5 to 14 heavy guns, could in competent hands and favourable conditions outrun any square-rigged warship. Ideally, Keats would have countered them with similar vessels but when the privateer schooner *Growler* was taken by the sloop *Electra* in July, he was not authorised to purchase and commission the prize.[14] With so few ships under his command, Keats had no choice but to work them hard and hope they were lucky.

Just eight days after Quilliam arrived, Keats, having provided a replacement for the invalided Lieutenant Thompson in the form of Lieutenant George Courtenay, sent *Crescent* back to sea to cruise in company with *Bellerophon,* while he as Governor remained in St John's to grapple with the problems posed by the economic boom and rapidly growing population generated by the war and the consequent acrimonious disputes over land tenure.[15] With *Bellerophon*'s Captain Edward Hawker as commodore, the two ships were to cruise some 350 miles south-east of Newfoundland to intercept American privateers or warships preying on inbound and outbound convoys or lone merchantmen, or seeking even richer pickings closer to Europe. Working together, they would be more than a match for even the most powerful super frigate, the lighter-armed *Crescent* an attractive bait to lure the predator under the battleship's guns.[16]

In the event, though they chased and stopped a number of American merchantmen, all, despite the war, were operating under licence to deliver vital grain supplies to Wellington's army in the Iberian Peninsula.[17] However, on the afternoon of 28 June a brig and a schooner were sighted and led the two men-of-war on divergent courses. *Crescent* 'Made sail after the Brig Bellerophon after the Schooner' and after more than six hours, with *Bellerophon* by now out of sight, 'At 8.40 she hove too'. When Quilliam 'shortened sail and sent a Boat on Board' they 'found her to be the Jane of Whitehaven from St Johns & in possession of the Americans taken on the 23rd off Cape Spear. Took the Prisoners out and sent 7 men on Board.'

With the schooner having predictably outrun *Bellerophon*, that proved to be their sole success. After working their way back through fog and icebergs, the two ships, together with the recaptured brig, warped back into St John's harbour on the morning of 9 July. Seven hours later, and without even having had time to replenish her water, *Crescent* was back at sea, patrolling some 60 miles south-west of St John's where, five days later, she met and 'spoke HMS *Rota*[18] with a convoy to Quebec'. Quilliam took the six merchantmen destined for St John's under convoy and two days later *Crescent* was 'working for the Harbour'.

This time she didn't even get into the Narrows. With the ship hove to, Quilliam 'Sent a Boat onshore to the Admiral' and within hours *Crescent* was headed south into the area she had patrolled with *Bellerophon* the previous month. In waters plagued by ice and fog, the only sail sighted in more than ten days was a Spanish brig from which they 'Received a Midshipman and one Man belonging to a Prize of the Narcissus[19] that had been carried into Savannah'.

Working her way back towards St John's *Crescent* had one of the most alarming encounters of the entire commission. In 'a very thick fog' in the very same waters in which the liner *Titanic* met her fate ninety-nine years later, they 'found the ship surrounded by a Quantity of loose Ice. Tacked and while in Stays heard the Sea break against an Ice Burg to windward which could not have been more than the Ships length from us as it becalmed the sails and the breaking of the Ice distinctly heard, though from the thick fog nothing could be seen.' After a further four days of continual fog, by the beginning of August *Crescent* was back at St John's. This time she was allowed to warp into the harbour and 'At sunset received Sir R.G. Keats Flag from the Pheasant'. Instead of keeping one of his already scarce ships permanently at anchor, Keats simply flew his flag on whatever ship was refitting, irrespective of her being a battleship, a frigate or, as in this case, a sloop.

Crescent spent seventeen days in St John's, taking on water and provisions and rectifying the wear and tear of four months at sea in the North Atlantic. By 20 August, however, she had 'Deliver'd the Admirals Flag to HMS Comet'[20] and 'made sail out of St Johns Harbour'. This third cruise took her round Cape Race and by the end of August as far west as Cape Breton Island at the extreme limit of Keats's station. As well as chasing, stopping and boarding a succession of vessels, including 'an American Cartel from Dartmouth bound to Newport in America', Quilliam again demonstrated his penchant for technical innovation as the log 'Remarked on foretopsail sent on board for trials. Observed the third reef of the Unbleached Canvass quite mildewed and the Patent bleached Canvass entirely free from Blemish.'

Largely uneventful, the cruise nevertheless concluded with two significant incidents. On the afternoon of 13 September, 'At Five thirty the Hands were turned up about ship in consequence of breakers being seen by the Captain off Deck which had been seen twenty three minutes before but were not reported to the Captain by Lieutenant Fortescue the officer of the Watch.' That was the only entry in the log during the entire commission and indeed in any of Quilliam's logs when an officer was named other than when joining or leaving the ship. He must have been furious that he had not been called to address such a serious issue. Moreover, it may be that his wrath was not just directed at the third lieutenant. It is possible that Fortescue had reported the breakers to the first lieutenant, and Bennett took it upon himself not to report them to the captain. Indeed the subsequent breakdown in relations between Quilliam and his first lieutenant may well be traced to this incident.

Any immediate ill feeling would, however, have been dispelled two days later when, 15 miles south-west of Cape Race, they 'Observed a Schooner on the Weather Bow' and 'Hauled up in Chase … Observed her make all Sail and sweeping. At One fired several shot at her and made all Sail to the best advantage … At two Observed the Schooner becalmed … At Two ten took possession of her. She proved to be an American Privateer of five guns and Sixty five Men Called the Elbridge Gerry[21] of Portland. Took the Prisoners out of the Prize … Sent a Midshipman & twelve men to take charge of her … At Six Ten Filled & made sail Prize in company.'

Two days later *Crescent* and her prize anchored in St John's and 'Sent forty prisoners to His Majestys Ship Dryad',[22] the first stage of a journey to Dartmoor Prison, whence some may never have returned.

Keats was delighted. The 160-ton privateer had only been commissioned in July and had yet to take a prize.[23] He sent Quilliam's report to the Admiralty, which, equally pleased, passed it to *The London Gazette* for publication. The dry, laconic report lacked any hint of self-glorification or drama: 'On the 16th instant, four miles off Cape Race, HM ship under my orders, captured the American Privateer Schooner Elbridge Gerry Pierced for 14 guns with a complement of 66 men, coppered and copper fastened, sails remarkably fast and capable of doing much mischief. Sailed on the 5th September from Portland Massachussetts, and intended to cruise in the English Channel.'[24]

Next day Quilliam had further intelligence to impart in a letter to Keats, which the admiral in turn forwarded to the Admiralty. Midshipman Charles Tobin had recognised the schooner's captain as Samuel Turner, 'master of the True American Schooner detained by the Niemen[25] before the American war, after parting with the Niemen Turner killed the midshipman in charge of her and took the schooner into Bordeaux, he was captured after sailing from thence by the Armide,[26] was a prisoner at large on board the Salvador del Mundo[27] last winter, Mr Tobin believes he was sent on board a Prison ship from thence. Since my letter of yesterday on the subject a Document has been found, that states his having been exchanged for three of the Java's men.' In his covering letter Keats added that Quilliam had since reported 'a Copy of our general Day Signals and Telegraphic signals has been discovered sewn up in his Bed, which he says was given him by an American seaman on board the San Antonio[28] prison ship, who had been discharged from a man-of-war and had been a signal man'.[29] Keats sent Turner to England on the sloop *Talbot*, which sailed with a convoy two weeks later but his ultimate fate is unknown.

A week after *Crescent*'s arrival back at St John's, a clerk from the prize agents Hunt, Stabb, Preston and Company came on board to pay prize money for the recaptured brig *Jane* and unwittingly triggered the next stage in the deterioration in the relationship between Quilliam and his first lieutenant. The sums were relatively trivial, even when two hundred years of inflation are taken into account. Lieutenant Bennett's share was just £1 9s, or about £85 in modern-day purchasing power, while individual seamen received sums of between one and two shillings, or in modern terms about £3.50. Crucial to their calculation in foreign ports was the rate of exchange between Sterling and the universal hard currency in which they were paid, Spanish dollars. That was determined by the price the agent had to pay to get dollars, at that time 'Ten Pounds per Centum making Five shillings and Six pence the dollar'.[30]

Despite the agent following standard practice at St John's, two of *Crescent*'s marines protested to their lieutenant, who in turn took the complaint to Quilliam. At that point Lieutenant Bennett also became involved and the issue was widely discussed among the officers, all of whom had accepted payment at the same rate in promissory notes or 'Bills' drawn on Hunt, Stabb, Preston that could be used as paper money on shore. Meanwhile, Quilliam undertook to raise the matter with the agents and there for the time being the matter rested.

Ten days later *Crescent* sailed in company with *Bellerophon* to shadow *Talbot* and her thirty-seven-strong convoy on the first stage of their passage to England. Rather than acting as part of the escort, they kept well to windward and for the most part out of sight, perhaps in the hope of ambushing a privateer or even a super frigate tempted by the rich prize. Keats may have had intelligence from Halifax that the super frigate *President*, which had taken two small prizes on the Grand Banks early in September, was under orders to sail from Newport, Rhode Island, where she had been refitting. With no predator appearing, however, after four days and 300 miles, they turned westward and, a week later, anchored back in St John's.

Hardly had *Crescent* come to rest before Quilliam 'Held a Survey on the Step of the fore Mast it being much decay'd' although remedial work was delayed to a later date, while another survey saw 'Several Old Sails Fore & Main Courses, & three Top Gallant Studding Sails Condemned' with remarkable if unforeseen consequences. Meanwhile, Keats was preparing to depart in accordance with his original instructions, which required him 'By the end of October ... to leave the station & repair to Spithead'.[31] Quilliam would be the senior officer on the station until the admiral returned in the spring.

Before *Bellerophon* left for England, however, *Crescent* had already departed 'in Company with Prometheus[32] & West Indies Convoy'. Quilliam's task as commodore was to see the nine-strong convoy through the first stage of its journey when it was most at risk from privateers, after which he would hand over responsibility to *Prometheus*' captain, Commander Hercules Robinson. It took them twelve days to reach the point some 600 miles north-east of Bermuda, where *Crescent* 'Haul'd to the Wind on the Larboard Tack' and 'Parted Company from the Prometheus & convoy'. Other than her charges, she had not sighted a single sail since leaving the Narrows on 28 October and she continued across an empty ocean as she headed back north-east, taking a wide sweep out into the Atlantic in the hope of intercepting American privateers or cruisers heading home from European waters. That was until ten minutes past four on the afternoon of Sunday, 28 November when the masthead lookout reported a strange sail to leeward.

On the quarterdeck, Quilliam immediately asked the officer of the watch, Lieutenant George Courtenay, to send a man aloft with a glass, while he went up to the main yard, where he was joined by Lieutenant Bennett. Because of the unusual spacing of her masts, opinions as to the identity of the stranger were divided. In the maintop, where the original lookout had been joined by a number of other observers, one group, which included Lieutenant Fortescue, thought she was a large frigate, possibly an American, while others, including the gunner, George Emblin, thought she was a merchantman, specifically 'a timber ship or Quebec man'.[33]

On the main yard, Quilliam and Bennett initially agreed that she was a frigate, Bennett later adding that he thought she was French, but by the time he reached the deck again and had talked to Emblin, Quilliam was fairly certain she was a merchantman. Nevertheless, he had to take into account the possibility that she was an enemy and even that she might be one of the American super frigates such as Commodore John Rodgers' *President*. His subsequent actions would therefore be governed by the Admiralty's 'secret and confidential' order of the previous July that 'they do not conceive that His Majestys Frigates should attempt to engage, single handed, the larger Class of American Ships' but 'should endeavour to manoeuvre, and keep company with her, without coming to action, in the hope of falling in with some other of His Majestys Ships'.[34] While maintaining the Admiralty's confidentiality and thus without informing his own officers of the order, that is essentially what he proceeded to do, giving Bennett permission to turn up the watch and make more sail and ordering a series of course alterations designed to keep in touch with the stranger without frightening her into making off but with the overriding objective of staying to windward of her and thus retaining the weather gauge. That resulted in a verbal altercation with the master who, in something approaching direct insubordination, implied that they should be steering straight for her.

There were no further sightings of the stranger before darkness fell other than by a group of topmen, who later claimed to have seen her from the main topsail yard but failed to report the fact. Nevertheless, the ship's company were kept at quarters throughout the evening. Quilliam paid repeated visits to the quarterdeck, telling the officer of the watch 'to look out for her', while the hammocks were not piped down and the guns secured until the following morning. Dawn revealed an empty horizon. Quilliam and Bennett briefly debated which way the stranger might have gone before *Crescent* resumed her north-easterly course. However, all thought of what might or might not have been sighted the previous afternoon was soon set aside as *Crescent* fought against a succession of gales, heavy seas, snow and hail over the ensuing more than three weeks that it took her to claw her way back to St John's. Finally, on 21 December, Quilliam having six days earlier been forced to cut the water allowance, they entered the Narrows and 'Came too with the Small Bower in St Johns harbour'.

21

Damnation to the Captain

The moment that Keats got back to Spithead in December 1813 he wrote to the Admiralty advising them 'that the Wear and Tear of Sails and Rope on that Station is particularly great in consequence of the American War rendering it necessary to keep the ships almost perpetually at Sea'.[1] *Crescent* had been at sea for 196 days, or 79 per cent of the total time since leaving Cork the previous April, and the wear and tear did not just extend to sails and rope or indeed to ships. The surgeon, William Hillman, had been invalided in late October, while Quilliam, ill during the stay at St John's in September, suffered recurring bouts of sickness over the next few months, possibly a return of malaria contracted in Batavia twenty years before. Moreover, Bennett at some point contracted the pneumonia that led to his being invalided home in 1814.

Meanwhile *Crescent* and her crew hunkered down for a long cold winter. Warm clothing including 'Mersey Jackets One Hundred[2] Flannel Waistcoats Fifty Stockings One hundred & fifty pair Guernsey Frocks One hundred & twenty Blankets Twenty five' was received and issued, while Quilliam had a condemned 'Mizen top sail ... cut up for screens for his cabin' and ordered the use of canvas 'to cover the booms and hatchways to keep the ships company warm and comfortable' and 'canvas and twine ... to cover the chain plates' to protect the cast iron fittings from frost damage.[3] The ship herself had her topmasts struck down and was 'moored with the Chain Cable head & stern & the Stream cable to the shore'. Justifying the preparations, 1814 began with 'Heavy Gales with Snow' on 3 January and a 'heavy fall of Snow' on the 8th, while the 6th dawned with 'At daylight the Harbour Frozen all over'.[4]

Although the last warships, *Dryad* and *Pheasant*, had sailed after Christmas with convoys for England and Portugal, *Crescent* and her ship's company were not entirely isolated. The naval yard could supply most of the ship's material needs, while St John's, undergoing something of a boom and comparable in size of population with Portsmouth, offered plenty to relieve the monotony. Quilliam and his officers were welcome in St John's society and regularly entertained their new acquaintances on board. Meanwhile, despite the conditions which at one point saw the frost so hard that the officer of the watch 'Sent the Rope Makers & Sawyers on the Ice to the Prison Ship' which was being used as a floating workshop, the ship underwent a full refit.

What would normally have been a welcome interruption to harbour routine came in early January when Hunt, Stabb, Preston's clerk came on board again to pay prize money for the *Elbridge Gerry*. Most of the ship's company accepted payment on the same terms as before but all but one of the officers refused. The issue came to a head five weeks later when Quilliam received a letter from Thomas Stabb, in whose house he had stayed when ill and with whom he had dined regularly, advising him that 'The first, second and fourth Lieutenants, the Master and the two Officers of Marines of His Majestys Ship Crescent under your Command' had refused payment on what he claimed were the normal terms for prize money in Newfoundland 'when the other Officers and Ships Company's Shares had been distributed and when such refusal might have tended to cause discontent throughout the Ship'. His name, he claimed further, had been treated 'in public in a very vindictive manner' and as a consequence, while he was happy to continue to act for the remainder of the officers and crew, the officers in question should appoint another agent and their names be removed from the agreement previously made between the ship and his firm.[5]

Quilliam passed Stabb's letter to Bennett, presumably expecting if not ordering him to make his peace with the agent. However, when he responded a week later, Bennett did so in a letter to Stabb so abusive that it could only further inflame the situation, accusing Stabb of an 'absolute Falsehood' and of impugning his own honour while implying that Stabb was not a gentleman.[6]

Quilliam, however, whether because of Stabb's suggestion of discontent or his own assessment of the mood in the gun room, had already had enough and decided to take the ship to sea, because, as he told Bennett, of 'a disturbance among the officers which had reached the Midshipmen and would soon be among the ship's company'.[7] Fully aware that it would take the best part of a month to get her ready for sea, he nevertheless anticipated that all would be far too fully occupied to continue the dispute.

Having announced his decision, Quilliam hardly behaved like a tyrant, allowing the officers of the gun room to continue to entertain their friends from the town on one evening each week. However, following one boisterous evening, Quilliam, who had been entertaining his own guests, placed an order in the Captain's Day Book, requiring the senior lieutenant present to 'put a stop to such undecorous conduct in the future'.[8] When the same company assembled the following week, some reports suggested that the visitors were invited to ridicule the entry while a subsequent anonymous allegation was made that, as the party broke up, Bennett proposed a toast with the wording either 'Damnation to the Captain' or 'Damn him who is the Occasion of your going away so soon'.[9] Bennett may or may not have used one or other form of words. What is certain is that, the following morning, he wrote to the commander-in-chief, relating the reason Quilliam had given him for going to sea early and requesting that he 'Order a Court of Enquiry upon my Conduct as First Lieutenant of this ship'.[10] The letter was handed to Quilliam but would not be delivered until Keats's return. In the meantime, five days later *Crescent* unmoored and made sail out of St John's harbour.

Keen to remove officers and crew from the temptations and influences of St John's, Quilliam took the ship down the coast to Aquaforte Harbour, one of the safest anchorages in Newfoundland, where she spent eleven days completing her winter refit and preparing for the new patrolling season. When she put to sea again on 8 April she embarked on what would prove to be the most intense period of activity since arriving on the station the previous summer.

In 1814 the main American threat came from the growing number of large, well-manned privateers preying on local and inshore shipping bringing from Prince Edward Island much of the cattle, corn and poultry on which Newfoundland depended.[11] Within hours, *Crescent* was chasing and firing several guns at a schooner. The next day she chased and boarded a brig, and on 12 April fell in with *Prometheus*, the first British warship she had seen for more than three months. Meanwhile, the effects of a winter diet devoid of fresh vegetables had become apparent as the log recorded serving 'one Ounce & half of L'Juice & an Ounce & half of Sugar in Do to each man per order of the Captain the Scurvy making its appearance among the Ships company'.

By the end of April, a few miles south of Cape Race, *Crescent* would have received her first news from Europe for some six months when she 'Boarded an English Brig from Odessa to Halifax'. The brig would have cleared the Straits of Gibraltar too soon to have heard of Napoleon's abdication on 6 April but she would almost certainly have passed on reports of the invasion of France from the east by the combined forces of Russia, Prussia, Austria and Sweden and from the south by Wellington's British, Spanish and Portuguese army, which had crossed the Pyrenees in late 1813.[12]

A few days later they once more linked up with *Prometheus* and late on the afternoon of 4 May sighted and chased a schooner and got close enough to fire a shot at her. Certain she was an American privateer, *Crescent* and *Prometheus* continued the pursuit through the night and the following day. Eventually, at eight in the evening, having 'Carried away the Tri sail mast' and 'the Fore Top Mast Studg Sail', they 'Lost sight of the Chase'. If that was an anticlimax, they had done their primary job of driving the enemy 250 miles south-east of the shipping lanes around Cape Race.

Ten days later, having parted company with *Prometheus*, *Crescent* was again in chase of a schooner off Cape Race but eventually in 'thick foggy weather lost sight of the Schnr apparently a Privateer'. Quilliam's luck finally changed on the morning of 17 May when *Crescent* 'Observed two sail to windward Wore ship & made all possible Sail in Chase of a Brig & Schooner'. Although he had also 'Set all steering sails', they lost sight of both vessels in the haze in the early afternoon but later sighted and 'Boarded a brig from Cork to Fortune Sent a Mid & 5 Men to take charge of her Recd 21 men from her taken out of vessels captured by the Amelia Privateer schooner'.

Amelia was one of the most successful American privateers of the war, credited with sixteen prizes totalling 2,270 tons.[13] Built in Baltimore, she had only been commissioned the previous March under the command of Alexander Adams. She was almost certainly the schooner that *Crescent* and *Prometheus* had chased for more than twenty-four hours on 4 May and *Crescent* had chased again on the 14th. Nor had they seen the last of her. Two days later, late in the evening and about halfway between Cape Race and St John's, *Crescent* 'hove too & boarded a Brig having lost her main mast ... which had been captured by the Amelia A Privateer Recd 10 men from her belonging to other Captured vessels'. Early the following afternoon they 'Obsd the Privateer we chased on the 14 and 15[14] to leeward', clearly stalking a group of five merchantmen ahead. On Quilliam's order, *Crescent* 'made all possible sail in chase', at the same time warning the other vessels of the danger as she 'made several signals for an Enemy'. The chase continued all afternoon but once again Adams' luck held as *Crescent* at '9.30 lost sight of the chase' and 'wore ship', heading back to place herself between the privateer and the merchantmen.

Adams did not give up easily. Next morning, as *Crescent* headed south in 'Moderate & foggy Wr', she sighted three merchantmen ahead and shortly afterwards 'Obsd the Privateer Schnr which we chased yesterday bore up & made all possible sail in Chase'. Once again she 'Made the Convoy Sigl for an enemy' and, chasing SSW away from the merchantmen, it was late afternoon before she 'Short'd sail Chase out of sight'. The following afternoon, 40 miles southeast of Cape Race, they 'saw a Sail on the Lee Bow' close by through a gap in the fog. *Crescent* immediately 'made Sail in Chase' and 'beat to quarters' but only a quarter of an hour later they 'lost sight of the Chase WbN when last seen'.

Quilliam was just as determined as Adams. Five days later, on the afternoon of 27 May, *Crescent* 'Exchd Nos with HM Brig Sabine'[15] and shortly afterwards both ships 'made all Sail in Chase of a Schr'. However, in contrast with previous encounters, an hour and a half later Quilliam 'Ansd Signal frm Horatio NW', having 'made Schnr out to be the same we chased on the 14th, 17th, 20th & 21st'. The appearance of the 38-gun frigate *Horatio,* on passage from Portsmouth to Halifax, must have been a nasty shock for Adams. Yet again it was the combination of the elements and his skill that came to *Amelia*'s aid as she ran for her life to the southeast. With the light winds favouring the schooner over the square-rigged men-of-war, *Crescent* had by '8.30 lost sight of the Schr' and at '9 shrtd sail' and turned back to the NW.

That was the last definite sighting *Crescent* had of the privateer. Although she had failed to catch *Amelia*, she had amply fulfilled her purpose of preventing her from plundering merchant or fishing vessels. Indeed, it is a measure of Quilliam's focus on that primary objective, rather than being lured away in fruitless pursuit of glory or prize money outside his immediate cruising ground, that Alexander Adams was forced to cross the Atlantic in search of richer pickings.

Twelve days later, with the 'Icy islands all around us' more of a hazard than the enemy, she called into Caplin Bay[16] for water and, having heard that Keats and *Bellerophon* had returned, on 12 June moored in St John's harbour. Next morning Quilliam went on board *Bellerophon* to report to Keats and to deliver Bennett's letter requesting a Court of Enquiry into his conduct. Keats had left Spithead on 26 April and would have brought Quilliam up to date on events in Europe, where twenty-two years of war had come to an end with the Treaty of Fontainebleau that stripped Napoleon of his powers and banished him to the island of Elba in the Mediterranean.[17]

Keats turned down Bennett's request in a letter dated the same day on the grounds that Quilliam had not 'made any representation to me calculated to reflect on the Conduct of the Officers of any denomination of the Crescent'.[18] Two days later he was surprised to receive an application for a survey on Bennett's health. Keats suspected it 'might be only a pretext to go from his duty'[19] but Quilliam assured him that Bennett had indeed been ill for some time. The survey was granted and Bennett was 'invalided for Pneumonia' and left the ship. William Chasman took over as first lieutenant while 'Lieut. Daly Joined' on Keats's orders.

Crescent left St John's four days later with a twenty-three-strong convoy comprised primarily of transports bound for Quebec to resupply British troops then facing a renewed threat of invasion by reorganised and reinvigorated United States forces. Just nine days later, in the mouth of the St Lawrence river, 'Transports parted Co' and she headed back eastward to patrol the waters south-west of Cape Race. There, on 12 July, she 'Shortd sail hove too boarded a Transport from Bordeaux to Quibec with Troops'. It was the first of four troop transports seen over the next two days as some of the veterans of Wellington's Peninsular army were redeployed to Canada, ready for a planned invasion of the northern United States.

Crescent was back in St John's on Sunday, 17 July where Quilliam found that the Bennett affair had resurfaced. Keats, in his absence, had been informed not only of the infamous toast made in *Crescent*'s gun room before she left St John's the previous March, but also of a further allegation that Bennett had 'beat the Captain's servants'. Keats was in a difficult position. If the story of the toast was credible, Bennett should be tried by court martial, but the witness who had given him the story refused to testify and he could only assemble the necessary quorum of senior officers to try the case by immobilising a large part of his forces. Instead he decided to kick the problem upstairs to the Admiralty, setting out in a letter how 'circumstances not compatible with proper discipline and regularity had transpired in the Crescent'.[20] Quilliam was charged with the letter's delivery and four days later, on 1 August, *Crescent,* which had acted as Keats's flagship for the previous week, 'Resigned the Flag of Adml Sir R Keats to H. M. Sloop Sabine' and 'weighed and made sail'. She had '10 sail of convoy in Company', one of which was the brig *Matilda* in which Bennett had secured a passage home.[21]

Ten days out they picked up a south-westerly breeze and by 17 August were in the Western Approaches where *Matilda* and the other ships bound for west coast and Scottish ports parted company. Three days later, on Saturday, 20 August, *Crescent* anchored at Spithead.

22

Courts Martial

Keats's letter reached the Admiralty two days after *Crescent*'s arrival at Spithead along with a letter from Quilliam explaining his reasons for not having himself initiated a court martial on Bennett over the gun room toast. The information had come to him in confidence via a third party and the actual witness with whom the story had originated 'declined saying any thing on the subject and indeed partly denied what had been at first advanced'. He therefore 'had not the means of obtaining proof to conviction'.[1] Bennett, who in the meantime had been promoted commander and henceforth enjoyed the courtesy title of Captain, had failed to report his arrival at Greenock to the Admiralty, leading Second Secretary John Barrow to enquire of Quilliam about his whereabouts.[2] That failure may have contributed to their Lordships' decision on 7 September to issue an order to establish a court martial on him.[3]

Bennett protested at the short notice but nonetheless had time to get his retaliation in first, writing to the Admiralty to request a court martial on Quilliam on four charges: first, neglect of duty in failing to close with a suspicious sail 'having the appearance of an Enemy'; second 'Wasteful expenditure of His Majesty's Stores in cutting up a Mizen topsail for screens for his Cabbin', allowing seamen 'to cut up Hammocks to make trousers of' and using canvas and twine for 'unnecessarily covering the chains with'; third unofficerlike conduct in calling 'the Boatswain a Savage and a Negro'; and fourth 'Neglecting to see the ship's Company righted' over the prize money for the *Jane*.[4] The letter was annotated on the reverse with the instruction to 'hand over till the other Court Martial is over'.

Bennett's court martial assembled on the morning of Saturday, 10 September 1814 and was presided over by Rear Admiral Edward Foote, 'Second Officer in the Command of His Majesty's Ships and Vessels at

Spithead and in Portsmouth Harbour'.[5] It was unusual in a number of ways. First, because of the number of witnesses likely to be called from the ship's company, it began in the *Crescent*'s cabin rather than in the great cabin of Foote's flagship, the Portsmouth guardship *Gladiator*; second there was no specific charge but simply a requirement to enquire into Bennett's conduct; and thirdly it was prosecuted by the Deputy Judge Advocate, since Quilliam had declined to do so and strongly argued against the trial in his earlier letter to the Admiralty. In his later description of the proceedings in Marshall's *Royal Naval Biography*,[6] which bears little resemblance to the official courts martial papers, Bennett gave the impression that Quilliam's refusal to prosecute came after the case had begun. As a result, in the Bennett/Marshall version, Admiral Foote declared that there was no need to proceed further and it was only after Bennett appealed for the opportunity to clear his name that the trial continued.

In fact, after the admiral and the twelve post-captains who would try the case had been sworn, the Deputy Judge Advocate began by asking Quilliam as the first witness to 'State the general Conduct of Captain Bennett' with regard to the 'circumstances alluded to in their Lordship's order', which had quoted Keats's letter verbatim. Even in the 200-year-old official record, Quilliam's discomfort can be plainly discerned as he had to justify complaints made in private that he had never intended to be made public. They included the allegation that Bennett had beaten his cook, that he had beaten the carpenter's yeoman, that his conduct over the issue of prize money had been 'likely to cause discontent in the Crescent' and, most importantly, that 'I was informed that the Toast as stated in my letter ... was proposed by the Prisoner'. However, while, 'There have been Complaints made to me of the Conduct of Mr Bennett, and I have had occasions to find fault with him ... they did not appear to me to be of a Nature to require a Court Martial.'

Quilliam was followed by each of *Crescent*'s officers. Predictably, none had ever heard Bennett comment on the captain's orders in a manner likely to bring him into contempt, had ever heard him propose either version of the notorious toast, knew of any irregularity or misconduct on his part, or had seen him beat anyone. Each, when asked whether Bennett did 'at all times zealously or not zealously support the Captain's Orders for the good Regulation of the ship', replied that, 'He did zealously.' Only two small chinks in Bennett's armour were revealed over the two days of the prosecution case. Lieutenant Fortescue conceded that Bennett might have made a comment on the infamous order in the Captain's Day Book on the evening of the alleged toast 'without my having heard', while Lieutenant Courtney admitted that, while he did not think the singing that had prompted that entry was offensive, it must have been so to the captain.

With the prosecution case concluded, day three opened with the prisoner's friend reading Bennett's defence. Characteristically it ran to 5,000 words and must have taken at least an hour to read. It began by questioning the legality of the proceedings, complaining that Quilliam was responsible for summoning 'the whole of the Ships Company as Witnesses' and sending the Master at Arms round the ship to 'enquire who could say anything against me' and detailing his '18 years in the Navy' prior to joining *Crescent*. Of the major allegation, he asserted 'as an Officer and a Gentleman that no such toast as that imputed to me was ever given by me either directly or indirectly'. On the other allegations, he was rather less convincing, claiming variously that they were inadmissible, that Quilliam had done the same or worse or, by way of justification for actions he nevertheless denied, that, 'I have thought I had good reason to complain of him.'

No sooner had Bennett's friend concluded with the rousing assertion that 'a British Officer is never safer than in the hands of a court martial' than 'The Court was cleared' and, as Quilliam had predicted, in a very short time 'agreed that the Charges had not been proved against the said Captain Thomas Bennett ... that the imputation against him were unfounded and vexatious and did adjudge the said Captain Thomas Bennett to be fully acquitted'.

Eleven days later, the Admiralty issued an order for Quilliam's court martial on the charges itemised in Bennett's letter of 7 September. When the trial opened on board *Gladiator* on the morning of Wednesday, 28 September, Rear Admiral Foote again presided with twelve captains, eight of whom had heard the previous case and one of whom was Quilliam's fellow Manxman and near contemporary Peter Heywood.[7]

Bennett, though the prosecutor, was first allowed to give his own evidence. He began by relating his version of the events on the afternoon and evening of the previous 28 November, painting a picture designed to contrast his own decisiveness with what he implied was Quilliam's hesitancy. It was he who had suggested to Quilliam that they should make more sail after the initial sighting while Quilliam had appeared disturbed, saying 'Nobody should get to windward of him' and, in a reference to the captain of the American super frigate *President*, 'Suppose that was

Rogers?' In fact, there is no evidence that any American frigate passed through the station that autumn.

Throughout his initial evidence and subsequent cross-examination of witnesses, Bennett sought to dispel any suspicion that his decision to seek the court martial dated from the announcement of his own prosecution. That strategy was seriously undermined when it became clear that he had every opportunity to report the incident to Keats as soon as he returned to St John's the previous June but had failed to do so. Quilliam proved himself adept at cross-examination, revealing inconsistencies in Bennett's estimates of how far and in what direction *Crescent* had travelled after the sighting, but his most significant success lay in raising the suspicion that the log for the day in question might be incorrect and that Bennett and Airey, the master, might even have altered it.

Bennett called a succession of witnesses ranging from Charles Peacock, the signalman who had been the first to be sent to the masthead when the stranger had been sighted, to William Chasman, the second and now first lieutenant. Despite his best efforts, he was unable to establish a clear narrative of Quilliam failing to act appropriately after the stranger was sighted. Moreover, when key witnesses were subjected to forensic cross-examination, they soon tied themselves in knots. Airey, for example, having stated categorically that, if all sail had been set and the correct course steered, *Crescent* would have been within signalling distance of the stranger before darkness fell, was then led through a series of questions and answers that clearly demonstrated the opposite. Similarly Lieutenant Fortescue, having conceded at the end of a detailed examination that, 'If they were the only courses steered the ships must close,' was then asked, 'How can you state then as you did in the former part of your evidence that we did not steer for her,' and could only bluster, 'Most undoubtedly we did not.'

Nor were Bennett's efforts on the other charges any more convincing. Not only were his witnesses unable to give reliable evidence even as to the date when the alleged offences occurred or, in the case of the boatswain, the exact language that had been used but, having failed to establish in advance what had happened to the screens made from the condemned sail, he later found that they had been in store all along.

Bennett took three days to conclude the prosecution case and Quilliam then successfully requested time to prepare his defence, so it was not until the morning of Monday, 3 October that his friend rose to address the court. Even when couched in the formal language of the time, Quilliam's defence statement conveys not only his contempt for the prosecutor and his allegations but his sense of suppressed outrage that the case should ever have been brought to court. That did not mean that he did not take the charges seriously, however. Quite the contrary, they were 'of a most opprobrious nature' and are 'seldom made against anyone without operating to the Prejudice of his Reputation'. As to the events of 28 November, 'as Commander of the ship I knew how to act and was alone competent to judge what was best to be done'. Bennett, however, had presumed 'to represent himself as more equal to the Direction and Management of the Ship entrusted to my Care and authority than her present Commander'. In a devastating critique of the evidence against his handling of the ship after nightfall, he accused Bennett of claiming to be 'not only capable of Demonstrating the Position and bearing of what had been once visible but the Position and Bearing of the same object, after it had been moving in an unknown Tract for an unknown Distance and had long since become invisible'. Two of the other charges were hardly worth considering, but the accusation of 'Connivance at Fraud practised on my Ship's Company' reflected on his honour and he was 'ready to meet the charge to the fullest extent'.

When his friend sat down, Quilliam called no fewer than eight defence witnesses, five of whom supported his version of events on 28 November and proved significantly more resilient under Bennett's cross-examination than had his own witnesses under Quilliam's. However, it was on the prize money charge that he went on the attack. First, he produced an affidavit sworn by the very clerk who had paid the prize money for the *Jane*, confirming that the price the agents had paid for dollars had indeed been 'Ten Pounds per Centum making Five Shillings and Sixpence the Dollar'. Next, he introduced a note from the Deputy Paymaster General of the Forces stating that 'the Lords of the Treasury have paid to the Newfoundland Squadron at the rate of 5/6 per dollar for the many captures by them' and then called as witness Mr John Preston of Hunt, Stabb, Preston & Co. He not only stated that the prize money for the *Jane* had been paid in strict compliance with standard practice at St John's, but that Quilliam had indeed raised his men's complaint with Stabb and had received the explanation that 'there could be no cause of complaint as the Dollar was worth five and six pence on shore'.

Quilliam's final flourish was to call Thomas Humphries, one of the men who had accepted the *Jane* prize money. 'What Officer superintended the Payment of the Prize money?' asked Quilliam. 'Mr Bennett was there when I was paid,' replied Humphries. 'He sat alongside the Table when I was paid.' Bennett, it was apparent, had known all along that his original complaint against Stabb had been based on a false premise. In even shorter time than had been required to acquit Bennett, the court 'agreed that the Charges had not been proved against the said Captain John Quilliam and did adjudge him to be acquitted'.

While both courts martial ended in acquittal, the threat they had posed to both Bennett and Quilliam had been real enough. Bennett had faced the possibility of being dismissed the service or worse, while Quilliam had risked being branded a coward and seeing twenty-three years of service end in disgrace. That both took the matter with the greatest seriousness is obvious from the court papers. Two questions therefore remain.

First, how did Bennett get himself into a situation where he was charged with something very like mutiny and then bring a charge in effect of cowardice against a commander with an impeccable record? Part of the answer is frustration. Bennett had served with distinction in the Mediterranean in the frigate *Seahorse* and had been recommended for promotion after she took the powerful Turkish frigate *Badere Zaffere* in 1808.[8] Unfortunately Admiral Collingwood died before confirming the appointment. It was his further misfortune to be posted to a ship that had been assigned to duties that offered little opportunity for the kind of derring do he saw as offering his best chance of winning promotion. In his view, *Crescent*'s 'captain seemed to have an antipathy to making prize-money, and a sort of horror at the idea of gaining a medal. Under these circumstances, Lieutenant Bennett considered that she would never make him a commander.'[9] Bennett had failed to appreciate that the war had changed. Quilliam, the older man, but the more modern professional, understood that completely, which was why Keats chose him. That, combined with Bennett's volatile character and an exaggerated sense of his own importance and social superiority, made some kind of explosion almost inevitable.

The second question is why the Admiralty ever allowed either case to come to court. The most likely explanation for Bennett's prosecution must be that the allegation that he had proposed the toast was so serious that it could only be dealt with by a full court martial. With Bennett's acquittal, however, it seems even stranger that the Admiralty allowed his entirely vindictive pursuit of Quilliam on the charge of neglect of duty, particularly since Quilliam had a 'get out of jail card' in the form of the 'secret and confidential' Admiralty order of July 1813.[10] Stranger still,

Quilliam did not choose to play the card. If it had become known to the enemy, the secret order would have effectively declared open season on British commerce. Equally, if it had been disclosed, it would have humiliated the service in the public eye, reinforcing the damage already done by the loss of three frigates in allegedly 'single' combat. That may be why their Lordships were prepared to see Quilliam face prosecution.

Four days after the trial ended, Quilliam sailed for Cork, his reputation intact. Bennett's reward was four long years 'on the beach' before being appointed to his first command, the tiny 10-gun brig *Cygnet,* in July 1819 and another ten-year wait before achieving the rank of captain in 1828.[11]

23

West Indian Swansong

By the time *Crescent* left Cork on 2 November, with the exception of Quilliam himself, all the significant participants in the events that had led to the two courts martial had left the ship.[1] All of the lieutenants, the lieutenant of marines and the master had been replaced and she had five new midshipmen.[2] Her assignment, along with the sloop *Forester* and the battleship *Sultan* whose captain would act as commodore, was to escort a 150-strong convoy bound for Barbados. *Crescent* would part company with the other warships short of Barbados and take a section of the merchantmen on to Surinam on the South American mainland.[3]

Britain had been at peace with France since March but, despite peace negotiations continuing with the Americans in Ghent, the naval war continued unabated.[4] As a reminder, two weeks out from Cork, *Crescent* chased and boarded a French ship bound for Guadeloupe that 'had been Boarded by an American Corvette of 20 guns on the 11th Inst'.[5]

It took a further month to reach the point where, with some 700 miles to run to the South American coast, *Crescent* and twenty of the merchantmen parted company, but by 18 December convoy and escort were 'At Anchor of the Entrance of the River Demerara', where they were joined by the sloop *Chanticleer*. The most significant event during the nine days *Crescent* spent anchored off the colony's capital, Georgetown, took place 4,500 miles away when, on Christmas Eve, Baron Gambier, the same Gambier under whom Quilliam had served twenty years before, and John Quincy Adams, the future sixth President of the United States, shook hands on the treaty that, once ratified by both sides, would end hostilities.[6] In the meantime, however, *Crescent* was still very much at war and on the morning of 29 December 'Observed a ship standing towards us with the Signal for an enemy in sight' pursued by another vessel that, shortly afterwards, 'hauled her wind and fired several shots at the ship'. *Crescent* had her fore topmast struck down for repairs, so Quilliam signalled 'HMS Chanticlear which vessel Weighed and made all sail in Chace' and 'Sent the Launch & Pinnace manned & armed'. Realising its danger, the enemy vessel turned tail and the boats returned having 'Chaced for 9 or 10 miles'.

Crescent finally dropped anchor in Carlisle Bay, Barbados on the afternoon of 7 January 1815 and 'Found lying here HMS Venerable Rear Admiral Durham'. Durham had commanded the battleship *Defiance* at Trafalgar and would have met Quilliam during that campaign, while they had also coincided briefly in the Baltic in 1811. Appointed commander-in-chief of the Leeward Islands station in November 1813, Durham had largely purged the area of American privateers by the end of the year, taking no less than eighty-four of them in the process.[7]

Like Keats in Newfoundland, Durham believed in working his ships hard. By 12 February *Crescent* was back off the Demerara River, where she transferred 'a Company of the 60th Regt'[8] to *Chanticleer* for the final stage of their journey to Georgetown before heading north with '44 Sail of Convoy in co'. Five days later she 'Obsd Swiftsure[9] & convoy to windward' and, having merged her by now forty-six merchantmen into the battleship's larger homeward-bound convoy, headed back to Carlisle Bay. Durham then sent her back on patrol to the west of the island in company with the schooner *Grecian*[10] but by 3 March she was back in Carlisle Bay, preparing to escort a convoy of transports carrying troops to the Virgin Islands and 'receiving Gun Carriages on board & Ammunition with Field Pieces &c'.

Back at sea on the afternoon of 7 March with '6 Sail of Convoy in Co', Quilliam chivvied his charges north, taking *British Hero*, a particularly poor sailer, in tow. By 16 March they had reached 'Mount Serrat' or modern-day Montserrat where, concerned about the state of the ship, he left the transports at anchor to beat up through the Guadeloupe Passage to English Harbour, Antigua, where 'Came on board the Officers of the Dock Yard Surveyed the Main Mast found it Serviceable'. With that reassurance, he turned the ship around and in eight hours had re-joined the transports.

A little over a week later convoy and escort dropped anchor off St Thomas in the Virgin Islands.[11] They had been there only an hour when they 'spoke a Scho from Martinique to St Thomas gave Intelligence of Treaty of Peace between Great Britain & America signed on 17 February'. The reaction to this momentous news made its mark in the log as they headed back to Barbados and Quilliam punished various seamen for 'fighting' and 'Riotous Conduct & Drunkenness' and a marine for 'neglect of Duty and allowing the Spirits to be Broached'. What they did not know was that their celebrations were premature. Almost a month earlier Bonaparte had escaped from Elba and on 20 March had triumphantly re-entered Paris.[12]

Arriving back in Carlisle Bay on 6 April, *Crescent* 'found lying here HM Ships Leander, Newcastle, Acasta, Barossa, Redwing & Raven'.[13] *Leander* and *Newcastle* were 50-gun heavy frigates built specifically to counter the American super frigates. Together with the 40-gun frigate *Acasta*, and under the command of Commodore Sir George Collier, they encountered the super frigate USS *Constitution* on 10 March off the Cape Verde Islands. Unfortunately, the American had escaped and only *Levant*, one of two prizes taken off Madeira a month earlier, had been recaptured. Collier was subsequently pilloried by naval historian William James[14] over the debacle and eventually took his own life.[15] Charges of cowardice or dereliction of duty were taken seriously.

Crescent was on her way again in a matter of days and in the last week of April anchored off Road Town, Tortola, in the modern-day British Virgin Islands. There, on the morning of 26 April, 'Came on Board His Excellency Lieut Genl Sir James Leith … Saluted him with 17 guns … weighed & made sail.' A twice-wounded Peninsular veteran,[16] Leith was governor and commander-in-chief of the Leeward Islands.[17] As such he was not just Durham's military opposite number but his equal as a decisive and occasionally impatient man of action. Quilliam was to provide his personal transport for the next month and a half.

After a brief visit to St Thomas, *Crescent* headed for Antigua. Leith already had some intimation of the latest events in Europe and was so keen to consult with Durham that, rather than wait for the frigate to work her way round Antigua to English Harbour, on the evening of 8 May had Quilliam put him ashore at St John's so that he could complete his journey overland. Next morning *Crescent* anchored in Falmouth Harbour, rather than the adjacent English Harbour, but not before she came under friendly fire. Perhaps mistaken for a Bonapartist frigate, 'The Fort Fired several Musquets & a Great Gun at us … found the Try sail mast wounded in two places by Musquet Balls.' Quilliam had to send the jolly boat on shore to establish their identity.

Bonaparte's return had put the British in the Caribbean in a difficult position. French possessions occupied during the war had been restored to France after his abdication.[18] Now it was unclear whether they would remain loyal to King Louis. Durham and Leith therefore decided personally to assess the situation in Guadeloupe and Martinique.[19] By 12 May *Crescent,* together with the 36-gun frigate *Barrosa* flying Durham's flag, was off Basse-Terre, the capital of Guadeloupe, in company with two brigs and two schooners and four days later made a similar show of strength 'Beating into Fort Royal Bay', Martinique.[20] *Crescent* then parted company to take Leith back to Barbados where, while Quilliam carried out a rapid refit, Leith assembled a 'disposable force of near 2000 men'. By the end of May *Crescent* had begun embarking troops and, with Leith back on board, on 2 June rendezvoused with Durham, now flying his flag in the battleship *Venerable*, in Gros Islet Bay, St Lucia, completing a squadron that now comprised a battleship, three frigates, two sloops and a schooner in addition to several troop transports.

Durham had, in the meantime, sent an officer to Martinique in disguise to establish whether the royalist governor was still in control. He reported the position precarious but still retrievable if troops were landed immediately. Accordingly, before dawn on 5 June, the entire squadron was under way and by 8am was 'beating into Fort Royal Bay'. Half an hour later, as the ship's boats began landing troops, 'The general then dashed on shore and took possession of the forts.'[21]

The squadron stayed five days before moving on to Guadeloupe where, in contrast, they found the Bonapartist tricolour flying. Durham, assuming that Governor Linois had been forcibly restrained, offered the squadron's protection but Linois pointed to the tricolour cockade in his hat and told him that, 'I have taken up my position and I shall maintain it.'[22] Leith, 'not deeming the force sufficient to attack the island', decided to return to Barbados to collect the 6,000 troops he believed he needed and, on the morning of 18 June, *Crescent* left for Carlisle Bay. At almost the same moment, more than 4,000 miles away, the first shots were being fired in the battle that would decide the fate of Europe and render Leith's efforts superfluous.

Twenty-four hours after Leith had been put ashore in Barbados, *Crescent* was under way again and on the afternoon of 20 June anchored in St George's Bay, Grenada. Major General Sir Charles Shipley, the sixty-year-old acting Lieutenant Governor,[23] came on board the next morning and Quilliam delivered Leith's request to assemble as many troops as he could afford for the Guadeloupe expedition.[24] However, *Crescent*'s next assignment was already off shore and by evening she was steering due north with 'Columbine[25] & 10 sail of Convoy in Co'.

Six days later they arrived off St Thomas and merged their by now fifteen merchantmen with a larger homeward-bound convoy for which *Crescent* would provide the escort, along with *Levant*, the prize recaptured from *Constitution*. On the afternoon of Thursday, 29 June they 'Weighed and made sail ... 72 sail of Convoy in Co' and by noon the following day were clear of the Virgin Passage with 'Bermuda Island N7E 790 miles'. *Crescent* and Quilliam were on their way home.[26]

Slow progress initially forced Quilliam to set 'The allowance of water 1 pint per man'. Nevertheless, by the first week of August they were in typically foggy weather in the Western Approaches, where *Levant* and twenty of the merchantmen parted company, bound for Irish sea ports, and on the afternoon of 11 August *Crescent* 'saw the land ... St Agnes Light House NbE½E 4 leagues'. A fresh north-westerly breeze ensured a fast passage up Channel and on Sunday, 13 August in the Downs Quilliam reported to the Admiralty 'the Arrival of His Majestys Ship under my Command at this Anchorage with the Homeward bound Trade from the Leeward Islands'.[27] Three days later *Crescent* headed back down Channel and, on the afternoon of 18 August, 'Came Too with the best Bower in Spithead'. Her arrival ensured that Quilliam was just in time to give a reference in person on the following day for Joseph Robertson at the court martial arising from the capture of the British squadron on Lake Champlain in September 1814. Robertson, a midshipman on *Crescent*, had volunteered to serve on the Lakes, which Quilliam said he 'thought was a very laudable thing'. Robertson was acquitted, along with all the other officers and men involved, with the exception of one lieutenant who had failed to appear.[28]

With the long war finally over, ships were being paid off and laid up with almost indecent haste. The next day *Crescent*'s ship's company were 'getting out the Powder' and two days later she 'stood into Portsmouth Harbour' and 'took in the Moorings'. By the end of August, without guns, sails or running rigging, *Crescent* was little more than an empty shell. Finally on the morning of Sunday, 3 September the ship's company 'Mustered by Divisions' for the last time and on the Monday morning were 'Employed paying the Ship off'.[29] Nearly three weeks later, Quilliam wrote the last letter of his seagoing career from his usual Great Russell Street address in London, requesting 'their Lordships to cause my Name to be inserted on the Half Pay List'.[30] The oldest frigate captain afloat had come ashore.

24

Manx Worthy

Three weeks after sending in his request to join the half pay list, Quilliam was writing to the Admiralty again, this time from Whitehaven, the Cumbrian port for Isle of Man packet boats. In a typically generous response to a request from the father of Midshipman and Acting Lieutenant Charles Tobin, he described his 'correct, diligent and officerlike conduct' and took the 'liberty in recommending him to their Lordships consideration for promotion',[1] despite Tobin having embarrassed Quilliam two years earlier by his behaviour at a dinner at Thomas Stabb's house in Newfoundland. In one of his last letters written on board *Crescent*, Quilliam had been similarly generous in recommending early promotion for Thomas Aynsworth, a 'passed' master's mate who would 'from his good Conduct, do every possible Credit to the Service'.[2]

One meeting Quilliam may have had before reaching Whitehaven was with Captain Samuel Brown, inventor of the iron cable whose use he had successfully pioneered on the *Crescent*. Responding to an Admiralty request for a report on the cable's 'general efficacy' from Whitehaven on 4 November, Quilliam demonstrated his professionalism, describing how it reduced the 'Strain on the Cable, the anchor and also the ship itself' and its advantages 'in the West Indies where the Bottom in general is Coral' while giving detailed advice for its implementation and providing further suggestions for other applications.[3]

These letters show that Quilliam spent more than three weeks in Whitehaven, perhaps delayed by bad weather. When he actually returned to the Island or where he initially took up residence when he got there is unclear, but the following March he was again writing to the Admiralty, giving his address simply as 'Isle of Man', in response to a request for information about Thomas Whatman, who had deserted from *Crescent* in Newfoundland. Despite the interval of nearly three years, Quilliam remembered Whatman all too well, advising their Lordships that he was 'one of the most useless persons in the Ship'.[4]

Within two years of his return to the Island, Quilliam had regained a seat in the House of Keys and won the hand of local heiress Margaret Christian Stevenson. The second daughter of Richard Ambrose Stevenson, Margaret was a member of one of the oldest and most distinguished families on the Island. Her father had died in 1785 when she was fifteen, dividing his property between his widow and his two surviving daughters. The family home and estate at Balladoole outside Castletown eventually passed to the elder sister, Charlotte, who had married Thomas Woods, a captain in the 59th Regiment. Margaret's mother had remarried and also outlived her second husband, inheriting further properties, some of which also came to Margaret on her mother's death.[5]

Quite what brought Margaret Stevenson and John Quilliam together is impossible to say, although they would have met as members of the Island's comparatively small military, naval and landowning circle. Neither was marrying for money or for social status. Quilliam, with his carefully invested prize money, was more than comfortably off, while Margaret was wealthy in her own right with a number of properties including Ballakeigan in the same Arbory parish as Balladoole and Balcony House on The Parade in Castletown.[6] Similarly, while Margaret had pedigree, Captain Quilliam had status: if he lived long enough he would become an admiral and was, arguably, the island's greatest celebrity. Nor was this a conventional liaison for a returning well-heeled hero who could have had his pick of the pretty young daughters of the local gentry. Margaret, at forty-seven, was a year older than Quilliam and neither was in the first flush of youth: it is difficult to avoid the conclusion that this was nothing more nor less than a late flowering of genuine affection. What is certain is that they were married by Special Licence on 21 December 1817 in the conservatory at Ballakeigan with the Government Chaplain officiating and Robert Kelly, High Bailiff of Castletown, as one of the witnesses.[7]

On the day before the wedding, the bride's properties were put into a trust, the trustees including neighbouring landowner Colonel William Cunninghame and local banker George Quayle, both of whom were members of the House of Keys (MHK).[8] Earlier in the year, Quilliam had come to Quayle's aid when one of the partners in his bank, formally The Isle of Man Bank but normally known simply as 'Quayle's Bank, Castletown', withdrew, leaving Quayle and the bank in difficulties.[9] Quilliam, with a list of other supporters, advertised that they still used and honoured the bank's notes and he and a small number of others also became trustee directors, enabling the bank to withdraw all the notes and copper penny tokens and repay all depositors in full.[10]

The newly married couple set up home at 'the Estate House' at Ballakeigan, where they kept a 'common dog', but they maintained a separate establishment just a few miles away at the 'Town House', Balcony House in Castletown, where a gig and a carriage were registered.[11] Castletown was then the Island's capital and Balcony House was convenient both for social occasions and for the House of Keys and Tynwald meetings. Four months before the wedding, Quilliam's had been one of two names put forward to the Lieutenant Governor to fill a newly created vacancy on the Keys and on 31 July 1817 he had re-joined their ranks on Tynwald Hill for the promulgation of Acts concerning bank notes, criminal law and herring fisheries.[12] His selection may have caused some temporary family coolness since the defeated candidate was his future wife's brother-in-law, Captain Thomas Woods.[13] Ironically, one of the first meetings of the Keys Quilliam attended after his reappointment received a report from architect Thomas Brine that their building was 'unfit and iminently unsafe'. Members immediately adjourned, reconvening at the nearby George Hotel, where they continued to meet until their new building opened in January 1821.[14]

In the meantime, unfinished business from the past continued to claim Quilliam's attention. Three months before the wedding, he had responded to the Admiralty's request for a 'Statement of my Services in His Majesty's Navy according to my best recollection up to Sepr 1815',[15] although, given his other preoccupations at the time, it is perhaps not surprising that, not only had it taken him a month and a half to compile the resultant 'Memorandum', but it contained a number of minor inaccuracies.[16] A year later the Admiralty wrote again, forwarding a claim that he had taken into safe keeping prize money paid to one of *Crescent*'s former marines and failed to return it. Quilliam responded brusquely that it had been his 'rule, never to keep in my hand Seamans money ... and surely not the Money of Marines'[17] and that in any case the prize mentioned had not been taken by *Crescent*. Nevertheless, perhaps aware of the shadow of Thomas Bennett and the possibility of scandal if the story was not firmly scotched, he wrote again three months later to report that, 'after considerable Trouble and Expence', he had established that the prize agents named had never made the payment referred to.[18]

While such echoes of past service gradually died away, Quilliam maintained his interest in naval affairs in general and in technological innovation in particular. In 1820, he wrote to the Admiralty on behalf of his friend and fellow MHK George Quayle, enclosing, at the latter's request, proposals for 'a new Mode of applying the Power of Steam to Steam Vessels'[19] which Quilliam believed was 'of that plain and simple nature that I have no doubt but it will fully answer the report given of it'.[20] In addition to his other interests, Quayle was an enthusiastic inventor and innovator with a proven track record, having thirty years earlier commissioned the schooner-rigged shallop *Peggy*, one of the first vessels to incorporate sliding keels or dagger boards.[21] Unfortunately, he played his cards so close to his chest that he failed to reveal the actual nature of his 'Improvement', with the result that their Lordships did 'not feel called upon to give any response on this subject'. However, it seems very likely that he was proposing screw propulsion, some fifteen years before Francis Pettit Smith filed the first patent. Both his and Quilliam's interest in steam propulsion would have been heightened by the steam ships that visited the Island periodically from 1815 onwards, at least one of which got into difficulties and came into Ramsey for repair.[22] By 1819 Douglas had become a 'call point' on a regular steamer service between Liverpool and Greenock and on 24 April 1821 Quilliam, together with Colonel Cunninghame, took passage from Douglas to Scotland on the steam packet *Superb*.[23]

Quilliam also kept up a correspondence with his former lieutenant William Parry, after Nelson the most distinguished of all his former shipmates. Parry's expedition in search of the North West Passage had succeeded in getting further west than anyone would manage for another thirty years. In late 1820 Quilliam congratulated him on his safe return, prompting a fulsome response in which Parry thanked him not just for the 'very kind and friendly congratulations' but for the 'hints you have been good enough to give me respecting the harpoon gun'. Parry was already preparing yet another expedition and invited Quilliam to 'come and have a look at our ships which will be fitting out ... till the middle of April'.[24] There is no record of Quilliam visiting the ships before they sailed but Parry did him the honour of naming Quilliam Creek, also now known as Quilliam Bay, at 69° 30' N, 82° 45'W in Nunavut, northern Canada after him.[25]

Nor was Parry the only former shipmate with whom Quilliam remained in touch. In May 1825 he received a letter from Captain, shortly to be Admiral, Hardy, responding to an earlier letter and regretting that they had missed each other in London. Hardy added that he was 'excessively sorry to hear so bad an account of your health',[26] the first indication of any deterioration in Quilliam's condition since his coming ashore.

Quilliam's post-war maritime activity also included initiatives aimed at reducing the loss of life through shipwreck in Manx waters. In this he supported the efforts of Sir William Hillary, an English baronet who had originally sought refuge from his creditors on the Island in 1808. Following the loss of the 16-gun sloop *Racehorse*, commanded by Nelson's nephew Maurice Suckling, off Langness Point in 1822, Hillary launched 'An Appeal to the British Navy on the Humanity and Policy of Forming a National Institution for the Preservation of Lives and Property from Shipwreck'. Although the initial response was disappointing, he persisted and, in March 1824, an inaugural meeting was held in London of 'The National Institution for the Preservation of Life from Shipwreck'. The new body soon attracted royal patronage but it was not until 1854 that it changed its name to the Royal National Lifeboat Institution.[27]

Shortly after that first meeting, Hillary arranged for the first lifeboat ordered by the Institution to be stationed at Douglas. However, he seems to have failed to tell the National Committee that he had already ordered a boat for Douglas, so that lifeboat, paid for by subscription largely from Lloyd's of London and insurance underwriters in Liverpool, was offered to Castletown. There, an organising committee of Quilliam and six others was appointed and suggested that the boats 'might be rendered more efficient by the addition of Capt. Manby's apparatus'.[28] Matters were put on a more formal basis in January 1826 when Lieutenant Governor Smelt chaired a meeting in the Courthouse at Castle Rushen, Castletown, 'for the purpose of … forming the Isle of Man into a District Association of the Royal National Institution for the Preservation of Life from Shipwreck'. Quilliam proposed that the name should be 'The Isle of Man District Association' of the Institution and suggested how and by whom it should be governed.[29] Two months later, a general meeting of the District Association established Local or Port Committees and appointed Quilliam vice-chairman of the Castletown Committee. Thomas Brine, the architect, was commissioned to design a boathouse and a carriage for the lifeboat. Quilliam's involvement continued until at least March 1827 when he chaired a meeting of 'The Committee for Shipwrecked Seamen' that authorised payments to ten men for services rendered in the lifeboat to vessels at Douglas, Port St Mary and Derbyhaven.[30]

Concern for improved maritime safety extended to a recognition of the inadequacy of the harbour at Douglas, outside which, as long ago as

1787, some fifty boats from the Manx fishing fleet had been wrecked in a storm with the loss of more than twenty lives.[31] A report in 1790 had called for the creation of a 'Deep Water Harbour of Refuge' and the issue was raised again in both 1822 and 1823. Quilliam then lent his weight to the campaign in 1824, sending a written report supported by plans to various government departments. Although it received complimentary comments, the lack of a practical response led Hillary to publish the information in a series of pamphlets.[32]

Quilliam also conceived several proposals for developing the port at Derbyhaven, one of which was for the construction of a canal across the narrow isthmus dividing it from Castletown Bay. This would allow ships detained by easterly winds to 'proceed on their voyage' when 'there was no tug to take them to the offing. Out of his own pocket, he employed several men with long iron bars probing the soil according to his directions. Failing health, however, caused him to abandon all his plans.'[33] Although that scheme was stillborn, another Quilliam proposal, for the erection of a breakwater at Derbyhaven, did go ahead, albeit thirteen years after his death.[34]

Quilliam's expertise was further exploited when, in 1826, he served on a committee set up to enquire into the state of the Manx herring fishery. Together with a number of colleagues, he set out to demonstrate how improving the boats themselves could transform the industry. The consortium bought and modified a boat, which they equipped with improved gear to enable her to be managed by a smaller crew than traditional Manx vessels. The *Davis* would be the prototype of the Manx 'Dandys' that formed the basis of a booming Manx herring fishery by the middle of the century.[35] In an almost certainly apocryphal anecdote, an eyewitness, who cannot have been more than six years old at the time, had Quilliam 'with his quarter deck dignity, seated in his arm chair on Castletown Pier', supervising his own carpenter, a Mr Fife, in setting up another vessel, the *Betsy*. When Quilliam directed Fife to 'see that the tabernacle is sufficiently roomy to allow of the easy lowering of the mast', the diminutive witness claims to have exclaimed, 'What! Are you about to make a Jewess of her Captain and allow her a tabernacle!' 'Stopper your jaw, you young landshark', Quilliam is claimed to have replied. 'I suppose you intended that for wit – you young powder monkey!'[36]

Meanwhile, Quilliam's membership of the House of Keys had placed him at the centre of its dispute with the Duke of Atholl and of the resulting unrest and hardship experienced by the wider community. The Duke had made himself increasingly unpopular, not least by appointing his thirty-year-old nephew George Murray to the Bishopric of Sodor and Mann and a number of other relatives to posts in the Island.[37] The Bishop had added to growing resentment in 1815 by attempting to commute tythes in kind due to the church to cash payments and ten years later precipitated the notorious 'Potato Riots' by attempting to levy a previously uncollected tythe on 'green crops'.[38]

That Quilliam was directly involved in the dispute as early as 1819 is indicated by a letter written by his sister-in-law Charlotte to her son George that June, quoting a letter from Margaret which observed that '... were it not for our Public Grievance I should be very happy, for Capt. Quilliam does all in his power to make me so'.[39] The dispute moved to a new level in late 1821 when, in the view of the Keys, a speech delivered by the Duke, 'made imputations on their honour and character as Gentlemen' and sought to 'degrade them in the eyes of the public'.[40] George Quayle and John Christian Curwen,[41] both long-standing members of the Keys and the latter also a member of the Westminster parliament, together with Quilliam, spearheaded opposition to the Duke. Quilliam was a signatory to a document embodying the Keys' response, which was forwarded to London and set in chain a sequence of events that eventually led to the House of Commons, with Curwen taking an active role, voting to enter into negotiations relating to the Duke's remaining rights and properties.[42]

Quilliam had been chosen by the Keys to be a member of a 'Committee of Communication'[43] and consequently stayed in London on numerous occasions during the middle years of the decade. On one such visit in May 1824 he wrote from London to John McHutchin, Deemster and head of the Isle of Man judiciary as Clerk of the Rolls.[44] The letter highlights two aspects of the older Quilliam, his willingness to go to considerable lengths to establish the right to a pension of the widow of a fellow officer, Captain Kelly, and his deep concern for the Island. In the context of the dispute with the Duke, he described the conduct of a recent trial in Castletown as involving 'the destruction of the Ancient Constitution of poor Mona ... by which a door has been opened to the most frightful oppression and injustice', adding that 'very soon Algiers will be a Paradise in comparison to my native Island'.[45]

Negotiations were eventually completed in 1828 when the British government purchased all the Duke's remaining rights and properties in the Island. By then, however, Quilliam's health was failing. In April of that year he made provision for his widow and siblings and their descendants, putting his Ballacallin and Ballakelly properties in trust, and signed a short will, itemising those properties that were in the hands of his trustees and leaving the remainder of his estate to his wife with her as sole executrix.[46] Perhaps it was at this time that he amended in pencil the first line of a prayer 'For a sick person' in Margaret's copy of *Prayers for The Use of Families*[47] to read 'I thy servant' in place of 'thy servant' in 'We offer up our supplications on behalf of Thy servant … let the consideration of thy goodness strengthen and comfort his soul in this time of affliction.'

Finally, in the autumn of 1829, the Quilliams moved to the supposedly healthier climate of the north-west of the island, taking up residence at the Whitehouse at Kirk Michael, a property leased by fellow MHK and future Speaker of the Keys General Goldie.[48] It was there that he died on 10 October 1829, less than a month after his fifty-eighth birthday.

25

An Honest Man, the Noblest Work of God

John Quilliam's funeral took place on Wednesday, 14 October 1829, four days after his death. Margaret Quilliam, who was to outlive her husband by another seventeen years, cut a few locks of his hair and wrapped them in a corner cut from his shroud[1] before he was buried in the Stevenson family tomb in Arbory churchyard.[2] Among the mourners was a group of 'poor widows who had been receiving weekly alms from Mrs Quilliam' and who came to 'pay their last respects to Captain Quilliam'. Margaret subsequently acknowledged their presence with an increase in their weekly alms. In a further mark of her deep and genuine affection for her husband, she left an endowment in the hands of trustees for the instruction of boys and young men in navigation, which is thought to have subsequently been applied to the support of King William's College.[3]

Except where they impugned his honour, Quilliam was not given to correcting even the most outrageously erroneous versions of his life story circulated during his lifetime, with the result that the obituary published in the *Manx Sun* on the day before the funeral perpetuated many of the myths that have been repeated assiduously down the years. His career aside, however, the *Sun* recorded that 'those only who knew his philanthropy, his uncompromising firmness of character in support of justice and truth, and the singleness of his views in promoting the welfare and best interests of this his native country, can only appreciate his value when living, and the loss sustained by his death'.[4] To the *Manx Advertiser* a week later he was simply 'a sensible, social, pleasing companion' and to 'his domestics a kind and good master'.[5]

It was left to Margaret to record the details of his career in the epitaph she had carved on the memorial tablet she placed in St Columba's church at Arbory. The work of a devoted wife, it reads:

Sacred to the memory of John Quilliam Esq, Captain in the Royal Navy. In his early service he was appointed by Adml. Lord Duncan to act as lieutenant at the Battle of Camperdown; after the victory was achieved, this appointment was confirmed. His gallantry and professional skill at the Battle of Copenhagen attracted the notice of Lord Nelson, who subsequently sought for his services on board his own ship, and as his lordship's first lieut. He steered the Victory into action at the Battle of Trafalgar.

By the example of Duncan and Nelson he learnt to conquer. By his own merit he rose to command; above all this he was an honest man, the noblest work of God. After many years of honourable and distinguished professional service, he retired to this land of his affectionate solicitude and birth, where in his public station as a member of the House of Keys, and in private life he was in arduous times the uncompromising defender of the rights and privileges of his countrymen, and the zealous and able supporter of every measure tending to promote the welfare and the best interests of his country. He departed this life on the 10th of October 1829 in the 59th year of his age.

This monument is erected by MARGARET. C. QUILLIAM to the memory of her beloved husband.

Notes

Quilliam in Context
1 Bourne, John M, *Patronage and Society in Nineteenth Century England*, Arnold, London, 1986. 2 Lewis, Michael, *A Social History of the Navy, 1793–1815* (London, 1960) is the standard work. 3 Wilson, Evan, 'Social Background and Promotion Prospects in the Royal Navy, 1775–1815'. *The English Historical Review*, 2016, Vol. 131 (550), pp. 570–595, at p. 587. 4 For a full-length study see: Wilson, Evan, *A Social History of British Naval Officers, 1775–1815*, Boydell, Woodbridge, 2017.

Chapter 1 Land of his Birth
1 'O Land of our birth' is the opening line of the Manx National Anthem. 2 The name Quilliam is a combination of the Gaelic Mac, meaning son of, and William. Mac fell out of usage on the Island in the seventeenth century although the final 'c' was retained. 3 Marown Parish Church Baptism Register. However, the Baptism certificate provided by the Minister at Kirk Marown in May 1798 and held with Lieutenants' Passing Certificates at the National Archives appears to give the date as 30 September 1772. See ADM 107/22. 4 The Isle of Man, 227 square miles in area and set in the centre of the Irish Sea from where England, Wales, Scotland, Northern Ireland and the Irish Republic can all be seen on a clear day, is not and never has been part of the United Kingdom. Despite being first and foremost Manx, however, it considers itself British and is a member of the British Commonwealth in its own right, having, often at great cost, supported Britain against its enemies over the centuries. Under the Vikings it became the capital of the Kingdom of Mann and the Isles with its own parliament, Tynwald, the world's oldest parliamentary assembly in continuous existence. Overlordship of the kingdom was sold by the King of Norway to the King of Scotland in 1266 and was eventually taken by England in the fourteenth century. It was subsequently granted to the Lords Stanley, later the Earls of Derby, in the early fifteenth century and eventually to the Dukes of Atholl. 5 In both earlier generations the first born was named John but when that child died the next male child was again named John, a common practice in Manx families, which tended to use a very selective range of names. As a result, in Quilliam's lifetime there may well have been in excess of 100 other John Quilliams. Nor was he the only Captain John Quilliam R.N. Another died in 1714 having purchased several properties on the island, perhaps investing prize money (Marown Parish Burial Register, 13 February 1714) while a John Quilliam died in Liverpool in 1810, shortly after receiving prize money gained while master of HMS *San Pareil* (Will NA Prerogative Court of Canterbury 24 July 1810, PROB 11/.1513/380. Collingwood Queue Numbers 354–400). 6 Marown Parish Burial Register. 7 Manx Museum (MM) Deeds October 1783 Marown 44. 8 At least two John Quilliams were pressed, however, one apprenticed to Captain P Quayle of the brig *Ellan Vannin* (the Manx language name for the Isle of Man) along with five other Manxmen in September 1789, another from the *Vede*, Captain Maxwell, in January 1794. (BT 98/54 pp. 212, 127, 181). 9 Isle of Man Government Harbours History, www.gov.im/about-the-

government/departments/infrastructure/harbours-information/harbours-history. **10** Gill, J F, ed., *The Statutes of the Isle of Man*, Vol. 1, Eyre & Spottiswoode, London, 1883, reprinted 1992, Clauses 9–12, pp. 155–161. **11** MM MS 65A.
12 *Journal of the House of Keys*, 1761–1852, MM MS 9191/2/2/1, p. 238. **13** Fannin had served as a master on the Irish Sea Station and in 1789 published one of the first detailed maps of the Island. His school was held in a building on Douglas Harbour Side that still exists and was then occupied by Peter John Heywood, father of *Bounty* mutineer Peter Heywood. The newly married William Bligh, who had been master of HMS *Resolution* on Cook's third expedition, lived just 200yd away, as did the family of Fletcher Christian. **14** *Cumberland Pacquet, 12* October, 1779. See also Clowes, W L, *The Royal Navy*, Chatham reprint 1997, Vol. 14, pp. 10–12. **15** For a general account of smuggling see Wilkins, F, *The Isle of Man in Smuggling History*, Wyre Forest Press, 1992, p. 1. **16** Nicolas, Sir Nicholas Harris, ed., *The Dispatches and Letters of Vice Admiral Lord Viscount Nelson*, Vol. 4, Henry Colburn, London, 1845, p. 534. **17** *A Six Days Tour of the Isle of Man by A Stranger*, attributed to Welch, John, William Dillon, 1836, p. 61. **18** Crimmin, P K, *Pasley, Sir Thomas*, in *Oxford Dictionary of National Biography*, Online edition, 2008. **19** Cowin, F, *The Lady on the Stamp, Isle of Man Natural History and Antiquarian Society* Vol. 12, No. 3, 2013. pp. 522–575. His brother, Captain Thomas Dundas, commanded the frigate *Naiad* at Trafalgar. **20** Hore, Peter, *Nelson's Band of Brothers: Lives and Memorials*, Seaforth Publishing, Barnsley, 2015, p. 56. **21** *The Revestment Act 1765*, www.tynwald.org.im/education/history/1867/Pages/1765.aspx.

Chapter 2 Ship Keeper

1 Portsmouth Ordinary Dockyard Paybook 1785, ADM 42/1122. **2** Ibid. **3** John Crane had been master of the 74-gun battleship *Courageux*, which had been captured from the French in 1761. When she was paid off at the end of the American War of Independence in 1783, Crane sought to enter the dockyard service, a common choice of second career for retired sailing masters. He was one of two candidates for the newly created post of Master Attendant at Harwich but lost out to the master of *Victory*. He was almost certainly in the dockyard service from 1783 and was Master Attendant at Sheerness from April 1790 before being appointed Second Master Attendant at Portsmouth in April 1791. He eventually retired as First Master Attendant in 1810 having, according to his pension claim, served a total of fifty-three years, three months, two weeks and five days. It is surely more than just coincidence that, in 1786, he was master of *Romulus* for three weeks up to the day before Quilliam transferred to her and of *Fox* for a further two weeks, starting the day after Quilliam left her. **4** Pre-decimalisation of British currency, £1 = 20s (shillings), 1s = 12d (old pence), hence post-decimalisation 1p (new penny) = 2.4d. **5** Portsmouth Ordinary Dockyard Paybook 1785, ADM 42/1122. **6** HMS *Lion*, Captain's Log, 20.06.1790–15.09.1791, ADM 51/523. **7** HMS *Lion*, Muster Book 01.02.1791–30.09.1791, ADM 36/11037. **8** HMS *Lion*, Muster Book 01.05.1792–31.10.1793, ADM 36/11208. **9** Rodger, N A M, *The Wooden World*, William Collins, London, 1986. **10** Ibid. **11** Laughton, John Knox, *Hardy, Thomas Masterman*, in Lee, Sidney. *Dictionary of National Biography*, 24, Smith, Elder & Co., London, 1890. **12** Barrow, John, *Some Account of the Public Life, and a Selection from the Unpublished Writings, of the Earl of Macartney*, T Cadell and W Davies, London, 1807. **13** Head, C G, *Gower, Sir Erasmus*, in *Dictionary of Canadian Biography*, Vol. 5, online edition at www.biographi.ca/en/bio/gower_erasmus_5E.html. **14** HMS *Lion*, Captain's Log, 05.05.1792–13.10.1794, ADM 51/1154.

Chapter 3 China

1 ADM 51/1154. **2** Staunton, Sir George, *An Authentic Account of An Embassy from the King of Great Britain to the Emperor of China, Volume 1*. C Nicol, Bookseller to His Majesty, London, 1797. Assisted by Barrow, Staunton described the expedition from its departure from Portsmouth in 1792 to its eventual arrival back there in 1794 in great detail in three volumes published in 1797. However, he was beaten to publication by one of the valets, Aeneas Anderson, whose account was so popular that it went to a second edition and generated sufficient funds to buy him a commission in the Royal Manx Fencibles. See Sargeant, B E, *The Royal Manx Fencibles*, Gale and Polden, Aldershot, 1947, p. 80. **3** ADM 51/1154. **4** Staunton, 1797. **5** ADM 51/1154. **6** The brig was named for William, Duke of Clarence, the third son of George III. He joined the Navy as a midshipman at the age of thirteen, becoming successively lieutenant, captain and, in 1789, rear admiral. He was a close friend of Nelson and gave away the bride at the latter's wedding. He effectively retired from the Navy in 1790 when he was created Duke of Clarence and in 1830 became King William IV on the death of his oldest brother, George IV, his elder brother Frederick, Duke of York having died earlier. Because of his naval background, he was known as 'The Sailor King'. He had no legitimate heir, despite having eight illegitimate children, and on his death in 1837 was succeeded by his niece, Victoria. **7** ADM 51/1154. **8** Staunton, 1797. **9** ADM 51/1154. **10** The British colony of Hong Kong was not established until the cession by China of Hong Kong Island to the UK government in 1842. **11** Macao or Macau was the oldest European foothold in China, having originally been established by the Portuguese in the 1550s. At the time of *Lion*'s visits, all trade with China had to be conducted through Canton, some 50 miles upriver, but Europeans were only permitted to remain in the city during the period between the arrival of the East Indiamen of various nations with the south-west monsoon in the autumn and their departure in the spring. For the rest of the year the various European trade missions or 'factories' had to return to Macao. In 1999 Macao was handed back to China, two years after the British left Hong Kong. **12** Staunton, Vol. 2, 1791. **13** Ibid. **14** The 1,100-mile-long Grand Canal was completed in the seventh century CE and connected Pekin and Hangzhou, passing through Tien-Sing. **15** It seems likely that Gower's most pressing requirement was for what was then called Peruvian or Jesuit Bark, a natural source of quinine and the preferred treatment for malaria and other forms of fever. The expedition almost certainly brought its own supplies of bark, but these had presumably already been exhausted with the higher than expected number of cases. The fever-reducing properties of the bark of the cinchona tree, which grew wild in the Western Andes, were first discovered by Peruvian Indians and brought to Europe by Jesuit missionaries, hence the term Peruvian or Jesuit Bark, Jesuit's Tree, Jesuit's Powder or Pulvis Patrum. Cinchona plantations were subsequently established in Java, Ceylon and India.

Chapter 4 War
1 Staunton, Vol. 3, 1791. **2** ADM 51/1154. **3** Mostert, Noel, *The Line Upon a Wind*, Vintage, London, 2008, pp. 130–152. Howe, with twenty-five sail of the line, had been seeking to intercept a large French grain convoy inbound from the United States when he encountered the twenty-six-strong main French fleet under Vice Admiral Louis Thomas Villaret de Joyeuse. Although only a minority of Howe's ships obeyed or understood his instructions to break the French line, twelve of the French ships were crippled and seven were taken by the British. Both sides nevertheless claimed victory, the French because the convoy escaped. **4** The Cape was originally named the Cape of Storms by the Portuguese explorer Bartolomeu Dias, who became the first European to reach it in 1488. It is not strictly the most southern point of Africa, that honour going to Cape Agulhas (Portuguese for 'Cape of the Needles') some 90 miles to the south-east. **5** ADM 51/1154. **6** The hospital would have been the Royal Hospital Haslar in Gosport, opened in 1753 and on completion in 1761 the largest brick building in England. **7** See Bates, I M, *Champion of the Quarterdeck, Admiral Sir Erasmus Gower (1742–1814)*, Sage Old Books, 2017. In addition to Quilliam, Bates names two of his future commanding officers, Edward Riou and Robert Stopford, as having benefitted from Gower's patronage.

Chapter 5 Quartermaster's Mate
1 *Threedecks database* https://threedecks.org. **2** HMS *Prince George*, Muster Book 01.10.1794–31.03.1796, ADM 36/11346. **3** Central England Temperature (CET) Record. **4** HMS *Prince George*, Captain's Log, 11.10.1794–23.03.1795, ADM 51/1158. **5** HMS *Prince George*, Captain's Log, 23.03.1795–03.06.1795, ADM 51/1157. **6** ADM 36/11346. **7** Rodger,

N A M, *The Command of the Ocean: A Naval History of Britain 1649-1815*, Allen Lane, London, 2004. **8** HMS *Prince George*, Captain's Log, 04.06.1795–14.09.1795, ADM 51/1151. **9** Warren was a native of Nottinghamshire and very much a local hero, with the result that several pubs in and around Nottingham were and still are named after him. Perhaps the best known is the Admiral Sir John Borlase Warren in Ilkeston Road, Nottingham, which, at least in the 1960s, was known affectionately, pace The Beach Boys, as 'The Sloop John B'. **10** ADM 51/1151. **11** Marshall, John, *Royal Naval Biography*, Vol. 2, Longman, Rees, Orme, Brown and Green, London, 1823. **12** Rear Admiral Sir Hugh Clobery Christian (1747–98) and his son Rear Admiral Hood Hanway Christian (1784–1849) were members of the Christian 'Milntown' family and are commemorated on a large brass family monument in the former Lezayre Parish Church in the Isle of Man, along with 'Charles Christian of Moreland Close, Cumberland, 1729–1768 whose son Fletcher Christian RN 1764–1793 was leader of the mutiny of the Bounty'. **13** HMS *Prince George*, Captain's Log, 14.09.1795–23.11.1795, ADM 51/1119. **14** James, William, *Naval History of Great Britain*, Vol. 1, 1826. pp. 253–4 and 368–370.

Chapter 6 Master's Mate
1 *Threedecks database* https://threedecks.org. **2** HMS *Triumph*, Muster Book 01.12.1794–30.11.1795, ADM 36/11938. **3** Rodger, N A M, *The Wooden World*, Fontana edition, 1988. pp. 24–26. **4** HMS *Triumph*, Captain's Log, 27.11.1794–30.11.1795, ADM 51/1107. **5** Mostert, 2008, pp. 184–6. **6** James, Vol. 2, 1822, pp. 2–4. **7** HMS *Triumph*, Captain's Log, 01.12.1796–04.06.1797, ADM 51/1184. **8** In addition to *Séduisant*, the other French line of battle ship wrecked was *Droits-de-l'Homme*, which was lost on the Brittany coast at the end of a famous action with two British frigates, *Amazon* and Sir Edward Pellew's *Indefatigable*. All three ships found themselves embayed on a lee shore but while *Indefatigable* managed to claw her way clear, both *Droits-de-l'Homme* and *Amazon* were wrecked. Most of the crew of *Amazon* got ashore and were taken prisoner but the majority of the crew and passengers on the French ship were lost. **9** *The Naval Chronicle*, Vol. 2, 1799, p. 369. **10** James, Vol. 2, 1822, p. 23. **11** Ibid.

Chapter 7 Camperdown
1 Texel is the largest of the string of islands off the north-west coast of Holland, separating the Waddenzee from the North Sea and providing a well-protected anchorage sheltered from the prevailing westerlies. It is this anchorage, rather than the island, which was referred to by the British as 'the Texel'. **2** Pakenham, T F D, *The Year of Liberty: The Story of the Great Irish Rebellion of 1798*, Abacus, London, 1997. **3** Manwaring, G E, Dobrée, Bonamy, *The Floating Republic*, Pelican Books, London, 1935. **4** HMS *Triumph*, Captain's Log, 04.06.1797–03.06.1798, ADM 51/1212. **5** James, Vol. 2, 1822, pp. 66–70. **6** *The London Gazette*, No. 14075, 19–23, 12, 1797, pp. 1209–1210. **7** Lloyd, Christopher, *St. Vincent & Camperdown*, Batsford, London, 1963. **8** HMS *Triumph*, Muster Book 01.04.1798–31.10.1798, ADM 36/11942. **9** HMS *Neptune* Muster Book 01.08.1798–31.01.1799, ADM 36/12567. **10** Bates, I M, 2017, p. 101. **11** ADM 36/12567. **12** Keen to Admiralty, 01.10.1798, ADM 1/2018.

Chapter 8 Lieutenant Quilliam
1 HMS *Chapman* Captain's Log 01.05.1798–30.04.1799, ADM 51/1247. **2** 'Garrons Bay' is known today as Gerrans Bay and 'Nare Point' is today's Nare Head. From the position given in Keen's log, *Chapman* had finished up just yards off what are today Carne and Pendower Beaches, popular holiday beaches on the Roseland Peninsular a few miles east of Falmouth and even today a notorious ship's graveyard. **3** Keen to Admiralty, 15.10.1798, ADM 1/2018. **4** The Battle of Tory Island was fought off the coast of Donegal on 12 October 1798 between Sir John Borlase Warren's squadron, which included the frigates *Ethalion* and *Melampus* and the 74-gun third rate *Canada*, and a French force making the final attempt of the war to land an invasion force on the coast of Ireland. The French lost

seven ships, including *La Bellone*, from a force of one ship of the line and nine frigates. See James, Vol. 2, 1822, pp. 124–145. **5** The Catwater or, more commonly now, Cattewater is the sheltered anchorage where the River Plym meets Plymouth Sound to the east of Plymouth Hoe. **6** HMS *Chapman* Muster Book 01.02.1798–31.08.1799, ADM 36/12980. **7** HMS *Ethalion* Pay Book 01.11.1798–10.01.1800, ADM 35/600. **8** *Threedecks database* https://threedecks.org. **9** Ibid. **10** HMS *Ethalion* Captain's Log 01.05.1798–09.04.1799, ADM 51/1265. **11** Countess to Bridport, 07.04.1799, ADM 1/1626, 1627. **12** HMS *Ethalion*, Master's Log, 01.07.1798–30.06.1799, ADM 52/2983. Countess went on to command the third-rate 74 *Robust*.

Chapter 9 Spanish Gold
1 Marshall, Vol. 1, part 2, 1823. **2** ADM 52/2983. **3** James, Vol. 2, 1822, pp. 254–256. **4** On 1 August 1798, in what became known as the Battle of the Nile, Nelson, with thirteen ships of the line, surprised the French fleet, also comprising thirteen ships of the line, at anchor in Aboukir Bay, destroying two of them and capturing another nine as well as destroying two frigates. Only two of the French ships of the line and two frigates escaped, leaving Napoleon's army marooned in Egypt. **5** James, Vol. 2, 1822, p. 260. **6** Dragonera is a small uninhabited island off the western extremity of Majorca. **7** James, Vol. 2, 1822, p. 264. **8** Ibid, p. 265. **9** Ibid, p. 267. **10** HMS *Triton* Captain's Log 12.09.1799–11.9.1800, ADM 51/1329. **11** Young to Bridport, *The London Gazette*, No. 15197, 22–26, 10, 1799, pp. 1093–4. **12** Pierrepoint to Bridport, Ibid, pp. 1094–5. **13** James, Vol. 2, 1822, p. 358.

Chapter 10 Shipwreck
1 Marshall, Vol. 1, part 2, 1823, p. 727. **2** HMS *Fisgard* Captain's Log 15.08.1799–15.08.1800, ADM 51/1317. **3** *Index of 19th Century Naval Vessels and some of their movements*, https://sites.rootsweb.com/~pbtyc/18-1900/Index.html **4** Courts Martial Papers 11.1799–01.1800 ADM 1/5351. **5** Ibid. **6** Ibid. **7** *Danae* achieved notoriety only three months later when her crew mutinied and handed her over to a French corvette, which took her into Brest. Captain Proby and those members of the crew who had stayed loyal were exchanged on parole. **8** *The Naval Chronicle*, July to December 1799, Vol. 1. **9** ADM 1/5351. **10** Officer and Williamson's 'Measuring Worth' comparison (www.measuringworth.com) would suggest that their equivalent economic status would today require nearly £40 million and their equivalent economic power, effectively a measure based on a comparison with national Gross Domestic Product (GDP), would be a staggering £161 million. **11** James, Vol. 2, 1822, p. 358. **12** Henderson, James, *The Frigates*, Leo Cooper, London, 1994. £180 would be equivalent in modern-day comparative purchasing power terms to some £14,500 at 2011 prices and equated to around ten years wages for an able seaman. **13** The distribution of the prize money caused a rift between Nelson and St Vincent as to who should get the Admiral's share, the courts eventually deciding in Nelson's favour. See Aldous, Grahame, QC, *Lord Nelson and Earl St Vincent: Prize Fighters* in *The Mariners' Mirror* 101:2, pp. 135–155, published online 30 April 2015. **14** *The Naval Chronicle*, January to July 1800, Vol. 3, p. 150. **15** James, Vol. 2, 1822, p. 358. Applying the same comparison as the captain's shares, that represents an economic status equivalent to little under a modern-day £5 million and economic power related to GDP equivalent to some £20 million in early twenty-first-century terms. Translated to the much smaller, largely closed economy of the Isle of Man where he would invest the majority of his new-found capital, its impact would almost certainly have been even greater. **16** Quilliam to Admiralty, 15.01.1800, ADM 1/3090. **17** Cowin, F, 'Captain John Quilliam R.N.', in the *Isle of Man Natural History and Antiquarian Society* Vol. 7, 1970–72, at pp. 522–575.

Chapter 11 HMS *Amazon*
1 *Amazon* and her sister ship *Hussar*, both launched in 1799, were designed by Sir William Rule, Surveyor of the Navy, 1793–1806. **2** Tracy, N, *Who's Who in Nelson's Navy*, Chatham

Publishing, London, 2005, p. 305. Laughton, John Knox, *Riou, Edward* in Lee, Sidney, *Dictionary of National Biography*, 48, Smith, Elder & Co., London, 1890, p. 315. **3** *The London Gazette*, No. 13226, 07-10.08 1790, p. 502. **4** *Laughton, 1890.* **5** Tracy, 2005. **6** Ibid. **7** ADM 1/3090. **8** Head, C G, *Dictionary of Canadian Biography*, Vol. 5. **9** HMS *Amazon* Muster Book 01.06.1799–30.04.1800, ADM 36/12944. **10** HMS *Amazon* Captain's Log 01.07.1800–02.04.1801, ADM 51/1354. **11** Riou to Admiralty, 08.07.1800, ADM 1/2403. **12** Ibid. **13** English colours union downwards – *ie* upside down – is usually taken to be a distress signal or urgent request for assistance but in this case may have been meant to indicate that she had been captured by the enemy. **14** ADM 51/1354. **15** Denloo and Deneloo are English corruptions of Deurloo, one of the two main deep-water channels or passages through the mouth of the Western Scheldt to Flushing (Vlissingen), the other being the Spleet. In Quilliam's day the Scheldt had two separate mouths, the Eastern and the Western Scheldt (Oosterschelde and Westerschelde), but in the mid-nineteenth century a dyke was built diverting the entire flow of the river into the Western Scheldt and leaving the Eastern as effectively an inlet rather than an estuary. **16** James, Vol. 3, 1837, p. 64. Norway and Denmark comprised a single united kingdom until 1814, when Norway was ceded to Sweden under the Treaty of Kiel. It finally became fully independent in 1905. **17** Southey, Robert, *The Life of Nelson*, Bickers & Son, London, 1877 edition, p. 231. **18** Rodger, N A M, 2004. **19** The Acts of Union were passed by the British and Irish Parliaments in respectively July and August 1800 and came into effect on 1 January 1801, creating the United Kingdom of Great Britain and Ireland. **20** ADM 51/1354. **21** The sixty-one-year-old Hyde Parker had, only the previous year, married Frances, the eighteen-year-old daughter of Admiral Sir Richard Onslow, who had been Duncan's deputy at Camperdown. The marriage had given rise to considerable ribaldry with the somewhat plump Frances being variously referred to as Hyde Parker's 'batter pudding' and, rather more wittily, his 'sheet-anchor'. **22** Nicolas, 1845, p. 290. **23** Willis, Sam, *In the Hour of Victory*, Atlantic Books, London, 2013, p. 132. **24** Lambert, Andrew, *Nelson: Britannia's God of War*, Faber and Faber, London, 2004. **25** ADM 51/1354.

Chapter 12 Copenhagen
1 ADM 51/1354. **2** James, Vol. 3, 1837, pp. 68–69. **3** Mostert, 2008, pp. 392–3. **4** Willis, 2013, p. 224. **5** Nicolas, 1845, p. 307. **6** Mostert, 2008, p. 393. **7** Willis, 2013, pp. 230–1. **8** ADM 51/1354. **9** Mostert, 2008, p. 395. **10** Ibid. **11** ADM 51/1354. **12** HMS *Amazon* Master's Log 23.11.1800–20.11.1801, ADM 52/4018. **13** Lambert, 2004. **14** Moore, A W, *Manx Worthies or Biographies of Notable Manx Men and Women*, Broadbent & Co, Douglas, 1901. The Megaws give another version of the story, substituting Riou for Nelson and moving the scene to the action itself: 'In the heat of the engagement Rion (sic) sent someone "for'ard" to enquire how things were going on. As a matter of fact, things were going on very badly. All the men at one gun had been killed with the exception of Quilliam himself, who was just training the gun at the moment when the messenger delivered the question to him. Quilliam's answer was: "Augh! Middlin-Middlin."' See Megaw, Basil & Eleanor, *John Quilliam of the 'Victory'* in *The Journal of the Manx Museum*, Volume 5, No. 67, December 1942. **15** HMS *Amazon*, Captain's Log, 04.04.1801–04.04.1802, ADM 51/4409. **16** Marshall, Vol. 1, Part 2, 1823, pp. 831–3. **17** HMS *Amazon* Muster Book 01.03.1801–31.12.1801, ADM 36/14681. **18** Southey, Robert, *The Life of Nelson*, Bickers & Son, London, 1877 edition, p. 275. **19** James, Vol. 3, 1837, p. 83. **20** Lambert, 2004. **21** White, Colin, ed., *Nelson: The New Letters*, The Boydell Press, Woodbridge, 2005. **22** Nelson had reconnoitred the Welling Channel leading to Flushing on board the hired cutter *St George*, whose master was the former Irish Sea smuggler Yawkins, described by him as 'a knowing one'. Yawkins was on sufficiently familiar terms with Nelson to some months later ask to be remembered to Lady Hamilton and Sir William. See Nicolas, Vol. 4, 1845, p. 479 and Rawson, Geoffrey, *Nelson's Letters*, Everyman's Library, J M Dent, London, 1960, pp. 350, 351. **23** ADM 51/4409. **24** Nicolas, Vol. 4, 1845, p. 489. Nelson completed the initial purchase of Merton Place in October 1801 and extended the estate further in 1802. **25** *Treaty of London* in *The Napoleon*

Series at www.napoleon-series.org/research/government/diplomatic/c_london.html. **26** White, 2005. **27** Nicolas, Vol. 4, 1845, p.534. **28** Vice Admiral Skeffington Lutwidge, under whom Nelson had served as a midshipman, was Commander in Chief in The Downs. He had served on the Irish Sea Station in the 1760s and his brother Charles was a Preventative Officer and wrote an extensive report on Irish Sea smuggling for the Treasury. After Revestment, and despite not being averse to 'trading' himself, he was appointed Receiver General and Collector of Revenues for the Isle of Man, in which post he nearly caused a riot. See Gawne, C W, *The Isle of Man and Britain: Controversy, 1651–1895, from Smuggling to the Common Purse*, Manx Heritage Foundation, Douglas, 2009. **29** Admiralty to Sutton, 07.06.1802, ADM 2/815. **30** Sutton to Admiralty, 04.08.1802, ADM 1/2503, 2504. The reply was written on the reverse of Sutton's letter. **31** HMS *Amazon* Captain's Log 20.11.1802–31.12.1803, ADM 51/1454.

Chapter 13 Mediterranean
1 Lambert, 2004. **2** Nicolas, Vol. 5, 1845, p.50. **3** Nelson to Admiral Charles Hamilton in White, 2005, p.99. It has been suggested that Nelson was spelling phonetically Quilliam's own pronunciation of his surname, making allowance for Nelson's Norfolk accent. **4** Quilliam to William Marsden, 23.04.1803, ADM 1/3090. Quilliam says that he received the letter 'of the 4th Inst … this day'. **5** HMS *Victory*, Muster Book 01.03.1803–31.07.1803, ADM 36/15895. The actual Muster Book entries have Pettit arriving on the 9th and the other four on the 10th. Quilliam's log also has Pettit putting the ship into commission on the 10th. However, because of the then naval convention of the date changing at midday rather than midnight, it seems likely that Pettit arrived on the morning of the calendar 9th and the other four the same afternoon when the ship was put in commission. **6** HMS *Victory*, Lieutenant's Log, kept by John Quilliam, 10.04.1803–10.04.1805, ADM/L/V/57. All lieutenants were required to keep their own logs throughout the time spent on a ship. These had to be signed off by the captain and lodged with the Admiralty when they were discharged. Unlike his logs for his time on *Chapman*, *Ethalion* and *Amazon*, Quilliam's lieutenants' logs for the whole of his time on *Victory* have survived. Surviving captains' logs and masters' logs from the period are held at the National Archives at Kew but, as a result of some quirk of nineteenth-century naval administration, lieutenants' logs are held by the Caird Library at the National Maritime Museum at Greenwich. Quilliam's logs for the two years from 10 April 1803 to 10 April 1805 are at Greenwich. However, his log covering the period from 11 April to 3 November 1805, and therefore including Trafalgar and its aftermath, is at Kew, bound in with Hardy's Captain's Log covering the Trafalgar campaign. Conversely, Samuel Sutton's captain's log for his time on *Victory* from 11 April to 31 July 1803, which should by rights be at Kew, is bound in with Quilliam's lieutenants' logs at Greenwich. **7** Some idea of what *Victory* may have looked like before she received her ballast and her guns can, rather surprisingly, be gained from J M W Turner's painting of 'The Battle of Trafalgar', now at the National Maritime Museum at Greenwich. It has often been remarked that Turner's depiction of the ship appears to show her unusually high in the water and it has been suggested that he may have based the painting on sketches of her made at Chatham where she eventually returned for repair in early 1806 and, crucially, after her guns and ballast had been removed. **8** HMS *Victory*, Captain's Log, 11.04.1803–30.07.1803, ADM 51/1467. **9** ADM/L/V/57. **10** ADM 36/15895. In fact, by the June muster, the number of lieutenants had increased to nine, pushing Bligh down to ninth, while Layman was one of two who had been 'Lent' to other ships. **11** Nicolas, Vol. 5, 1845, pp.66–7. **12** Modern-day Cap Haitien in Haiti. **13** Quilliam's log spells it Villett, Sutton's Villete or La Villete. However, by the time they leave two days later, Quilliam's is spelling it Valette and finally Valetta. **14** Cape Sicie is the southernmost point on the French coast immediately to the west of Toulon. **15** ADM 51/1467. **16** *Donegal, Renown, Belleisle* and the absent *Kent* were all 74s, *Gibraltar* an 80 and *Monmouth* and the absent *Agincourt* 64s. *Active, Amphion* and *Phoebe* were all frigates. **17** James, Vol. 3, 1837, pp.182–3. **18** Nicolas, Vol. 5, 1845, pp.308–9. **19** Hardy to Admiralty, 19.12.1805, ADM 1/1931. **20** Marshall, Vol. 2, Part 2, 1823, pp.962–3. **21** Megaw, Basil & Eleanor,

'*John Quilliam of the "Victory"*' in *The Journal of the Manx Museum*, Vol. 5, No. 67, December 1942. **22** ADM 36/15895. **23** ADM/L/V/57. **24** Nicolas, Vol. 5, 1845, pp. 247, 254. **25** James, Vol. 3, 1837, pp. 184, 277–8. **26** Ibid, p. 274. **27** Modern-day Cape Cépet, to the west of the entrance to Toulon. **28** Gardiner, Robert, ed., *The Campaign of Trafalgar 1803–1805*, Caxton Editions, 2001, p. 109. **29** The arrival of the 74-gun, third rate *Leviathan* further increased the number of line of battle ships available to Nelson. The three bomb vessels each had a 13in and a 10in mortar, as well as a conventional armament of eight 24pdrs. In the event no opportunity to use the 'bombs' in their specialist role arose during 1804 and 1805 and Nelson added them to his inadequate stock of smaller vessels, deploying them as convoy escorts and on anti-gun boat patrols. **30** ADM/L/V/57. **31** Ibid. **32** Nicolas, Vol. 6, 1845, pp. 150–1. **33** Nicolas, Vol. 2, 1845, p. 444. **34** Nicolas, Vol. 6, 1845, p. 214. **35** Nicolas, Vol. 6, 1845, pp. 271–2.

Chapter 14 The Chase
1 ADM/L/V/57. **2** James, Vol. 3, 1837, pp. 322–3. **3** Nicolas, Vol. 6, 1845, p. 325. **4** The Morea – contemporary name for the Peloponnese peninsular of southern Greece. **5** Nicolas, Vol. 6, 1845, p. 328. **6** 'The Pharos of Messina' seems to have been used interchangeably as the name of the headland on the Sicilian side of the entrance to the Straits of Messina, today known as Torre Faro, and the straits themselves. Hence Quilliam gives *Victory*'s position as 'Pharos of Messina SbWt Dist 6 leagues' on the 29th but then on the 31st has her 'Tacking thro' ye Pharos of Messina'. Torre Faro and, on the Italian mainland, Scilla, are said to be the locations of the classical Scylla and Charybdis. **7** Nicolas, Vol. 6, 1845, p. 336. **8** This was *Victory*'s closest approach to Malta during the entire period when both Nelson and Quilliam were on board. The Megaws, Cowin and Wozencroft (*Captain John Quilliam R.N., Trafalgar Chronicle,* 1805 Club, No. 12, 2002) all quote an anecdote from the Rev. F W Stubbs, first published in the *Isle of Man Times* of 1929, claiming that 'some of the officers, junior to Quilliam, were a bit restless – probably they were jealous of his position. In any case one night Nelson and Quilliam were together on deck, and the latter mentioned the matter to Nelson. Apparently they were then off the coast of Malta. Nelson gave orders for certain ranks to go ashore. In due course they paraded, Quilliam with the rest. Nelson walked down the line, halted and looking at Quilliam, called out, "Quilliam come and take my arm." This incident, no doubt, produced a "great calm".' However, there is no evidence that anyone went ashore when *Victory* was 'off the coast of Malta' and no reason for them to do so. Nelson himself did not set foot on shore between 15 June 1803, when *Amphion* was at Malta, and 19 July 1805, when *Victory* called at Gibraltar. Stubbs, Rev. F W, *Isle of Man Times*, 12 October 1929, see *Journal of the Manx Museum*, Vol. 3, June 1936, p. 108. **9** Nicolas, Vol. 6, 1845, p. 345. **10** James, Vol. 3, 1837, p. 325. **11** Nicolas, Vol. 6, 1845, p. 348. **12** Ibid., p. 360. **13** James, Vol. 3, 1837, pp. 327–8. **14** The Republic of Ragusa comprised the modern city of Dubrovnik and its surroundings on the Dalmatian coast of the Adriatic and existed under the protection of the Ottoman Empire, for which it provided valuable trading links throughout the Mediterranean and beyond. It came to an end in 1808 when Napoleon invaded and incorporated it into the newly created kingdom of Italy. **15** James, Vol. 3, 1837, p. 328. **16** Nicolas, Vol. 6, 1845, pp. 402–407. **17** HMS *Victory*, Lieutenant's Log, 11.04.1805–03.11.1805, ADM 51/4514 NB. Incorrectly archived as a captain's log. **18** James, Vol. 3, 1837, p. 333. Campbell's assistance cost him his job. Once the French heard of what they claimed was a breach of Portugal's neutrality, they pressured the Portuguese government and had him dismissed. **19** Ibid., pp. 330–1. **20** Ibid., p. 335. **21** Nicolas, Vol. 6, 1845, pp. 445–6. **22** Ibid., 1845, pp. 472, 478. **23** In this context the Saints are the Iles des Saintes, a group of smaller islands some 10 miles to the south of Basse-Terre, the western section of the island of Guadeloupe. **24** Nicolas, Vol. 6, 1845, pp. 451–475. **25** Gardiner, 2001, pp. 127–9. **26** Nicolas, Vol. 7, 1846, pp. 11–12. **27** Ibid., p. 23. **28** Lambert, 2004. **29** Nicolas, Vol. 7, 1846, p. 26. **30** Ibid., p. 33.

Chapter 15 Quilliam's Trafalgar

1 ADM 51/4514. **2** Nicolas, Vol. 7, 1846, pp. 48–53. **3** Adkin, Mark, *The Trafalgar Companion*, Aurum Press, London, 2005, pp. 422–430. **4** For a further explanation of how the day was measured, see *Time at Sea in Nelson's Day*, Society for Nautical Research https://snr.org.uk/snr-forum/topic/time-at-sea-in-nelsons-day. **5** ADM 51/4514. **6** Rear Admiral the Earl of Northesk flew his flag in *Britannia* and became third in command when Calder left on 13 October. **7** Nicolas, Vol. 7, 1846, pp. 89–92. **8** Widely quoted including, for example, by Howarth, David and Howarth, Stephen, *Nelson: The Immortal Memory*, Conway Maritime Press, London, 2004. **9** Nicolas, Vol. 7, 1846, p. 126. **10** James, Vol. 4, 1837, p. 27. **11** Clayton, Tim; Craig, Phil, *Trafalgar: The Men, the Battle, the Storm*, Hodder & Stoughton, London, 2004. **12** Nicolas, Vol. 7, 1846, p. 133. **13** Adkin, 2005, p. 469. **14** Nicolas, Vol. 7, 1846, p. 80. **15** Adkin, 2005, p. 471. **16** Although most subsequent published descriptions of the battle use the term 'studding sails' for the sails rigged outboard of a ship's courses and top sails, Quilliam consistently uses the term 'steering sails', as does Atkinson and indeed Nelson himself in his Trafalgar Memorandum. **17** Gardiner, 2001, pp. 145–6. **18** Nicolas, Vol. 7, 1846, pp. 139–140. **19** Ibid., p. 140. **20** HMS *Victory*, Master's Log, kept by Mr Thomas Atkinson, 10.04.1803–16.01.1806, ADM 52/3711. **21** Captain, later Admiral, Home Popham's 'Talking Telegraph' or signal code used combinations of the numbers 0 to 9 to signify letters, words and whole sentences. The 1801 edition included 2,994 separate codes. **22** Gardiner, 2001, p. 146. **23** Adkin, 2005, pp. 449–50. **24** Frazer, Edward, *The Sailors Whom Nelson Led: Their Doings Described by Themselves*, Methuen, London, 1913. Westphal describes being with Quilliam when *Belleisle* (Captain William Hargood) reached the enemy line, engaging the ships on either side of her with both broadsides and prompting Nelson to exclaim 'Nobly done Hargood!' **25** James, Vol. 4, 1837, pp. 39–42. **26** *Bucentaure* and *Redoutable* were in fact 12th and 13th in the line but with some parts of the line doubled up, some ships would have been masked from view as *Victory* approached. **27** Beatty, William, M D, *Authentic Narrative of the Death of Lord Nelson*, T Cadell and W Davies, London, 1807. **28** Robert Blake (1598–1657) was England's pre-eminent 'General at Sea' during the Commonwealth. William Dampier (1651–1715) was an explorer and navigator, the first man to circumnavigate the globe three times and the rescuer of Alexander Selkirk, on whom Defoe's *Robinson Crusoe* was based. **29** Southey to Grosvenor C Bedford, 24.11.1807. Southey, C ed., *Life and Correspondence of Robert Southey* London 1848, pp. 119–22. www.rc.umd.edu/editions/southey_letters/Part_Three/HTML/letterEEd.26.1382.html. Southey's brother Thomas (Tom) was a lieutenant on *Bellona* at Copenhagen, where he was wounded. That may have been when he met Quilliam, who clearly knew him well enough to call on the Southeys on his way to or from the Island. Tom was promoted commander in 1811. Southey incorporated detail supplied both by his brother and by Quilliam in his descriptions of Copenhagen and Trafalgar but seems only to have used what they told him they saw, rather than what they did. It may be that their involvement inhibited him since, in a letter dated 5 December 1807, he wrote, 'Oh Grosvenor Bedford, what a pamphlet would I write about the navy if my brother were not in it!' **30** Southey, Robert, 1877, pp. 337–9. **31** James, Vol. 4, 1837, p. 40. **32** *The Naval Chronicle*, Vol. 15, 1805, pp. 35, 40, 369. The Atkinson family account, as related in correspondence with F Cowin, broadly agrees with this version, while adding more detail and placing the incident on the approach, but makes no mention of Quilliam. **33** Beatty, 1807, p. 56. **34** Goodwin, Peter, *HMS Victory, Owners' Workshop Manual*, J H Haynes & Co., Sparkford, 2012, p. 69. **35** Southey, Robert, 1877, pp. 337–9. **36** James, Vol. 4, 1837, pp. 72–3. **37** Atkinson's personal log, from which his Master's Log and all of the other logs including Quilliam's would have subsequently been written up, is now held at the McGowin Library of Pembroke College, Oxford. It contains much more detail than the other logs up to 9.15, after which all the logs are clearly from a common source until their arrival at Gibraltar. Opinions differ as to how much of Quilliam's logs are actually written in his own hand but his Trafalgar log is signed by him and was initialled TH by Hardy as passed on 4 September, presumably of 1806. **38** Megaw, 1942, p. 79. **39** Beatty, 1807. **40** Collingwood to Quilliam, 22.10.1805, ADM 1/2373. Collingwood's commission disproves the assertion in Marshall's *Royal Navy Biography* that Quilliam advanced to post rank 'without ever having been a Commander'. **41** Willis, 2013, p. 276. **42** Signal 314 – The ship is in distress and requires to be assisted immediately. **43** Quilliam's log, perhaps understandably, confuses 26 and 27 October. However, comparison with Atkinson's log makes clear that this entry refers to the 26th. **44** *Victory* had a slow and stormy passage home, not reaching Spithead until a month later on 4 December. There further urgent repairs to her rig were required before she made her way round to the Nore where, on 23 December, Nelson's body was transferred to the Admiralty yacht *Chatham* and conveyed to Greenwich. There it lay in state in the Painted Hall of the Royal Hospital. **45** HM Bomb *Aetna*, Captain's Log, 04.11.1805–29.03.1806, ADM 51/1536.

Chapter 16 Captain Quilliam

1 Bombs were traditionally given names reflecting their primary function and often named after volcanoes. In addition to *Aetna*, there were at different times also *Vesuvius* and *Stromboli*. There was some confusion over how the name *Aetna* was actually spelt, she being variously and interchangeably referred to as *Aetna*, *Ætna* and *Etna*, sometimes within the same document. **2** ADM 51/1536. **3** *Eurydice* was a sixth-rate post-ship, commanded by a post-captain who from December 1805 was Nelson's nephew, Sir William Bolton. He would have outranked Quilliam and would therefore have been in effective command when the two ships were working together. The designation of sixth rates appears to have been somewhat vague, those between 20 and 24 guns normally being designated sloops, although they were full-rigged ships, and those of 28 guns being referred to as frigates. However, it is clear they were virtually indistinguishable, at least at a distance, and Quilliam on a number of occasions refers to *Eurydice* as a frigate, particularly when she had not yet been identified. As a matter of interest, HMS *Surprise*, Jack Aubrey's fictional command in Patrick O'Brian's novels, was a sixth rate. **4** John Quilliam, Date of Seniority: 24 December 1805 as post-captain, ADM 9/2/321. **5** HMB *Aetna*, Muster Book 01.09.1805–31.07.1806, ADM 36/16087. **6** Corbett, J S, *The Campaign of Trafalgar*, Longmans, Green & Co., London, 1910, pp. 98, 104, 210, 326, 335. Flournoy, F R, *British Policy Towards Morocco in the age of Palmerston*, P S King & Co., London, 1935. **7** HMS *Ildefonso*, Captain's Log, 03.04.1806–19.06.1806, ADM 51/1539. **8** None of the Trafalgar prizes, all of which were 74s, became British ships of the line. *San Juan* remained at Gibraltar for the next ten years, serving first as a base hulk, second as a prison ship, third as a depot ship to a flotilla of gunboats covering the Straits and fourth as the flagship of the commander-in-chief of Gibraltar before reverting once again to a base hulk. She was finally paid off and sold at Gibraltar in 1816. **9** HMS *Ildefonso*, Muster Book, 01.04.1806–30.06.1806, ADM 36/16189. **10** Corbett, 1910. Contre-Admiral Zacharie Allemand had left Rochefort on 16 July 1805 with four battleships and several frigates and smaller craft. Having failed to rendezvous with Villeneuve or with the Brest fleet, he embarked on a commerce-raiding cruise, during which he took more than forty merchant ships before finally arriving back at Rochefort in December 1806. **11** Cowin, 1972, p. 545. See also Wozencroft, 2002, p. 149, Megaw, 1942, pp. 79–80. **12** Numbers 67 to 70 Great Russell Street are believed to be the earliest surviving work of the architect John Nash, who lived for a time at number 66. Built in 1777 just around the corner from the British Museum, their outward appearance is still very much as it would have been when Quilliam stayed at number 70. **13** Quilliam to Admiralty, 24.03.1807, ADM 1/2373. **14** Southey, writing to Bedford in December 1807, reported that Quilliam was 'at home on the Isle of Man' with 'no chance of being employed, having no interest to get a ship, and, what is better, no wish to have one'. See Southey to Grosvenor C Bedford, 05.12.1807. Southey, C ed., *Life and Correspondence of Robert Southey* London 1848, pp. 119–22. www.rc.umd.edu/editions/southey_letters/Part_Three/HTML/letterEEd.26.1389.html.

Chapter 17 Flag Captain
1 Cowin, 1972. **2** In Quilliam's time, when a vacancy occurred, the remaining members of The Keys were required to put forward the names of two suitable candidates to join their ranks, one of whom would then be selected by the Governor. Refusal to serve without good reason would incur a severe penalty. **3** Admiralty to Adml. Stopford, 21.04.1808, ADM 2/154. **4** HMS *Spencer*, Captain's Log, 05.6.1808–11.01.1809, ADM 51/1849. **5** Cowin, 1972. The Chapter Court, an ecclesiastical court, could order the father, if proved, to pay 'birth costs' and maintenance for the child. **6** Braddan burial register, 14 January 1809. Many people have been claimed to be Quilliam's direct descendants over the years but all have proved to be descended from his siblings or other relatives. **7** ADM 51/1849. **8** Quilliam to Admiralty, 24.07.1808, ADM 1/2373. **9** ADM 51/1849. **10** See Beaglehole, J G, *The Life of Captain James Cook*, A&C Black, London, 1974, pp. 238–9, for a famous example of this technique. **11** ADM 51/1849. **12** Admiralty to Navy Board, 8.11.1808, ADM 2/315. **13** Admiralty to Quilliam, 8.11.1808, ADM 2/653. **14** The precise meaning of the term 'stoop to her canvas' prompted a lively discussion on the online forum of the Society for Nautical Research (*www.snr.org.uk*). The consensus was that Quilliam was complaining of either excessive roll, pitch or yaw, or a combination of all three, resulting in the need to reduce sail earlier than would normally be expected and possibly resulting in her broaching or riding under. Quilliam's proposed solution could, it was suggested, increase the wetted area of her hull or its moment of inertia, both of which might be expected to decrease the violence of her movements. **15** Quilliam to Admiralty, 11.11.1808, ADM 1/2373. **16** Ibid. **17** Stopford eventually hoisted his flag in the battleship *Caesar*, where his arrival and the impact of his piety and objection to profane language were noted by William Richardson, a member of the ship's company. See Lewis, John. E, ed., *Life before the Mast*, Castle Books, 2002, p. 249. **18** Admiralty to Quilliam, 12.12.1808, ADM 2/654. **19** *Spencer* seems to have been laid up until October 1811, when a large repair began that lasted until early 1814. She was then recommissioned and sailed for America under Captain Richard Raggett. She was finally broken up at Plymouth in 1822. **20** Redding, Cyrus, *Fifty Years Recollections, Literary and Personal, with Observations of Men and Things*, Charles J Skeet, London, 1858, Vol. 1, pp. 107–9. **21** ADM 51/1849.

Chapter 18 Frigate Captain
1 Cowin, 1972. **2** Wareham, T, *The Star Captains: Frigate Command in the Napoleonic Wars*, Chatham Publishing, London, 2001. **3** Nathaniel Day Cochrane was the illegitimate son of the Hon John Cochrane and the grandson of the 8th Earl of Dundonald. He was thus first cousin to the more famous and dashing captain, Lord Thomas Cochrane, later 10th Earl of Dundonald. **4** Captain Nathaniel Cochrane to Admiralty, 9.12.1809, ADM 1/1654/15. **5** Admiralty to Quilliam et al 14.03.1810, ADM 2/158. **6** HMS *Alexandria*, Captain's Log, 09.2.1810–10.01.1814, ADM 51/2098. Joining next day was *Alexandria*'s new third lieutenant, eighteen-year-old William Parry, the future polar explorer. He established a friendship with his new captain that more than a decade later saw them corresponding about his voyages in search of the North West Passage. Parry may well have had Quilliam to thank for much of his hydrographic and navigational expertise, his charts of the coast of Norway and the Baltic Approaches being made under Quilliam's command. **7** Despite her nominal 32 guns, *Alexandria* carried 26 12pdrs on her main gun deck and another 12 24pdr Carronades on the quarterdeck and forecastle. **8** Quilliam to Admiralty, 13.03.1810, ADM 1/2373. **9** Admiralty to Master General of Ordnance, 15.03.1810, ADM 2/319. **10** Wingo – anglicisation of Vinga. **11** Hulm – anglicisation of Hjelm. **12** Reefness – anglicisation of Rosnaes, the headland at the north-west extremity of the island of Zealand marking the entrance to the Great Belt. **13** Admiral Dixon to Saumarez, 4.8.1810 in Ryan, A N, *The Saumarez Papers: The Baltic 1808–1812*. Navy Record Society, London, 1963, p. 144. **14** Quilliam to Admiralty, 20.07.1810, ADM 1/2373. **15** Response to Quilliam's request in Admiralty to Quilliam, 21.07.1810, ADM 2/863. **16** Wilkes Maurice was something of an island

fortress specialist, having as a lieutenant led the seventeen-month defence of Diamond Rock off Martinique between 1804 and 1805. More recently he had been appointed Governor of the newly captured tiny Caribbean island of Marie-Galante but had been forced to return to England by ill health. **17** Admiralty to Quilliam, 21.08.1810, ADM 2/863. **18** Three years younger than Quilliam, Cathcart had already had a distinguished career, having been a lieutenant on *Bellerophon* both during Cornwallis's Retreat and later at the Nile where, when all of the more senior officers were injured, his action in cutting her cable saved her from being destroyed when the French flagship *L'Orient* blew up. He was subsequently involved in a celebrated action in 1808 in which the brig *Seagull* was eventually forced to strike to a Danish brig and a swarm of gunboats. Cathcart was exonerated and commended at the court martial held on his return from imprisonment in Denmark and promoted post-captain. On taking over *Alexandria*, he was ordered to Leith and was subsequently deployed on the protection of the Spitzbergen whale fishery before, like Quilliam, being sent to America following the outbreak of the War of 1812.

Chapter 19 A Very Fast Ship

1 'She is a very fast ship.' Commander Thomas Bennett of the *Crescent* in Courts Martial Papers, September 1814, ADM1/5445. **2** Lambert, Andrew, *The Challenge: Britain versus America in the Naval War of 1812*, Faber, London 2012. **3** Threedecks database https://threedecks.org. **4** John Quilliam, Memorandum of Service, ADM 9/2/321. **5** Captain's Letters, 29.12.1810, ADM 1/2373. The original Commission, catalogued as MM MS05516, is on display together with Quilliam's uniform and other Quilliam memorabilia in the 'Mann at War Gallery' at the Manx Museum in Douglas, opened in 2018. **6** Quilliam to Admiralty, 03.01.1811, ADM 1/2373. **7** Quilliam to Admiralty, 10.01.1810, ADM 1/2373. **8** Cowin, 1972, pp. 536, 553. **9** HMS *Crescent*, Captain's Log, 11.01.1811–04.09.1815, ADM 51/2193. **10** Gardiner, Robert, *Frigates of the Napoleonic Wars*, Chatham Publishing, London, 2000. See also *Threedecks database*. **11** Admiralty to Navy Board, 19.01.1811, ADM 2/322. **12** Quilliam to Admiralty, 24.01.1811, ADM 1/2373. **13** Ibid. **14** *Erebus* was an 18-gun unrated fireship. *Cruiser* or *Cruizer* was the same 16-gun brig sloop that had worked with *Alexandria* in 1810. **15** On 12 June Quilliam wrote to the Admiralty enclosing his 'Report of Crimes and Punishments on board His Majesty's Ship Crescent under my Command between the 11th of January and 5th of April 1811'. The report was acknowledged in a standard letter that records not only *Crescent*'s punishments but also those of other ships for the same quarter acknowledged on the same day. They place Quilliam's regime in context, particularly as he is attempting to impose discipline on an entirely new ship's company. They are listed here together with each ship's name and, for comparison of size, nominal number of guns: *Leveret* (10) 5 men, *Dryad* (36) 34, *Bermuda* (10) 2, *Bellona* (74) 23, *Aboukir* (74) 23, *Medusa* (32) 10, *Mermaid* (18) 7, *Crescent* (38) 22, *Spitfire* (8) 10, *Andromache* (32) 26. Quilliam to Admiralty 12.06 1811, ADM 1/2373; Admiralty to Quilliam et al., 15.07.1811, ADM 2/160. **16** Hollesley Bay south of Orford Ness on the Suffolk coast was a popular anchorage for ships entering and leaving the Thames estuary. Quilliam and contemporaries usually spelled it phonetically as either Horsley or Horseley. **17** O'Byrne, W R, *A Naval Biographical Dictionary*, John Murray, London, 1849. See also *Threedecks database*. **18** Fleckwe – English corruption of Flekkefjorden, a fjord northwest of Kristiansand. **19** James, Vol. 6, 1859, pp. 349–350. Palle Uhd Jepsen *The Last Voyage: An Account of the British Ships of the Line HMS St. George and HMS Defence and their History until their stranding on the West Coast of Denmark on 24 December 1811*. Strandingmuseum St George, Vesterhavsgade Denmark, 2019. **20** Saumarez to Croker, 29.10.1811 in Ryan, 1963, pp. 201–2. **21** Dashwood had been in the Navy since the age of thirteen and as a midshipman had been at Rodney's side at the Battle of the Saintes in 1782. Made post-captain in 1801, from 1808 he commanded the frigates *Franchise* and *Belvidera*, distinguishing himself in numerous actions and cutting out operations. Following his time in the Baltic with *Pyramus*, he took command of the battleship *Cressy*. He would have been known, at least by name, to the novelist Jane Austen's two naval officer brothers, Charles and Francis. Although other explanations have been suggested, it is at least conceivable that she chose the name Dashwood for the family of the principal characters in her novel *Sense and Sensibility*, first published in 1811, having heard of Captain Dashwood and his exploits from her brothers. See O'Byrne, 1849. **22** Quilliam to Admiralty, 21.03.1812, ADM 1/2373. **23** *Helder* was a 32-gun frigate captured from the Dutch in 1808. **24** Admiralty to Navy Board 22.02.1812, ADM 2/324. **25** Saumarez to Croker, 20.3.1812 in Ryan, 1963, pp. 216–7. **26** Saumarez's instructions to Admiral Martin, 3.6.1812 in Ryan, 1963, p. 226. **27** Zamoyski, Adam, *Moscow 1812: Napoleon's Fatal March*, HarperCollins, London, 2004. **28** *British and Foreign State Papers* (1812–1814), Volume 1 Part 1, Great Britain, Foreign and Commonwealth Office, 1841.

Chapter 20 Newfoundland
1 Orders in Council were and still are the means by which the UK and some British Commonwealth countries introduce laws without having to obtain the approval of Parliament, particularly in times of emergency or war. They can, however, be overturned by the courts and the issues referred back to Parliament. The Orders in Council specifically at issue in 1812 had been introduced in November 1807. They forbade French trade with Britain and its allies and, more contentiously, with neutrals, and required all ships, including those of neutrals, to stop in English ports to be checked for contraband. Any ship, including those of neutrals, which did not stop in an English port to be checked or refused to stop when challenged on the high seas was liable to seizure. **2** Lambert, Andrew, 2012. pp. 37, 58 in paperback edition, 2013. **3** Ibid., pp. 98–101. **4** Admiralty to Sir Richard Keats, 13.03.1813, ADM 2/164. **5** Admiralty to Quilliam et al., 16.02.1813, ADM 2/163. **6** Admiralty to Navy Board, 28.12.1812, ADM 2/326. **7** Admiralty to Navy Board, 13.01.1813, ADM 2/326. **8** Admiralty to Master General of Ordnance, 13.01.1813, ADM 2/326. **9** Admiralty Circular to all Commanders-in-Chief, ADM2/1083. See Lambert, 2013, pp. 89–90. **10** ADM 51/2193. **11** HMS *Crescent* Muster Books, January 1811–August 1815, ADM 37/3546, 3547, 4253, 4254, 5359, 5260. **12** O'Flaherty, P, *Keats, Sir Richard Gordon* in *Dictionary of Canadian Biography*, Vol. 6. **13** Keats to Admiralty, 05.06.1813, ADM 1/478. **14** Keats to Admiralty, 20.7.1813, ADM 1/478. **15** O'Flaherty, *Dictionary of Canadian Biography*. **16** Almost certainly unbeknown to either Quilliam or Hawker before they left St John's, Captain Phillip Broke of the 38-gun frigate *Shannon* had restored British prestige by on 1 June deploying superior gunnery and seamanship to take the American 44-gun super frigate *Chesapeake*. Broke had been severely wounded in the encounter but *Shannon* had brought her prize into Halifax in triumph on 6 June. See Lambert, 2013, pp. 168–177. Singled out for mention by Broke after the action was Midshipman Cosnahan, the son of Deemster John Cosnahan, a fellow member of Tynwald with Quilliam. **17** On 21 June 1813, Wellington's 82,000-strong combined British, Portuguese and Spanish force had routed a 60,000-strong French army under Joseph Bonaparte and Marshal Jourdan at Vitoria in northern Spain, opening the way to the eventual invasion of France across the Pyrenees. **18** *Rota* – 38-gun frigate. **19** *Narcissus* – British 32-gun frigate. **20** *Comet* – 18-gun former fire ship. **21** The American privateer was named after Elbridge Thomas Gerry, the then Vice-President of the United States. Gerry was one of the original signatories of the Declaration of Independence and had financed privateers during the Revolutionary War. However, he is perhaps best if not only remembered for lending his name to the term 'gerrymander' as a result of the creation of some very odd legislative districts designed to give the Republican Party an inbuilt advantage during his time as Governor of Massachusetts. A local newspaper described one of the districts created as having the shape of a salamander and dubbed it a Gerry-mander. Gerry was President Maddison's vice-presidential running mate in the election of 1812 but died while in office in November 1814. See Austin, James Trecothick, *The Life of Elbridge Gerry*, Wells and Lilly, Boston, 1828, also Davis, Jennifer, *Elbridge Gerry and the Monstrous Gerrymander*, Library of Congress, 2017. **22** *Dryad* – 36-gun frigate. **23** Kert, F M, *Privateering: Patriots and Profits in the War of 1812*, John

Hopkins UP Baltimore, 2015. Appendix 2 records her as being commissioned on 17 August, only a month before her capture. **24** Keats to Admiralty, 19.9.1813, encl. Quilliam to Keats 18.9.1813 – rec'd 3.11.1813, St. John's, ADM1/478. **25** *Nieman* – 38-gun frigate, originally the French frigate *Niémen* taken in 1808. **26** *Armide* – 38-gun frigate, originally the French frigate *L'Armide* taken in 1804. **27** *Salvador del Mundo* – Spanish 112-gun battleship taken at the Battle of Cape St Vincent in 1797 and used as a harbour ship at Plymouth. **28** *San Antonio* – former French battleship *San Antoine*, taken in 1801 and used as a prison hulk in Portsmouth Harbour. **29** Keats to Admiralty, 27.9.1813, encl. Quilliam to Keats, 19.9.1813, ADM 1/478. **30** Courts Martial Papers, September 1814, ADM1/5445. **31** Admiralty to Sir Richard Keats, 13.03.1813, ADM 2/164. **32** *Prometheus* – sixth-rate former fire ship. **33** ADM 1/5445. **34** Admiralty General Order to all station commanders, 10 July 1813, ADM 2/1377. See Lambert, 2013, p. 189.

Chapter 21 Damnation to the Captain

1 Admiralty to Navy Board, 05.01.1814, ADM 2/328. **2** It has been suggested that Mersey in this context is a corruption of 'Mercerized', a process for the treatment of cotton fabrics developed by Lancashire chemist John Mercer. However, Mercer apparently only developed the process in 1844. It seems more likely that the term refers to a hooded jacket or coat similar to a duffle coat, perhaps originating on the River Mersey. It is worth noting that at least two vendors, Burberry and Gloverall, currently offer a 'Mersey Duffle Coat', although neither seemed able to explain the derivation of the term. **3** Courts Martial Papers, September 1814, ADM1/5445. **4** ADM 51/2193. **5** Stabb to Quilliam, 16.02.1814, ADM1/5445. **6** Bennett to Stabb, 23.02.1814, ADM1/5445. **7** ADM1/5445. **8** Ibid. **9** Ibid. **10** Bennett to Keats, 15.03.1814, ADM1/5445. **11** Keats to Admiralty, 31.3.1814, ADM 1/478. **12** Glover, Michael, *The Peninsular War 1807–1814*, David & Charles, London, 1974. **13** Coggeshall, George, *History of the American Privateers and Letters-of-Marque During our War with England in the years 1812, 13 and 14,* Published by the Author, New York, 1861. **14** Not for the first time, there is confusion in the log. The second chase seems to have occurred on the 17th. **15** *Sabine* was an 18-gun Brig Sloop newly arrived from Portugal. Her captain, Commander Edward Wrottesley, died only a little over a month later at St John's, aged twenty-nine. **16** Modern-day Calvert. **17** Alison, Archibald, *History of Europe from the Commencement of the French Revolution to the Restoration of the Bourbons in 1815,* W Blackwood, London, 1860. **18** Keats to Bennett, 13.06.1814, ADM1/5445. **19** Keats to Admiralty, 27.07.1814, ADM1/5445. **20** Keats to Admiralty, 27.07.1814, ADM1/5445. **21** *Crescent* also had a number of passengers including Mr Jno Burnes, late Master of *Comet*; Mr J C Hyde, late Surgeon of *Perseus*; Mr G. Cole, late Purser of *Prometheus*; and Jno Peterson, Seaman, *Bellerophon*, all of whom had been invalided; Lieutenant General Francis More, who had been superseded in the command of His Majesty's Forces in the island together with his servant; James Curley, a soldier under sentence of a General Court Martial to be transported for life, guarded as a prisoner; and Ensign Walker of the 93rd Regiment to return to England for the recovery of his health. See Keats to Quilliam, 19.07.1814, ADM 1/2373; Quilliam to Admiralty 20.08.1814, ADM 1/2373.

Chapter 22 Courts Martial

1 Quilliam to Admiralty, 01.08.1814, ADM 1/2373. **2** Quilliam to Admiralty, 23.08.1814, ADM 1/2373. John (later Sir John) Barrow was Second Secretary to the Admiralty from 1804 to 1845. **3** ADM1/5445. **4** Bennett to Admiralty 07.09.1814, ADM1/5445. **5** On the previous day, 9 September, Admiral Foote had presided over the court martial on *Gladiator* of Captain Robert Heriot Barclay for the loss of the squadron on Lake Erie on 10 September 1813. Quilliam was a member of the Board that found Barclay, who lost an arm in 1809 and a leg in the latest engagement, deserving of 'the highest praise' and 'most fully and honourably' acquitted him and his surviving officers and men. **6** Marshall, Vol. 3, Part 2, 1832, pp. 58–76. **7** ADM1/5445. **8** **Marshall,** Vol. 3, Part 2, 1832, pp. 58–76. **9** Ibid. **10** Admiralty General

Order to all station commanders, 10.07.1813, ADM 2/1377, p. 154. See Lambert, 2013, p. 189. **11** Marshall, Vol. 3, Part 2, 1832, pp. 58–76.

Chapter 23 West Indian Swansong
1 None of the lieutenants involved in the events on *Crescent* seem to have suffered permanent damage to their careers. Chasman joined Admiral Domett's flagship *Impregnable* in March 1815 and by 1818 was first lieutenant of *Superb*, bearing Sir Thomas Masterman Hardy's broad pendant on the South American station. He was made commander in 1821 but does not seem to have reached post-captain. (See O'Byrne, 1849). Courtney, perhaps the best connected, was appointed to Sir Richard Strachan's flagship *San Josef* in April 1815 and after a succession of appointments was promoted post-captain in 1828, the same year as Thomas Bennett despite being ten years his junior. His last seagoing appointment was in 1831, after which he became Consul General in Haiti. (See Ibid.) Least successful was Fortescue, who was still a lieutenant in 1838 commanding the naval packet *Nightingale*, on which he died 'four days after she left the West Indies'. (See *The Nautical Magazine and Naval Chronicle for 1838*, Simpkin, Marshall and Co., London.) **2** The change in personnel did not completely free Quilliam of problems with his officers and midshipmen. In June 1815, while in Martinique, he wrote to Admiral Durham, describing how Lieutenant John William Jones had 'caused several of the midshipmen to furnish him with written memorandums of my conduct and conversation when censoring him for an act of neglect and disobedience of orders ... Such conduct being calculated to cause discontent in this ship and also tending to lessen the respect due to me as his captain ... that you may take such steps as the case in your opinion may require'. See Rubinstein, Hilary L, ed., *The Durham Papers*, Routledge, London, for The Navy Records Society, 2019, p. 447. **3** In Quilliam's time Surinam could be used to refer to both the Dutch colony of that name, which later became known as Dutch Guiana, and then, after eventual independence, by its current name of Suriname, and to it and the other three neighbouring Dutch colonies of Demerara, Essequibo and Berbice, which had been taken over by the British in 1796 and were formally ceded to Britain in 1814. The latter three were subsequently merged to create British Guiana, which, after independence in 1966, was renamed Guyana. **4** Perkins, B, *Castlereagh and Adams, England and the United States*, University of California Press, Berkeley, 1964. **5** ADM 51/2193. **6** Perkins, 1964. **7** Lambert, 2012. **8** The 60th eventually became the King's Royal Rifle Corps (KRRC). See Forces War. **9** *Swiftsure* – 74-gun battleship. **10** *Grecian* – 10-gun American privateer schooner captured by HM Brig *Jasseur* in May 1814 and taken into British service. **11** St Thomas was a Danish colony but had been occupied by the British since 1807. It is now part of the US Virgin Islands. **12** Clayton, Tim, *Waterloo: Four Days that Changed Europe's Destiny*, Little, Brown, London, 2014. **13** *Redwing* and *Raven* were respectively 18- and 14-gun sloops. **14** James, Vol. 6, 1837, pp. 376–383. **15** Lambert, *The Challenge*, 2013, pp. 347–349. **16** Glover, 1974. **17** *The London Gazette*, 15.02.1814, Issue 16859, p. 367. **18** Howard, Martin R, *Death before Glory: The British Soldier in the West Indies in the French Revolutionary & Napoleonic Wars*, Pen & Sword Military, Barnsley, 2015, pp. 134–136. **19** Murray, Captain A, *Memoir of the Naval Life and Services of Admiral Sir Philip C.H.C. Durham*, John Murray, London, 1846, pp. 96–98. **20** Martinique's capital was renamed Fort-de-France after the revolution of 1789 but the British continued to use its pre-revolutionary name, Fort Royal. **21** Murray, 1846. **22** Ibid. **23** Vetch, Robert Hamilton, *Shipley, Charles*, in Lee, Sidney, *Dictionary of National Biography*, 52, Smith, Elder & Co., London, 1897, p. 109. **24** Leith's 6,000-strong force attacked Guadeloupe on 8 August in three columns, one of which was commanded by Sir Charles Shipley, forcing the island's complete capitulation two days later. However, neither Leith nor Shipley were spared much time to enjoy their triumph. Shipley died three months later of an infection contracted on the expedition while Leith succumbed to yellow fever the following year. **25** *Columbine* – 16-gun sloop. **26** In January 1816 Quilliam was paid £77 2s 10d for Freight of Specie from Barbados to St Lucia, Dominica and Martinique. **27** Quilliam to Admiralty, 13.08.1815,

ADM 1/2373. **28** Wood, William, ed., *Select British Documents of the Canadian War of 1812*, Vol. 3, Part 1, The Champlain Society, Toronto, 1926, p. 458. **29** *Crescent* was laid up for the next twenty-five years. She was recommissioned in 1840 as a receiving ship for freed slaves at Rio de Janeiro, where she was eventually sold in 1854. **30** Quilliam to Admiralty, 22.09.1815, ADM 1/2373.

Chapter 24 Manx Worthy
1 Quilliam to Admiralty, 16.10.1815, ADM 1/2373. **2** Quilliam to Admiralty, 22.08.1815, ADM 1/2373. **3** Quilliam to Admiralty, 04.11.1815, ADM 1/2373. Partly as a result of Quilliam's report no doubt, the Admiralty shortly afterwards adopted iron cables for all new vessels. Brown's company supplied the chains for Brunel's *Great Eastern* and all the Royal Navy's chains for the next 100 years. **4** Quilliam to Admiralty, 23.03.1816, ADM 1/2373. **5** Moore, A W, *Old Manx Families*, 1889. Charlotte and Thomas had one son, George Augustus Maxwell Woods, who inherited Balladoole. He, however, married twice, first to Elizabeth Coney, by whom he had eight children, and second to Charlotte Hepenstall, by whom he had a further four, of which the eldest, Richard Ambrose Woods, is joint author Andrew Bond's great grandfather. George Woods' eldest son by his first marriage, William Baring Woods, changed his name back to Stevenson on inheriting Balladoole on his father's death in 1866. As a result, there continued to be Stevensons at Balladoole until his grandson, retired ambassador Sir Ralph Stevenson, sold the house and estate in 1973. See also George Augustus Woods v. HE the Hon Charles Hope, Lieutenant Governor and others, Trustees for the time being of the Academic Fund (later Trustees of King William's College). *Manx Liberal*, 11.03.1843, p. 3. **6** Cowin, 1972, p. 561. Both Balladoole House and Balcony House still exist much as they would have appeared in Quilliam's time. Balcony House had fallen into disrepair in recent times but has since been restored. **7** Isle of Man Parish Registers, Arbory, Marriage, 1817–1848, MS 10400-2. Gelling, Canon J D, *A History of the Manx Church*, 1698–1911, Manx Heritage Foundation 1998, p. 223. Two people of such standing in the community might have expected to have been married by the Bishop, perhaps in the church in Castletown adjacent to Balcony House. However, the church was in urgent need of repair and the Bishop was out of favour, so much so that he felt it wise to absent himself from the island for three months the following year. The Government Chaplain, Joseph Brown, however, was in effect Quilliam's colleague in the House of Keys as well as Master of the Grammar School and was shortly to be appointed Diocesan Registrar. **8** Colonel Cunninghame had been colonel of the 50th Regiment and had served in the defence of Gibraltar with Margaret Stevenson's brother in law, Thomas Woods. Both he and his son Robert, who was also a trustee of Margaret's trust, are commemorated on monuments in Arbory Parish Church close by Quilliam's own memorial. See Richardson, Matthew, *Isle of Man in the Age of Sail and Musket*, Manx National Heritage 2019. **9** Manx National Heritage iMuseum Manuscript Archive MM MS04953. See also MNHi museum, Banking Records of George Quayle and Co, also known as the Isle of Man Bank Company and Quayle's Bank of Bridge House, Castletown. **10** *Manks Advertiser*, 20.03.1817, p. 2. See also *The Journal of the House of Keys*. **11** *Manx Advertiser*, 22.02.1821, p. 4. List and account of Duties on Sprung Carriages and Dogs. **12** Gill, J F, *The Statutes of the Isle of Man*, 1883, reprinted 1992, Vol. 1417–1824, p. 392. **13** Cowin, 1972, p. 562. **14** *The Journal of the House of Keys*. The new building was designed by Brine, at that time Clerk of Works to the Barracks, and used by the Keys until they moved to Douglas in 1874. It is now a museum. **15** Quilliam to Admiralty, 15.09.1817, ADM 1/2373. **16** The original Memorandum is filed with Quilliam's covering letter at the National Archives at Kew. **17** Quilliam to Admiralty, 03.09.1818, ADM 1/2373. **18** Quilliam to Admiralty, 16.12.1818, ADM 1/2373. **19** Enclosure with Quilliam to Admiralty, 06.09.1820, ADM 1/2373. **20** Quilliam to Admiralty, 06.09.1820, ADM 1/2373. **21** *Peggy* still exists, having been walled up in George Quayle's boat house, now a museum, for nigh on two hundred years. See www.nationalhistoricships.org.uk/register/1125/peggy. At the same time as *Peggy* was being built on the Island, the Admiralty was building two cutters, each of approximately 13 tons burthen, or

roughly twice her size, the one of conventional design and the other with three dagger boards. Not only did the innovative design prove a better sailer but she had the added advantage that she could be beached. 22 Wardle, A C, *Early Steam Ships on the Mersey 1815–1820*, Proceedings of the Historic Society of Lancashire and Cheshire, 1940, pp. 85–100. 23 *Manks Advertiser*, 26.04.1821, p. 3. 24 Parry to Quilliam, 03.01.1821, Manx National Heritage iMuseum Manuscript Archive MS 06775. 25 Parry, Captain W E, *Journal of Second Voyage for the Discovery of a North-West Passage*, John Murray, London, 1824. There is also a Quilliam Shoal on Lake Huron but this could not have been named by Parry. 26 Hardy, T M, to Quilliam 17.05.1825, Manx National Heritage iMuseum Manuscript Archive MS 06775. 27 Kelly, Robert, *For Those in Peril; The Life and Times of Sir William Hillary, Founder of the RNLI*, Shearwater Press, London, 1979. 28 *Manx Rising Sun*. 14.12.1824. Captain Manby's apparatus, also known as the Manby Mortar, fired a shot with a line attached from the shore to a ship in distress to enable her crew to be brought ashore by breeches buoy. The service was later provided on the Island by the Rocket Brigade. The Douglas boat was ordered from Pellew Plenty of Newbury, the Castletown vessel from Bernard Ogden of Sunderland. 29 *Manks Advertiser*, 12.01.1826. 30 Ibid, 22.03.1827. 31 Kelly, 1979, p. 2. 32 *Manx Sun*, 18.03.1854, p. 4. 33 Megaw, 1942, p. 81, quoting as reference *Manx Sun*, 20.10.1900. 34 Ibid, quoting Margaret's great, great nephew, Surgeon General Henry Wickham Stevenson. 35 Megaw, 1942, pp. 80–81; Cowin, 1972, pp. 564–5. 36 *Mona's Herald*, 12.05.1931 quoting the earlier edition of 07.04.1858. The witness, James Gell, was born in 1823 and so was only six years old when Quilliam died. He was thus unlikely to have been articled to his uncle, John McHutchin, the Clerk of the Rolls, at the time of the anecdote as reported. He became High Bailiff of Castletown in 1854, Attorney General in 1866, knighted in 1877, Deemster in 1897 and was Acting Governor during the royal visit to the Island in 1902, when he was made C.V.O. He died in 1905. The report has Quilliam 'bringing with him his trusty carpenter, Mr. Fife' on his return to the Island, implying that Fife was *Crescent*'s carpenter. However, her last carpenter was a Phillip Stevenson and no one by the name of Fife was part of her ship's company when she was paid off nor does the name appear locally at that period. 37 Gelling, p. 52. 38 Gawne, C W, *The Isle of Man and Britain Controversy 1651–1895*, Manx Heritage Foundation, 2009, pp. 72–4. See also Gelling, pp. 54–7. Bishop Murray was eventually 'translated' to become Bishop of Rochester in October 1827, having left the Island for the last time the previous August. 39 Cowin, 1972, pp. 563–4. 40 *Rising Sun*, 30.03.1822. See also *Journal of the House of Keys*. 41 Moore, A W, *Manx Worthies or Biographies of Notable Manx Men and Women*, S K Broadbent & Co, Douglas, IoM, 1901, p. 135. See www.isle-of-man.com/manxnotebook/fulltext/worthies/p071a.htm. Quilliam also has his own entry: see www.isle-of-man.com/manxnotebook/fulltext/worthies/p135.htm Curwen had been born John Christian, a relative of Fletcher Christian of HMS *Bounty*. His first wife was Margaret Taubman, daughter of John Taubman, Speaker of the House of Keys, with the result that the group opposing the Duke of Atholl became known as the 'Taubman faction'. On his first wife's death he married his cousin, Isabella Curwen, owner of Workington Hall in Cumbria, and in 1791 took her surname. He was Member of Parliament for Carlisle from 1786 to 1812 and for Cumberland from 1820 to 1829. He is thought to have been one of only two people to have ever sat in both the House of Keys and the House of Commons, the other being Margaret Quilliam's ancestor, John Stevenson (1655–1737). 42 Gawne, 2009. 43 *Journal of the House of Keys*. 44 Moore, A W, 1901, p. 135. 45 Quilliam to John McHutchin, 02.06.1824, Manx National Heritage iMuseum Manuscript Archive MS 11770. McHutchin was appointed High Bailiff of Douglas in 1816, Deemster in 1821 and Clerk of the Rolls in 1822. He was said to be the only person holding the confidence of both sides in the disputes between the Duke and the Keys. 46 The deed made and signed 23.04.1829 was produced to the courts on 27.10 1829, seventeen days after Quilliam's death. For the will see National Archives, PROB 11/1764/179. 47 Enfield, William, *Prayers for The Use of Families*, Sixth Edition, J Johnson, London, 1809. The copy, now in a private collection, has Margaret's full maiden name in her own hand at the top of the title page, partially cropped when the book was rebound, and Quilliam's signature and address inside the front cover. **48** Clague, Mike, *Whitehouse: A Michael Gem*, Michael Heritage Trust, 2019.

Chapter 25 An Honest Man, the Noblest Work of God
1 Now part of the Manx Museum's collection of Quilliam memorabilia. **2** The tomb now bears a tablet with the inscription, 'Interred in this vault lie the remains of John Quilliam Captain in the Royal Navy Trafalgar 1805', presented by the 1805 Club to mark the bicentenary of the battle. **3** *Manx Sun*, 20.10.1900, p. 21. **4** Ibid, 13.10.1829. **5** *Manx Advertiser*, 20.10.1829.

Glossary

Aback: hove all aback – to turn a ship's sails so that the wind acts on their forward surfaces in order to bring her to a halt. Hence Taken Aback – brought to an abrupt stop by the wind shifting ahead of the ship.

Admiral – of the Red, White, Blue. In Nelson's time there were nine separate degrees of admiral in an order of precedence dating from the sixteenth century. The most senior grades were Admiral of the Red Squadron, otherwise known as Admiral of the Fleet, of which there was only one, Admiral of the White and Admiral of the Blue. These were followed by three grades of vice admiral viz Vice Admiral of the Red, Vice Admiral of the White and Vice Admiral of the Blue and these in turn by three grades of rear admiral, viz Rear Admiral of the Red, Rear Admiral of the White and Rear Admiral of the Blue. Originally there had only been one of each grade, but by the end of the Napoleonic Wars there were 190, although still just one Admiral of the Fleet. Ranks were held for life and promotion was by strict seniority, so it was only possible to join the list or move from one grade to the next when someone higher up died. Admirals, Vice Admirals and Rear Admirals of the Red flew a red flag from respectively the main, the fore or the mizzen mast and a red ensign from the stern. Those of the White flew a flag of St George (red cross on a white ground) from their respective masts and a white ensign at the stern, and those of the Blue a blue flag from their respective masts and a blue ensign from the stern. The entire system was reformed in 1864 with the abolition of the separate squadrons. The White Ensign was then adopted as the flag of the Royal Navy, the Blue Ensign was allocated to Royal Naval Reserve and auxiliary vessels and the Red Ensign was adopted for all other British-registered vessels.

Azimuth and amplitude – observations of the position of a heavenly body that can be used in conjunction with tables to calculate compass error.

Battleship – aka line of battle ship, ship of the line, sail of the line. A ship capable of taking her place in the line of battle, in practice a first, second or third rate.

Bore up – present tense bear up, to turn to put the wind astern.

Bearings – bearings and courses were normally given in terms of the points of the 32-wind compass rather than in degrees; thus a point is one 32nd of the full 360 degrees or 11.25 degrees. The points between north and east are referred to as north by east, north-north-east, north-east by north, north-east, north-east by east, east-north-east and east by north, similarly for the other three quadrants.

Beat – to make progress to windward by successive tacks.

Beat to quarters – drum signal to ship's company to move to their quarters or action stations.

Bend, bent – attaching the head of a square sail to the yard, or the luff of a triangular sail to a mast, stay or gaff; also to join a cable to, for example, an anchor.

GLOSSARY

Boatswain – warrant officer with responsibility for a ship's sails, rigging and ground tackle.

Bomb ship, bomb – a vessel equipped with one or two large mortars designed for coastal bombardment.

Boom – spar to which the foot of a gaff rigged sail, *eg* driver or spanker is attached.

Booms – area of the ship's deck where spare spars were stored; ship's boats would be stored on top of the spare spars.

Bower – a bow anchor and/or its cable. Ships usually carried two 'bower' anchors, the 'best bower' normally on the starboard bow and the 'small bower' on the port.

Bowsprit – a spar, strictly a mast, projecting forward from the bow to anchor the forestay.

Bridles – loops of hawser attaching a ship to permanent buoys rather than mooring with her own anchors.

Brig – a two-masted vessel, square rigged on both of its two masts. Brigs were reckoned to be fast and highly manoeuvrable and hence well adapted to act as tenders to larger men-of-war.

Cable – heavy hawser securing a ship to her anchor.

Cable length – often abbreviated simply to a cable, a tenth of a nautical mile or approximately 100 fathoms.

Captain – 1. Anyone in command of a naval vessel, irrespective of rank. 2. Courtesy title of a Commander 3. A post-captain, one who's promotion to command a rated vessel had been posted in *The London Gazette*.

Captain of the Fleet – an admiral's chief of staff.

Carronades – Originally developed by the Carron iron works in Falkirk, Scotland, carronades were lighter and had a shorter range than the equivalent long gun. Firing a heavy projectile, they proved devastating as anti-ship and anti-personnel weapons in close-range engagements.

Cartel – a vessel carrying prisoners to or from an agreed exchange and therefore immune from capture provided she did not take part in any commerce or warlike action such as carrying dispatches.

Caulking – sealing the joints between planks by driving in oakum; hence caulkers.

Chace guns – Guns, typically 9pdr cannon or 'long nines', mounted on a ship's foc's'le, which could be trained forward and fired at the 'chace' with the aim of disabling her sails and rig. Further guns on the quarterdeck could perform the same function against a potential pursuer.

Chains, chain plates – the iron fittings securing the shrouds to the ship's sides.

Clear(ed) for action – clearing for action involved removing all impedimenta from the gun ducks, either striking it down into the hold or casting it over board and removing all the temporary screens forming the officers' cabins including the captain's and admiral's, to create a clean sweep on each deck from stem to stern.

Colours – a ship's national ensign.

Come to (or too) – to anchor.

Commander – rank between lieutenant and captain, but normally given courtesy title of **Captain**.

Commodore – temporary rank of a captain in command of a group of warships and/or a convoy.

Convoy – a collection of merchant ships under the protection of one or more warships.

Corvette – French term for a brig-sloop.

Course – 1. the direction set to be steered by a vessel; 2. the lowest and largest square sail on a ship's main or foremast.

Cutter – a small vessel fore and aft rigged with a single mainsail and a jib and a staysail. See also **Ship's boats**.

Dandy-rig – fishing boat rig with a larger than normal mizzen sail.

Downs – The Downs or Downes is the sheltered anchorage off Deal between the Goodwin Sands and the Kent coast where ships would wait for favourable wind and tide to take them either into the Thames estuary or down Channel. Even today ships can be seen waiting in the Downs for the tide or sheltering from westerly gales in the Channel.

East Indiamen – ships operated by or under licence to the various European East India companies. In effect armed merchantmen, capable of defending themselves against anything but a man-of-war, British East Indiamen carried both goods and passengers between England, the Cape of Good Hope, India and China. They typically measured between 1100 and 1400 tons burthen.

Fathom, fm – 6ft or 1.8m

First rate – see **Rates**.

Fish, fishing – strengthening a damaged spar by fixing long 'fishes' or splints around the damaged section to provide extra stiffening.

Flag captain – Captain of an admiral's flagship.

Forecastle – raised deck over the forward portion of a ship.

Foremast – the nearest to the bow of a ship's three masts.

Foresail or fore course – the largest and lowest square sail on the foremast.

Fothering – passing a sail filled with oakum under a ship's bottom to stem a leak.

Frigate – a cruising warship typically of from 28 to 44 guns on a single deck. See **Rates**.

Full rigged ship – A ship with three masts and square rigged on all three.

Gaff – spar supporting the head of a quadrilateral sail *eg* a driver or spanker.

Gallery, sometimes Quarter Gallery – Balcony-like extension on either side of the stern of a ship housing, in particular, the captain's and officers' latrines.

Galliot – A galliot, galiot or galiote could be a French bomb vessel or a Dutch or German ketch-rigged flat-bottomed merchant vessel.

Gig – a smaller ship's boat.

Great guns – a ship's main armament.

Hamoaze – the estuarine section of the River Tamar leading up from Plymouth Sound.

Hauled up, hauled her wind – came closer to the wind.

Hawse – anchor cable, hence **hawse hole** – hole in the bow of a ship through which the anchor cable passes.

Hove to – past tense of heave to, to bring a ship to a stop by backing certain of its sails.

Hoy(e) – a small sloop rigged merchant vessel or a lighter.

Hulk – a ship whose masts have been removed, often used for accommodation of prisoners of war or of a ship's company while their ship is under repair.

Jib – fore-and-aft sail set between the foremast and the bowsprit or jib-boom.

Jib-boom – spar rigged to extend the bowsprit.

Jolly boat – see **Ship's boats**

Judge Advocate – civilian lawyer appointed to advise a court martial on points of law.

GLOSSARY

Junk – Asian trading vessel.

Kedge anchor – small anchor that could be carried out in a small boat and lowered so that the ship could be hauled towards it.

Knot – One nautical mile per hour. A ship's speed was measured by counting the number of knots of the log line paid out in a thirty-second period, timed by a glass. Knots in the log line were spaced at 48ft or 8 fathom intervals (1 fathom = 6ft). Hence fractions of a knot were recorded in fathoms, 4 fathoms being half a knot.

Larboard – the left-hand side of a vessel when viewed by someone on board facing her bow. Modern-day port.

Launch, see **ship's boats**

League – 1 league = 3 nautical miles.

Leeward – direction towards which the wind is blowing.

Lee Shore – a coastline towards which the wind is blowing.

Letter of Marque – a privateer's licence or a privateer.

Lieutenant – the lowest rank of commissioned officer.

Line of battle ship – see **Battleship**

Log – 1. Hourly and daily record kept of a ship's position, course, distance run, sail changes and details of proceedings. Logs were kept by or on behalf of the captain, master and each of the lieutenants. 2. The means by which a ship's speed and hence distance run is measured.

Lugger – a vessel with two or more masts with lug sails, fore and aft sails suspended from yards and extending ahead and astern of their respective masts.

Main course – lowest square sail on a ship's main mast.

Main mast – the middle and tallest of a ships three masts.

Mainsail – see **Main Course**

Man-of-war – a warship.

Master – the most senior warrant officer rank, responsible for a warship's navigation.

Master's mate – senior petty officer reporting to the master. After seven years at sea and three as either master's mate or **midshipman**, a candidate could sit the examination for **lieutenant**.

Midshipman or Mid – a trainee officer, by Quilliam's time a rank effectively interchangeable with **master's mate.**

Mizzen mast – the nearest to the stern of a ship's three masts.

Moor, Mooring ship – A ship would come to anchor by dropping a single anchor and might remain 'at single anchor'. However, more usually she would be moored by deploying a second anchor at the same distance from the bow of the ship but at an angle approaching 90 degrees to it. Unmooring would involve raising one of the two anchors, leaving her once more at single anchor.

Muster – to assemble the entire ship's company *eg* for divine service, to witness punishment, etc.

Muster book – monthly record of an entire ship's company including officers, seamen and supernumeraries.

Navy Board – Ship construction and maintenance, victualing and the provision of naval stores were the responsibility of the Navy Board or Navy Office, based from 1789 at Somerset House on the Strand in London. It was abolished and its functions absorbed into the new Admiralty Board in 1832.

Ocham, Oakum – fibres unpicked from tarred rope and used primarily for caulking planking.

Packet Boat – small fast sailing brig, schooner or similar vessel providing scheduled service for mail, passengers and goods.

Petty officer – non-commissioned officer appointment entirely in the gift of a ship's captain.

Pilot – specialist warrant officer grade although normally civilian seaman engaged for his detailed local knowledge of the approaches to a harbour such as the Thames below Woolwich or the Medway below Chatham or of a particularly dangerous cruising ground such as the approaches to Brest.

Pinnace – see **ship's boats**

Post-captain – see **Captain**

Powder monkey – boy sailor tasked with carrying powder or cartridges from a warship's magazine to the guns.

Press – abbreviation of Impressment: forced recruitment, especially of trained seamen. Hence the press gang.

Privateer – private warship operating under a licence or Letter of Marque to prey on enemy commerce for profit.

Prize – a captured ship.

Prize crew – small detachment of seamen sent under an officer or warrant or petty officer to take a prize into a friendly port.

Prize money – money paid to a ship's officers and crew as a result of the sale of a captured merchant ship or of the government purchasing a captured warship.

Quarterdeck – deck above the main deck over the stern section of a ship from which the captain and officers exercised command.

Rates – Ships were rated by their number of guns. First rates, such as *Victory*, carried 100 guns or more on three decks, second rates between 90 and 98 guns on three decks and third rates more than 60 guns on two decks. Fourth rates were originally ships of the line of between 50 and 60 guns but by Quilliam's time these were generally regarded as too small to take their place in the line of battle. The large frigates introduced to counter the American super frigates after 1812 were classified as fourth rates. Fifth rates were frigates from 32 to 44 guns. Sixth rates were frigates of 28 or more guns or Post-ships of 20 to 24 guns, also often referred to as frigates.

Reef – a fold taken in a sail to reduce its size commensurate with the strength of the wind.

Road, roads – an anchorage open to the sea.

Royal sail – sail set above a topgallant sail.

Running rigging – the lines controlling a vessel's sails.

Sail of the line – see **Battleship**

Schooner – a two-masted vessel fore and aft rigged on both masts.

Settee – A small lateen-rigged single-masted fishing or trading vessel.

Shallop – small usually two-masted vessel propelled by oars or sails and used chiefly in shallow coastal waters.

Sheer hulk – a hulk equipped with sheer legs for lifting ship's masts in and out.

Sheer legs – an A-frame formed of two spars rigged to provide a crane, for example to lift out a mast.

Ship of the line – see **Battleship**

Ship's boats – Ships of the line and frigates normally carried as many as six ship's boats including, roughly in order of size, a launch, a barge, a pinnace, a cutter and a jolly boat, most of which could be propelled by oar or sail.

Shrouds – the standing rigging securing a vessel's masts laterally.

Sixth rate – see **Rates**

Sloop – any armed vessel of less than 20 guns and therefore unrated. A brig-sloop was thus a brig-rigged sloop with just two masts; a ship-sloop ship-rigged with three masts.

Slow match – guns were fired by a flint-lock igniting the powder in the touch hole. However, as a precaution against the mechanism failing, a slow match was kept burning in a tub beside the gun, ready to be applied directly to the touch hole if necessary.

Sound – to measure the depth of water with a lead weighted line.

Soundings – coastal waters sufficiently shallow for the depth to be measured with a lead line.

Spar – a mast, yard, boom, gaff, etc.

Spritsail Yard – spar athwart or horizontally perpendicular across the bowsprit, originally used to support the obsolete spritsail but retained to provide anchorages for the guys supporting the jib boom.

Springs – additional lines led astern from an anchor cable to enable the ship to be turned, for example to bring her broadside to bear when at anchor.

Sprung – of mast or spar, weakened by partial fracture.

Squadron – a group of warships normally smaller than, although occasionally referred to alternatively as, a fleet.

Standing rigging – the shrouds and stays supporting a vessel's masts.

Starboard – the right-hand side of a vessel when viewed by someone on board facing forward.

Stays – 1. Standing rigging securing a vessel's masts longitudinally. 2. A ship is in stays when, while tacking, the wind is directly ahead.

Steering sails – Quilliam's and contemporaries' term for sails rigged outboard of a ship's courses (main sails) and top sails, otherwise known as studding sails.

Stern sashes – stern windows of the captain's and/or admiral's cabins in a frigate or battleship.

Storm Force – devised by Captain (later Admiral Sir Francis) Beaufort when commanding HMS *Woolwich* in 1805 but not officially adopted by the Royal Navy until the 1830s, the Beaufort Scale measures wind strength on a 12-point scale from Force 0 – flat calm – through Force 1 – 3 knots – to Storm Force 10 – 48 to 55 knots – and Hurricane Force 12 – winds in excess of 64 knots.

Stream anchor – a lighter anchor, typically between 1 and 2 tons in weight, used for anchoring the vessel in a tidal stream or for warping her and could be deployed at the stern.

Strike, strike colours – to lower the national ensign, hence to surrender.

Studding sails – see **Steering sails**

Supernumeraries – naval and civilian personnel on board a ship but not part of the regular ship's company.

Sweeps – long oars deployed typically through the gun ports to row the ship forward; hence **Sweeping**.

Tabernacle – Timber assembly supporting a mast at deck level, allowing it to be raised or lowered.

Tack, starboard or larboard – A ship is on the starboard tack when the wind is coming over her starboard side. To 'haul the starboard tack' is to bring the ship's head closer to the wind on the starboard tack. Similarly larboard tack.

Tacking and wearing – Tacking ship brings the ship's head through the wind and thus brings the wind on to the other side of the ship. Wearing ship achieves the same result but by turning the ship's head away from the wind until her stern passes through the wind, the equivalent of a gybe in a modern yacht. Given enough space, square rigged ships frequently preferred to wear rather than tack because, particularly in light airs, they were at risk of 'missing stays' when tacking and finding themselves 'in irons', that is dead in the water with the ship's head into the wind and unable to turn either to starboard or port in order to pick up way again.

Tartan – a small usually two-masted Mediterranean vessel with a modified lateen rig.

Third rate – see **Rates**

Thrum – *Naut*. To sew or fasten bunches of rope-yarn over (a mat or sail) so as to produce a shaggy surface ... to stop a leak. *Shorter Oxford English Dictionary.*

Topgallant mast – third stage mast above a topmast carrying topgallant yard and sail. Topgallant masts could be struck down on deck in severe weather.

Topgallant sail – sail set above a topsail.

Topmast – second stage mast carrying topsail yard and topsail.

Topmasts pointed to the cap – topmasts in position on the lower masts but without the standing rigging set up.

Topsail – second lowest sail on each of a ship's masts, set above the course.

Tri sail or try sail – loose-footed sail bent to a gaff known as the 'tri sail mast'.

Under way – a vessel is said to be under way when it is moving under control; hence getting under way for beginning to move. Sometimes erroneously spelt 'under weigh' as a result of confusion with weighing anchor.

Unmooring – see **mooring**

Van or vanguard – the leading division of a fleet.

Warp – To move a vessel by hauling on a cable or cables attached to a stationary object.

Warrant officer – non-commissioned officer holding his appointment under warrant from the Navy Board.

Watches – a ship's company would be divided into two watches, starboard and larboard, one of which would be on deck and on duty while the other was off duty and below. Each watch lasted four hours, except for the two two-hour dog watches between four and eight in the evening. The resultant seven watches making up the full twenty-four hours being an odd number ensured that routine duties alternated between the two watches. At the end of each half hour during a watch the quartermaster turned the half hour sandglass and struck the ships bell; at eight bells the watch changed, that on duty going below and the watch below turning out.

Wear ship – see **tacking**

Weather – the direction from which the wind is blowing, for example the weather bow.

Weigh – to raise an anchor.

Woulding – Reinforcing or repairing a sprung or fished yard by wrapping it with a length of suitable rope.

Yard – horizontal spar to which the head of a square sail is attached.

Bibliography

Archive Sources

National Archives

Letters from Senior Officers, Newfoundland ADM 1/478
Letters from Captains ADM 1/1435-2733
Letters from Lieutenants, Surnames Q, ADM 1/3090
Courts Martial Papers ADM 1/5351, 5445
Admiralty Out Letters ADM 2 series
Admiralty Survey Returns of Officers' Services ADM 9 series
Ships' Pay Books ADM 35 series
Ships' Musters ADM 36 series
Dockyard Paybooks ADM 42 series
Captains' Logs ADM 51 series
Masters' Logs ADM 52 series
Lieutenants' Passing Certificates ADM 107 series

Manx National Heritage iMuseum Manuscript Archive

MS 06775
MS 11770
Manx Museum (MM) Deeds
MM MS 9191/2/2/1

Other Manx sources

Marown, Braddan, Arbory parish burial registers
Journal of the Isle of Man Natural History and Antiquarian Society
Journal of the House of Keys 1761–1852, Manx National Heritage MS9191/2/2/1

National Maritime Museum, Caird Library

Lieutenants' Logs ADM/L/V/57

Online Sources

Central England Temperature (CET) Record, www.metoffice.gov.uk/hadobs/hadcet but see also www.pascalbonenfant.com/18c/weather.html
Forces War Records, www.forces-war-records.co.uk
Index of 19th Century Naval Vessels and some of their movements, www.pbenyon.plus.com/18-1900/F/01873c.html
Isle of Man Government Harbours History, www.gov.im/about-the-government/departments/infrastructure/harbours-information/harbours-history

Manx Worthies, www.isle-of-man.com/manxnotebook/fulltext/worthies/index.htm
Measuring Worth, www.measuringworth.com
National Historic Ships, UK www.nationalhistoricships.org.uk
The Society for Nautical Research, www.snr.org.uk
Threedecks database, https://threedecks.org
The Treaty of London in The Napoleon Series, www.napoleon-series.org/research/government/diplomatic/c_london.html
Tynwald: The Parliament of the Isle of Man, www.tynwald.org.im

Periodicals

The Manx (Manks) Advertiser
The Manx Liberal
The Manx Sun
The Rising Sun
N.B. All Manx newspapers of the period are fully searchable online at the Manx National Heritage iMuseum website, manxnationalheritage.im
The Cumberland Pacquet. British Newspaper Archive, www.british newspaperarchive.co.uk
The London Gazette. Searchable online at www.thegazette.co.uk
The Mariners' Mirror, quarterly journal of the Society for Nautical Research
The Nautical Magazine and Naval Chronicle for 1838, Simpkin, Marshall and Co., London.
The Naval Chronicle, published monthly from January 1799 to December 1818. 38 Volumes. Searchable online at various locations including https://archive.org and https://books.google.co.uk
Proceedings of the Historic Society of Lancashire and Cheshire, 1940

Books

Adkin, M, *The Trafalgar Companion*, Aurum Press, London, 2005.
Alison, A, *History of Europe from the Commencement of the French Revolution to the Restoration of the Bourbons in 1815*, W Blackwood, London, 1860.
Austin, J T, *The Life of Elbridge Gerry*, Wells and Lilly, Boston, 1828.
Barrow, J, *Some Account of the Public Life, and a Selection from the Unpublished Writings, of the Earl of Macartney*, T Cadell and W Davies, London, 1807.
Bates, I M, *Champion of the Quarterdeck, Admiral Sir Erasmus Gower (1742–1814)*, Sage Old Books, 2017.
Beaglehole, J G, *The Life of Captain James Cook*, A&C Black, London, 1974.
Beatty, W, *Authentic Narrative of the Death of Lord Nelson*, T Cadell and W Davies, London, 1807.
British and Foreign State Papers (1812–1814), Volume 1 Part 1, Foreign and Commonwealth Office, London, 1841.
Clague, Mike, *Whitehouse: A Michael Gem*, Michael Heritage Trust, 2019.
Bourne, John M, *Patronage and Society in Nineteenth Century England*, Arnold, London, 1986.
Clayton, T, Craig, P, *Trafalgar: The Men, The Battle, The Storm*, Hodder & Stoughton, London, 2004.
Clayton, T, *Waterloo: Four Days that Changed Europe's Destiny*, Little, Brown, London, 2014.
Coggeshall, G, *History of the American Privateers and Letters-of-Marque During our War with England in the years 1812, '13 and '14*, Published by the Author, New York, 1861.
Corbett, J S, *The Campaign of Trafalgar*, Longmans, Green & Co., London, 1910.
Cowin, F, *Captain John Quilliam R.N.* in *Journal of the Isle of Man Natural History and Antiquarian Society*, Vol. 7, 1970–72.
Davis, J, *Elbridge Gerry and the Monstrous Gerrymander*, Library of Congress, Washington, 2017, at https://blogs.loc.gov/law/2017/02/elbridge-gerry-and-the-monstrous-gerrymander.

Enfield, William, *Prayers for The Use of Families*, Sixth Edition, J Johnson, London, 1809
Flournoy, F R, *British Policy Towards Morocco in the age of Palmerston*. P S King & Co., London, 1935.
Frazer, Edward, *The Sailors Whom Nelson Led: Their Doings Described by Themselves*, Methuen, London, 1913.
Gardiner, R., ed., *The Campaign of Trafalgar 1803–1805*, Caxton Editions, 2001.
——, *Frigates of the Napoleonic Wars*, Chatham Publishing, London, 2000.
Gawne, C W, *The Isle of Man and Britain: Controversy, 1651–1895, from Smuggling to the Common Purse*, Manx Heritage Foundation, Douglas, 2009.
Gelling, Canon J D, *A History of the Manx Church 1698–1911*, Manx Heritage Foundation, 1998.
Gill, J F, ed., *The Statutes of the Isle of Man*, Vol. 1, Eyre & Spottiswoode, London, 1883, reprinted 1992.
Glover, M, *The Peninsular War 1807–1814*, David & Charles, London, 1974.
Goodwin, Peter, *HMS Victory, Owner's Workshop Manual*, J H Haynes & Co, Sparkford, 2012.
Head, C G, *Gower, Sir Erasmus*, in *Dictionary of Canadian Biography*, Vol. 5, online edition at www.biographi.ca/en/bio/gower_erasmus_5E.html
Henderson, J, *The Frigates*, Leo Cooper, London, 1994.
Howard, M R, *Death before Glory: The British Soldier in the West Indies in the French Revolutionary & Napoleonic Wars*, Pen & Sword Military, Barnsley, 2015.
Howarth, D J, Howarth, S, *Nelson: The Immortal Memory*, Conway Maritime Press, London, 2004.
Hore, Peter, *Nelson's Band of Brothers: Lives and Memorials*, Seaforth Publishing, Barnsley, 2015.
James, W M, *The Naval History of Great Britain from the Declaration of War by France, In February 1793, to the Accession of George IV, in January 1820*, Five Volumes, Baldwin, Cradock & Joy, London, 1822–1824.
Kert, F M, *Privateering: Patriots and Profits in the War of 1812*, John Hopkins UP, Baltimore, 2015.
Kelly, Robert, *For Those in Peril; The Life and Times of Sir William Hillary, Founder of the RNLI*, Shearwater Press, London, 1979.
Lambert, A D, *Nelson: Britannia's God of War*, Faber and Faber, London, 2004.
——, *The Challenge: Britain versus America in the Naval War of 1812*. Faber and Faber, London, 2012.
Laughton, J K, *Hardy, Thomas Masterman*, in Lee, S, *Dictionary of National Biography*, 24, Smith, Elder & Co., London, 1890.
——, *Riou, Edward*, in Lee, S, *Dictionary of National Biography*, 24, Smith, Elder & Co., London, 1890.
Lewis, John E, ed., *Life before the Mast*, Castle Books, 2002.
Lewis, Michael, *A Social History of the Navy, 1793–1815*, George Allen & Unwin, London, 1960.
Lloyd, C C. *St Vincent & Camperdown*, Batsford, London, 1963.
Manwaring, G E, Dobrée, B, *The Floating Republic: An Account of the Mutinies at Spithead and the Nore in 1797*, Pelican Books, London, 1935.
Marshall, J, *Royal Naval Biography; or Memoirs of the Services of all the Flag-Officers, Superannuated Rear-Admirals, Retired-Captains, Post-Captains and Commanders Whose names appeared on the Admiralty List of Sea Officers at the commencement of the present year or have since been promoted*, Twelve Volumes, Longman, Rees, Orme, Brown and Green, London, 1823–1835.
Megaw, B & E, *John Quilliam of the 'Victory'* in *The Journal of the Manx Museum*, Vol. 5, No. 67, December 1942.

Moore, A W, *Old Manx Families*, MS, 1889, see www.isle-of-man.com/manxnotebook/famhist/families/awm1889/index.htm
——, *Manx Worthies or Biographies of Notable Manx Men and Women*, S K Broadbent & Co, Douglas, IoM, 1901.
Mostert, N, *The Line Upon A Wind*, Vintage, London, 2008.
Murray, A, *Memoir of the Naval Life and Services of Admiral Sir Philip C H C Durham*, John Murray, London, 1846.
Nicolas, N H, ed., *The Dispatches and Letters of Vice Admiral Lord Viscount Nelson*, Seven Volumes, Henry Colburn, London, 1844–46.
O'Byrne, W R, *A Naval Biographical Dictionary*, John Murray, London, 1849.
O'Flaherty, P, *Keats, Sir Richard Gordon* in *Dictionary of Canadian Biography*, Vol. 6, online edition at www.biographi.ca/en/bio/keats_richard_goodwin_6E.html
Pakenham, T F D, *The Year of Liberty: The Story of the Great Irish Rebellion of 1798*, Abacus, London, 1997.
Perkins, B, *Castlereagh and Adams: England and the United States*, University of California Press, Berkeley, 1964.
Rawson, Geoffrey, *Nelson's Letters*, Everyman's Library, J M Dent, London, 1960.
Redding, Cyrus, *Fifty Years Recollections, Literary and Personal, with Observations of Men and Things*, Charles J Skeet, London, 1858.
Richardson, Matthew, *The Isle of Man in the Age of Sail and Musket*, Manx National Heritage, 2019.
Rodger, N A M, *The Wooden World*, William Collins, London, 1986.
——, *The Command of the Ocean: A Naval History of Britain 1649–1815*, Allen Lane, London, 2004.
Rubinstein, Hilary L, ed., *The Durham Papers*, Routledge, London, for The Navy Records Society, 2019.
Ryan., A N, *The Saumarez Papers: The Baltic 1808–1812*, Navy Records Society, London, 1963.
Sargeant, B E, *The Royal Manx Fencibles*, Gale and Polden, Aldershot, 1947.
Southey, R, *The Life of Nelson*, John Murray, London, 1813.
Southey, C C, ed., *Life and Correspondence of Robert Southey, Six Volumes*, Longman, Brown, Green & Longmans, 1849–1850, London.
Staunton, G T, *An Authentic Account of An Embassy from the King of Great Britain to the Emperor of China*, Three Volumes, C Nicol, Bookseller to His Majesty, London, 1797.
Tracy, N, *Who's Who in Nelson's Navy. Chatham Publishing, London, 2005.*
Vetch, R H, *Shipley, Charles*, in Lee, S., *Dictionary of National Biography*, 52, Smith, Elder & Co., London, 1897.
Wareham, T, *The Star Captains. Frigate Command in the Napoleonic Wars*, Chatham Publishing, *London*, 2001.
White, C S, *Nelson: The New Letters*, The Boydell Press, Woodbridge, 2005.
Willis, S B A, *In The Hour of Victory*, Atlantic Books, London, 2013.
Wilson, E, *A Social History of British Naval Officers, 1775–1815*, Boydell, Woodbridge, 2017.
Winfield, R F, *British Warships in the Age of Sail 1714–1792*, Seaforth Publishing, Barnsley, 2007.
Wood, William, ed., *Select British Documents of the Canadian War of 1812*, Vol. 3, Part 1, The Champlain Society, Toronto, 1926.
Wozencroft. A, *Captain John Quilliam R.N., A Manxman at Trafalgar*, in *Trafalgar Chronicle*, 1805 Club, No. 12, 2002.
Zamoyski, A S, *Moscow 1812: Napoleon's Fatal March*, HarperCollins, London, 2004.

Index

Plate numbers are given in italics.

Aboukir 107
Aboukir Bay 35
Acasta 135
Acheron 64
Achille 85
Actaeon 108
Active 61, 63, 65, 67, 70
Adams
   Captain Alexander 123, 124
   John Quincy 133
Aetna 64, 83,85, 87
Africa 76, 84
Agamemnon 52, 76
Agincourt 63
Agincourt Sound 67, 69
Airey, John, Master 129
Alcmene 37, 52, 54, *Pl 13*
Alexander, William *Pl 5*
Alexandre 22, *Pl 11*
Alexandria
   Alexandria, city 66, 67, 69
   Alexandria, ship 94–102, *Pl 18, 22*
Algiers 144
Amazon 42, 43–56, 58, 63, 64, 71, 95, 99 *Pl 7, 8, 9, 13, 19, 27*
Ambuscade 60
Amelia
   Amelia, British merchantman 45
   Amelia, Privateer schooner 123
   Amelia, frigate 101
Amiens 57
Amphion 58, 60, 61, 74, 86
Anger Point 17
Anholt 96, 98, 99, 103, 107, 108
Anson 33
Antigua 68, 72, 134, 135
Aquaforte Harbour 111, 122
Arbory ii, 81, 139, 146, *Pl 16, 31*
Ardent 46
Argo 17, 18

Ariel 107
Armide 116
Atholl, Duke of 2, 31, 143, *Pl 3, 15, 28*
Atkinson, Thomas, Master 78, 79–81, 83, 85
Austen
   Jane 21
   Francis, Lieutenant 21
Aynsworth, Thomas, Master's Mate 138
Azores 26, 72, 110

Balcony House 139, 140, *Pl 26*
Balearics 67, 70
Ballacallin ii, 89, 145
Balladoole ii, 139
Ballakeigan ii, 139, 140, *Pl 26*
Ballakelly ii, 1, 5, 42, 145
Banca Straits 12
Bantry Bay 25, 26
Barbados 68, 71, 133, 134, 136, *Pl 4*
Barber, Henry *Pl 1*
Barcelona 36, 65
Barossa 135, 136
Barrow, John 6, 126
Basque Roads 25, 91
Basse Terre 136
Batavia 9, 12, 16
Bayonnaise 60
Beatty, William, Surgeon 80, 81
Beaulieu 43
Beechy, Sir William *Pl 9*
Belle Isle 25, 33, 34, 91
Belle Poule Pl 19
Belleisle 61, 64, 76
Bellerophon 111, 113, 114, 117, 124
Bengal 17
Bennett, Thomas, Lieutenant 106, 115, 117, 118–122, 125–131, 140
Bermuda 68, 72, 111, 117, 137
Berry, Sir Edward, Captain 76
Betsy 143

Bickerton, Sir Richard, Admiral 70
Biscay 25, 60
Blackstakes 19
Blackwood, Henry, Captain 73, 74, 76
Blanche 52, *Pl 13*
Bligh
   William, Captain 3, 29, *Pl 3*
   George, Lieutenant 59, 61, 84
Bocca Tigris 14
Bolt Head 18
Bonaparte, Napoleon 46, 55, 58, 64, 74, 124, 135
Bonifacio, Straits of 63, 70
Bordeaux 45, 60, 116, 125
Boreas 113
Borneo 14
Botany Bay 43
Boulogne 20, 55, 56
Bounty 2, *Pl 24*
Bovernbergen 20, 103
Bowen, James, Captain 23
Boyle, Courtenay, Captain 66
Brereton, Robert, Brigadier General 71
Brest 22, 25, 26, 30, 33, 35, 37, 39–41, 60, 61, 69, 72, 90
Bridport, Admiral Lord 21–24, 37, *Pl 11*
Brine, Thomas 140, 142, *Pl 30*
Briseis 107
Britannia 87
British Hero 134
Brown, Samuel, Captain 106, 138
Bruix, Étienne, Vice Admiral 35, 36
Bucentaure 64, 65, 79, 80, *Pl 14*

Cadiz 35, 36, 69–70, 72–76, 78, 82, 86
Cagliari, Gulf of 66
Calcutta 17

Calder, Sir Robert, Admiral 75
Cambridge 41
Campbell
  Donald, Rear Admiral 64
  George, Rear Admiral 70
Camperdown xiii, 20, 28–30, 147, Pl 12
Canopus 64
Canton 14, 15
Cape Breton Island 111, 115
Cape Carbonara 66
Cape de Gatte 70
Cape of Good Hope 10, 17, 43
Cape Ortegal 25, 26, 37
Cape Race 111, 112, 115, 116, 122–124
Cape San Sebastian 63, 65, 67
Cape Sepet 63
Cape Sicie 61, 65
Cape Spartel 86
Cape Spear 114
Cape St Vincent 70, 87
Cape Verde Islands 7, 135
Carden, John Surman, Captain 101
Carlisle Bay 71, 134–136
Caroline 35
Carrick Roads 32, 33
Cartagena 35, 65, 69, 70
Castletown ii, 94, 139, 140, 142–144, Pl 26, 30
Cathcart, Robert, Captain 100
Catwater 33
Cawsand Bay 22, 25, 30, 31, 60, 89, 90
Celebes 14
Chanticleer 133, 134
Chapman 31–33, 44, Pl 7
Chasman, William, Lieutenant 125, 129
Chatham 18–20, 58, 59
Christian, Sir Hugh, Admiral 23, 24
Chu-San 9, 13–15
Circe 28
Clacton 103
Clarence 12, 13, 15, Pl 5
Clark, Edward, Captain 88
Clucas
  Christian 1
  Thomas 1
Clyde 39, 41
Cochrane, Nathaniel, Captain 94, 95
Colberg 105
Collier, Sir George, Commodore 135
Collingwood, Cuthbert, Admiral 41, 74–76, 82–84, 131
Columbine 136
Comet 115
Conn, John, Captain 73
Conqueror 85
Constitution 110, 135, 137
Cook, James, Captain 2, 14, 43

Copenhagen xiii, 47–50, 53–55, 58, 71, 96, 106, 147, Pl 13
Corbett, Colleen Pl 16
Corge Bay 108
Cork 25, 112, 113, 120, 123, 132, 133
Cornwallis, William, Admiral 24, 60, 61, 72
Corsica 63, 70
Countess, George, Captain 33, 34, 41
Courageux 108
Court Martial viii, xiii, xvi, 41, 43, 92, 103, 125–133, 137, Pl 25
Courtenay, George, Lieutenant 113, 118
Crane
  John, Master Attendant 5, 6, 31
  Thomas, Lieutenant 101, 102
  Thomas 1, 5
Crenon, James 103, 104
Crescent 101–137, 140, Pl 8, 25
Cressy 104, 105, 107
Cruizer 99, 104
Cunningham, Captain 41
Cunninghame, William, Colonel 139, 141
Curwen, John Christian 144, Pl 15
Cygnet 132

Da Nang 9, 12
Dager Ort 97, 107
Daly, Cuthbert, Lieutenant 125
Danae 40
Dandys 143
Daphne 104
Dartmoor Prison 116
Dartmouth 115
Dashwood, Charles, Captain 105, 106
Davis 143
de Winter, Jan, Vice Admiral 28, 29
Deal 56
Defence 19, 85, 105
Defiance 52, 76, 134, Pl 13
Demerara, River 133, 134
Denloo Passage 46
Derbyhaven ii, 142, 143
Dickson, Archibald, Admiral 47
Digby, Henry, Captain 41
Director 29
Dixon, Manley, Admiral 105
Dockyard, Royal viii, 5, 6, 41, 42, 53 Pl 4
Dodds, Robert Pl 4
Dogger Bank 23
Domett, William, Captain 48
Donegal
  Donegal, Ship 61, 63, 64
  Donegal, Ireland 33

Douglas ii, 1–3, 89, 141, 142, Pl 3, 24
Downs, The 20, 55, 56, 100, 101, 137
Dragon 91
Dragon's Mouth 71
Dragonera 36
Dreadnought 60, 87, 88, 90
Dryad 116, 120
Duke of Athol 88
Dumanoir, Pierre, Rear Admiral 82
Duncan, Adam, Admiral 27–29, 147
Dundas, George, Captain 3
Dungeness 56
Dunkirk 3, 33
Durham, Sir Philip, Admiral 134–136

Earnest 99, 106
Ebenezer 106
Edgar 95
Edge, William, Captain 21, 23
Egypt 62, 65–67
Elba 124, 135
Elbridge Gerry 115, 116, 121
Electra 113
Elephant 48, 51–53, Pl 13
Elsinore 105
Emblin, George, Gunner 118
Emilla 15, 16
Endeavour 13
Erebus 102, 103
Essington, William, Captain 28, 29
Ethalion 33–37, 39–44, 107, Pl 7, 27
Euryalus 73, 74, 83

Falmouth 25, 26, 32, 135
Fannin, Peter 2, Pl 24
Ferrol 25, 72, 73
Fisgard 39–41, 99
Flame 99
Fleckwe 20, 104
Flushing 3, 20, 46, 55
Fontainebleau. Treaty of 124
Foote, Edward, Admiral 126, 127
Forester 133
Formidable 22, 26, 82, Pl 11
Formosa 13, 15
Fort de France 70, 71
Fortescue, George, Lieutenant 115, 118, 127, 129
Fortitude 30
Fox 5
Fremantle, Thomas, Captain 84
Funchal 7, 45

Gambier, Lord James, Admiral 19, 21, 89, 133
Gardner, Alan, Admiral 24

INDEX

Garrons (Gerrans) 32
Garth, The 1
Gazette, The London 30, 86, 116
Gelling, Elizabeth 90
Genoa 36
Georges Bay 72
Georgetown 68, 133, 134
Ghent 133
Gibraltar 35, 36, 60, 61, 69, 70, 72, 74, 75, 83, 85–87, 122
Gillingham Reach 19
Gironde, River 91
Gladiator 127, 128
Glénan, Isles de (Glenans) 25, 91, 92
Glorious First of June 17, 19, 21, 23
Glory 23
Goldie, Alexander John, General 145
Gore, John, Captain 41
Gothenburg 96, 98
Gower, Sir Erasmus, Admiral 6, 7, 10–18, 24, 27, 30, 31, 33, 44, 57, Pl 7
Gozo 67
Grand Canal 13, 14
Graves, Thomas, Admiral 52, Pl 13
Gravina, Frederico, Admiral 76
Great Belt 48, 55, 96, 98, 99, 105, 107, 108
Great Ladrone 13
Grecian 134
Greenhithe 56
Greenock 126, 141
Greensword, Edward, Master's Mate 29
Grenada 23, 136
Groix, Isle de 22–25, 91, Pl 11
Growler 113
Guadeloupe 72, 133, 136
Guardian 43
Guerriere 110

Halifax 68, 110–113, 117, 122, 124
Hamilton, Sir George and Lady Emma 55, 56
Hamoaze 33, 92, 109, 110
Handfield, Lieutenant 32
Hano, Hanö 96, 98–100, 107, 108
Hardy, Thomas Masterman, Admiral xiii, xiv, 6, 58, 61–62, 72, 75, 77, 80–83, 90, 141 Pl 2
Hawker, Edward, Captain 113
Hawkins-Whitshed, James, Admiral 35
Helder 106
Helsingborg 49
Hercule 30

Hercules 30, Pl 12
Hermione 78
Heureux Hazard 34
Heywood, Peter, Captain 2, 128, Pl 3, 24
Hillary, Sir William 142, 143
Hillman, William, Surgeon 120
Hindostan 6, 7, 10–15, 17 Pl 5
Hohenlinden 46
Hollesley Bay 20, 103, 106
Hong Kong 13
Hood, Lord Samuel, Admiral 21
Horatio 124
Howe, Lord Richard, Admiral 18, 21
Hulm 96, 98
Humber 20, 47
Humphries, Thomas 130, 131

Ildefonso, (*Ildelphonso*) 87, 88 Pl 2
Île Amsterdam 11
Île Saint-Paul 11
Impétueux 37
Inconstant 101
Ireland ii, 2, 3, 26, 28, 33, 44, 47

Jackall 6,7, 12, 13, 15, 17, Pl 5
Jakarta 9, 12
Jamaica 71, 72
Jane 114, 116, 126, 130
Japan 7, 14, 15
Jauncey, Henry, Lieutenant 37, 40
Java 11
Java 110, 116
Jervis, Admiral Sir John, Lord St Vincent 26, 35, 36, 48
Johnston, David, Lieutenant 44, 54
Jones, John Paul, Admiral 3
Judge Advocate 127
Jutland 48, 103, 105

Karlskrona 54, 96, 98
Kattegat 48, 96, 98, 99, 105
Keats, Sir Richard, Admiral xv, 89, 95, 110, 111, 113, 115–118, 120, 124, 125, 129, 131
Keen, Robert, Captain 31, 32
Keith, Lord, Admiral 35–37
Kelly
  William, Captain 144
  Robert 139
Keys, House of 89, 94, 139, 140, 143–145, 147, Pl 15, 22, 26
King William's College 146
King, Andrew, Lieutenant 59, 61

Kioge Bay 54
Kirk Michael ii, 145
Ki-San-Seu 14
Knuds Head 99
Koll, The 48, 96
Korea 13
Krakatoa 11
Kristiansand 20, 103
Kronberg (Cronenberg) Castle 49
Krondstadt 55

La Bellone 33
La Blonde 60
La Boulonnoise 33
La Indefatigable 34
La Julie 45
La Palma Pl 19
La Roche-Bonne 34
La Touche-Tréville, Vice Admiral 61, 64, 65
Lackey, Lieutenant 59
L'Aimable 76, 86
L'Amicable Agatha 60
Lantau Island 13
Layman, William, Lieutenant 59
Le Geyt, PC Pl 6
Le Renard 63
Leander 135
Leeward Islands 17, 134, 135, 137
Leith
  Leith, Scotland 20, 99
  Leith, Sir James, General 135, 136
Levant 31, 135, 137
Leviathan 64, 67, 76
Lifeboat
  at Castletown 142 Pl 30
  at Douglas 142
Linois, Charles-Alexandre, General 136
Lion 5–19, 31, 42, Pl 4, 5
Lisbon 74
Liverpool 1, 141, 142
Lizard 25, 32, 33
Loire 103, 104
London
  London 51–53
  London, City of 38, 45–47, 56, 73, 88, 137, 141, 142, 144
Long Reach 59
Lordship of Mann 2, 3
Lorient 22, 25
Louis, Thomas, Admiral 74. 76
Luneville, Treaty of 55

Macao 14–16
Macartney, George, Lord 6, 12–16
Macedonian 101, 110
Maddalena Islands 63, 66

Madeira 7, 8, 12, 27, 44, 71, 135
Magrath, George, Surgeon 64
Mahon 35, 36
Majorca 36
Malaria 12, 120
Malta 60, 61, 67, 69
Manby's apparatus 142
Marengo Pl 19
Marown ii, 1, 2, *Pl 17*
Mars 30, 107
Marshall, William 62, 127
Martin, Thomas Byam, Admiral 40, 41, 107
Martinique 60, 70–72, 134, 136
Masefield, Joseph Ore, Lieutenant 44, 52, 54
Matilda 125
Matvick 96, 108
Maurice, James Wilkes, Captain 99
Mauritius (Île de France) 11
Mazrie Bay 72
McHutchin, John 144
Medusa 55
Medway 19, 59
Merton Place 56, 73, 89
Messina 66
Milford Haven 25, 33
Minerve 45
Minorca 35, 62
Minotaur 82
Mischief Act 3
Moluccas 14
Monarch 29, 54
Monmouth 61
Montserrat 134
Moore's Mathematical School 2
Morea 66
Morocco 72
Murray
  George, Bishop 144, *Pl 15*
  George, Captain 58, 60–62, 73
  The Hon George, Captain 31
Mutiny
  Nore 27, 30
  Spithead 27

Naiad 34, 37
Nantes 22, 34, 60
Naples 66, 70, 74
Narcissus 114
Nare Head 32
Navy Board 30, 106
Nelson, Lord Horatio, Admiral xiv–xvi, 3, 30, 47, 48, 50–56, 58, 60–67, 70–84, 88, 89, 141, 147, *Pl 9, 13, 14*
Nepean, Evan *Pl 18*
Neptune 30, 31, 44, 78, 84, 85
Newcastle 135
Newfoundland 6, 110–119, 121, 122, 130, 134, 138, *Pl 6, 7, 23*
Newport 115, 117

Nicolas, Sir Nicholas Harris 78
Niemen, River 107, 116
Niemen 116
Nile 46
Nimrod 40
Nore 19–21, 27–28, 30, 55, 56, 59, 95, 98–100, 102, 106, 109
North Island 12
North Sea ii, 20, 27, 28, 46–48, 98, 103, 106, 109
North West Passage 141
Northesk. Lord William, Admiral 75
Northfleet 102
Northumberland 71
Norway 20, 46, 47, 103, 107

Onslow, Sir Richard, Admiral 29, 54
Orde, Sir John, Admiral 21
Örebro 108
Orion 95
Otway, Robert, Captain 48

Palma 65, 67
Paria, Gulf of 68, 71
Parker, Sir Hyde, Admiral 47, 48, 51, 52, 54, 55
Parker, Edward, Captain 56
Parker, William, Captain 63
Parry, William, Lieutenant 141
Parthian 92
Pasco, John, Lieutenant 59, 61, 62, 78, 84, *Pl 20*
Pasley, Sir Thomas, Admiral 3
Pater, Charles, Captain 107
Peacock, Charles, Signalman 129
Pearce (Pearse), Henry, Lieutenant 60, 62
Pearl River 13, 14
Peggy 141
Pei-Ho River 13
Pekin 9, 13–15
Penfret 91, 92
Penmarks 41
Pettit, Robert, Lieutenant 59, 61
Pheasant 115, 120
Philippines 14
Phoebe 61, 67, 70, 76, 86
Pierrepoint, William, Captain 37, 41
Plym, River 93
Plymouth 22, 23, 25, 30, 33–35, 37, 38, 41, 45, 89, 90, 92, 93, 109–112
Pocock, Nicholas *Pl 13, 19*
Pointe de Sainte Mathieu, *See* St Matthews
Pointe de Toulinguet 39
Pointe du Raz 22, 25
Polyphemus 46, 52, 84
Pomone 46

Pompée 37
Porquerolles 63
Portland 12, 23, 111, 115, 116
Portsmouth vii, xvi, 5–9, 12, 13, 20, 25, 41, 55, 58, 63, 69, 73, 86, 87, 101, 121, 124, 127, 137
Potato Riots 144
Powerful 29
President 117, 118, 128
Preston, John 130
Prevoyante 46
Prince Edward Island 111, 122
Prince George 18, 19, 21–23, 91, *Pl 11*
Prometheus 117, 118, 122, 123
Proselyte 32
Pulau Sangiang 12
Puloe Condore 12
Pym, Samuel, Lieutenant 37
Pyramus 105, 106, 108

Quayle, George 139, 141, 144, *Pl 15, 28, 29*
Quayle's Bank 139, *Pl 29*
Quebec 114, 118, 125
Queen Charlotte 23, 35
Quiberon Bay 21, 22
Quilliam Pl 32
Quilliam Creek 141

Racehorse 142
Raisonable 46
Raleigh 104
Ranger 3, 95
Redoutable 79–81, *Pl 14*
Renown 61
Reval 54, 97
Revestment Act 3
Reynard 99
Rio de Janeiro 7, 8, 10
Riou, Edward, Captain 43–47, 51, 52, 54, 95, *Pl 8*
Robertson, Joseph, Midshipman 137
Robinson, Hercules, Commander 117
Rochefort 25, 87, 91
Rodgers, John, Commodore 118
Rodney, George, Admiral 6
Ross, John, Captain 107
Rossia Bay 70, 72
Rota 114
Rotherham, Edward, Captain 83
Roundabout Island 14
Royal George 21, 27, 30, 90, *Pl 11*
Royal Sovereign 73, 76, 78, 82, 84, 85
Russell 29
Ryves, George, Captain 63

Sabine 124, 125
Saints, The (Chaussée de Sein) 39, 41, 72

INDEX

Salvador del Mundo 92, 116
Sampson 17
San Antonio 116
Santa Brigida 37, 41
Santiago, Cape Verde Islands (St Jago) 7, 8
Santissima Trinidad 81, 82 *Pl 14*
Sardinia 63, 65–67, 70
Saturn 91, 95
Saumarez, Sir James, Admiral xv, 94, 95, 99, 101, 103, 105, 107, 111, *Pl 10, 23*
Savannah, Georgia 45, 114
Scaw, The 20, 48, 96
Sceptre 28
Scheldt, River 20, 46, 55
Schomberg, Alexander, Captain 103
Scilly, Isles of 18, 25
Seahorse 65–67, 131
Searle, John Clarke, Captain 39–41
Séduisant 26
Serrell, John, Captain 106
Seymour, Lord Hugh, Admiral 26, 27
Shan-tung 13
Sheerness 19, 20, 55, 59, 95, 98, 101, 106
Sheldrake 95, 98
Shelley, Samuel *Pl 8*
Shipley, Sir Charles, General 136
Sicily 65, 66, 70
Sirius 60
Skagerrak 98, 103, 107, 109
Smelt, Cornelius, Lieutenant Governor 142, *Pl 22*
Smith, Francis Pettit 141
Sound, The (Øresund) 48, 50, 96, 99, 105, 108
Southey, Robert 80, 81
Spartiate 58, 82
Spencer 89–94
Spithead 6, 18, 20, 21, 23, 25–28, 30, 42, 44, 59, 60, 69, 72, 73, 88, 109, 112, 117, 120, 124–127, 137
St Agnes 137
St George 47, 48, 51, 105
St Helena 8, 17, 28
St Helens 26, 73
St John's 68, 111, 113, 114, 116, 120–122, 124, 125, 129, 135, *Pl 6*
St Lawrence River 111, 125
St Lucia 23, 71, 136
St Nazaire 91
St Paul 9, 11
St Thomas 134, 135, 137
St Vincent, Island of 23
St Matthew's 25, 39, 40
Stabb, Thomas 116, 117, 121, 130, 131, 138
Statira 91, 92

Staunton, Sir George 6, 10
Stevenson
 Margaret Christian vii, 139, 146, *Pl 24, 31*
 Richard Ambrose 139
Stopford, Sir Robert, Admiral 89–92
Sultan 133
Sumatra 11, 12
Sunda Strait 11, 16
Superb 89, 141
Surinam 133
Sutton, Evelyn, Commodore 56
Sutton, Samuel, Captain 54, 56–61, 74, 92
Swan 33
Swift 41
Swiftsure 85, 134
Sylph 39, 40

Tagus 26, 74
Taiwan 13
Talbot 116, 117
Tangier 86
Tartar 99, 100
Téméraire (Temeraire) 78, 81, 85, *Pl 14*
Ten-cheou-fou *Pl 5*
Tenerife 7, 8
Termagent 61
Terpsichore 35, 46
Texel 20, 28, 46, 47
Theseus 91
Thetis 37, 38, 41
Thomas, Richard, Captain 83, 85, 86
Thompson, WA, Lieutenant 113
Three Crowns battery. *See* Trekroner battery
Thunder 64
Thunderer 23
Thwart-the-Way Island 12
Tien-Sing 13
Tigre 22, *Pl 11*
Titanic 114
Tobago 71
Tobin, Charles, Midshipman 116, 138
Torbay 25, 30, 44, 90
Toro, Island of 67
Tory Island, Battle of 33
Toulon 21, 23, 24, 35, 36, 61
Trekroner battery 50–52, 54, *Pl 13*
Trelleborg 96, 108
Tremendous 39
Tresconnel 60
Tribune 99
Trinidad (Trinidada) 68, 71
Tristan da Cunha 8, 10, 11
Triton 37
Triumph 24, 26–30, 104, *Pl 7, 12*
Troubridge, Sir Thomas 48
True American 116
Tsar Paul 46, 54

Turner
 Samuel 116
 JMW *Pl 14*
Turon Bay 9
Tynwald ii, 2, 89, 140

United States 110
Upnor Castle 19, 59
Urgent 99
Ushant 22, 25, 30, 33, 36, 39, 60, 87, 90, 92

Valencia 36
Valletta (Villett) xvi, 61
Venerable 28, 29, 134, 136, *Pl 12*
Venezuela 71
Vera Cruz 37
Victory vii, xiii, 6, 53, 57–88, 90, 103, 104, 147, *Pl 9, 14, 20, 27*
Vietnam 12
Vigo 25, 72
Vigo 105, 108
Villaret de Joyeuse, Louis-Thomas, Admiral 22, 26
Villeneuve, Pierre de, Vice Admiral 65–67, 70, 72–74, 76–79
Virgin Islands 134, 135, 137
Vrijhead 29, *Pl 12*

Walpole, George, Lieutenant 54
Wampoo 15
Warren, Sir John Borlase, Admiral 21, 22, 110, *Pl 19*
Wassenaar 29
Wellington, Duke of 114, 123, 125
Wembury House 92
West Indies 6, 23, 24, 43, 44, 54, 70–72, 117, 138
West, Benjamin 88, *Pl 2*
Whatman, Thomas 138, 139
Whitcombe, Thomas *Pl 12*
Whitehouse, The 145
Whitehaven 3, 114, 138
Williams, Edward, Lieutenant 61
Wingo Sound 96, 99, 103–107, 109
Woods, Thomas, Captain 139, 140
Woods, Charlotte 139
Wrangler 99

Xebea Bay 36

Yarmouth 20, 28–30, 46, 47, 95
Yawkins, Captain 3
Young, James, Captain 34–39
Yule, John, Lieutenant 59, 61, 87

Zealand 48, 55, 96
Zhoushan. *See* Chu-San

THE QUILLIAM GROUP

The Quilliam Group was created in 2010 when a small group of like-minded naval enthusiasts on the Isle of Man responded to a call from the Rt Revd Robert Paterson, the then Bishop of Sodor and Man, for church buildings to be more widely used. They decided to host an annual Trafalgar Day lecture to commemorate Captain John Quilliam RN, in Arbory church, his final resting place. These lectures would celebrate Manx maritime heritage and subjects linked to the Royal Navy. The lectures quickly attracted capacity audiences and high-quality speakers. A Spring lecture was added to the Autumn event in 2013.

At the same time the Group began participating in other Island events, organising the Tynwald Week Royal Marine Band concerts, building partnerships with other organisations including the Friends of Manx National Heritage and attracting additional local support and sponsorship. The Group raised funds for charity, provided opportunities for local youngsters to perform with top-ranking musicians and raised the profile of Arbory church.

Though fund-raising was not the primary objective, local audiences provided generous financial support through donations at events while sponsorship from local businesses allowed the Group to bring in eminent speakers and support appropriate charities such as the Royal Naval Benevolent Fund, the local Sea Cadet unit at T.S. *Manxman* and projects in Arbory church. Links with visiting Royal Navy vessels included supplying hampers of local produce and enabling sailors to experience the famous TT motorcycle racing course and pit-lane.

In 2012 the Group decided to raise funds for a stained glass window in Arbory church to commemorate Captain Quilliam, designed by local artist Colleen Corlett. A Diocesan faculty approving the plan was obtained and the Quilliam Group secured additional funding from other agencies including the Manx Museum and the National Trust Donald Collister Bequest. The window was in place for the 2015 Trafalgar Day Lecture.

The same year saw two further developments for the Group. For the first time John Quilliam's birthday was celebrated on 28 September at a formal dinner organised by the Group and attended by His Excellency the Lieutenant Governor, the Chief of Staff from Naval Regional Headquarters in Liverpool and the Archdeacon of Man, who gave the post-dinner address. Later that year the existing members of the Quilliam Group, Dave Handscombe, Mike Berry, Quintin Gill and Phil Smith, formally recognised Colleen Corlett as a full member of the Group.

In recognition of recent research into Captain Quilliam's naval career, the Quilliam Group is delighted to support the publication of a book that will bring the Island's greatest naval hero to a far wider audience.

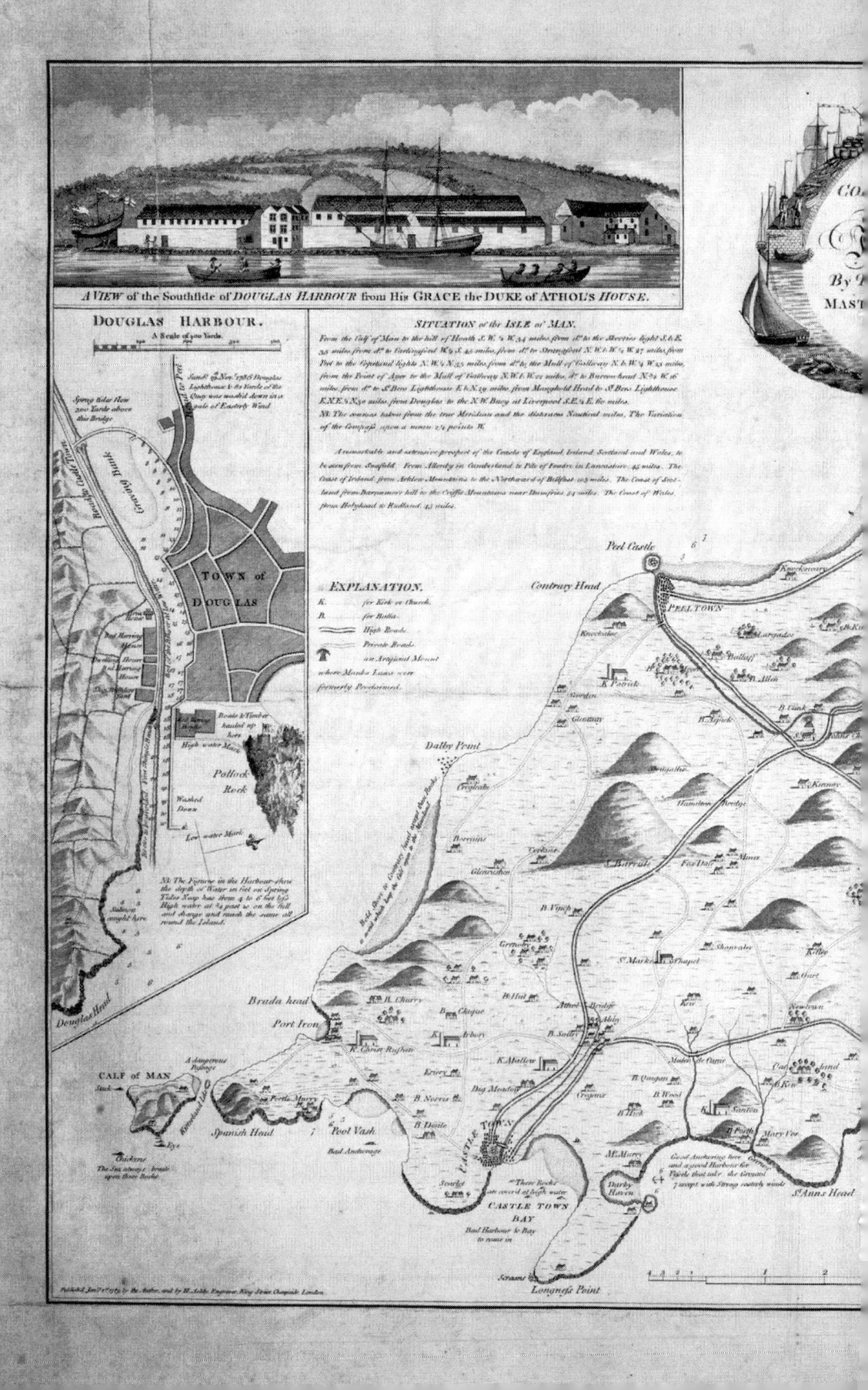

A VIEW of the Southside of DOUGLAS HARBOUR from His GRACE the DUKE of ATHOL'S HOUSE.

DOUGLAS HARBOUR.

A Scale of 500 Yards

Sunk 5 Nov. 1785 Douglas Lighthouse & 60 Yards of the Quay was washed down in a gale of Easterly Wind

Spring tides flow 20 Yards above this Bridge

TOWN of DOUGLAS

EXPLANATION.
K.......for Kirk or Church.
B.......for Rocks
≈≈≈.....High Roads
→.......Private Roads
△.......an Artificial Mount where Monks Laws were formerly Proclaimed.

N.B. The Figures in the Harbour shew the depth of Water in feet on Spring Tides Neap tides drop 4 to 6 feet less High water at 12 past 11 on the Hill and changes and runs the same all round the Island.

SITUATION of the ISLE of MAN.

From the Calf of Man to the hill of Howth S.W. ¼ W. 54 miles, from d° to the Skerries light S.& E. 54 miles from d° to Carlingford N.¼ ¾ 45 miles, from d° to Strangford N.W.¼ W. 27 miles from D°t to the Copeland lights N.W.¼ N. 35 miles, from d° by the Mull of Galloway N. b.W. ¼ W.13 miles, from the Point of Ayer to the Mull of Galloway N.N.E. ¾ W. 22 miles, d° to Burrowhead N.24. W. 16 miles, from d° to S.t Bees Lighthouse E.N.E. 39 miles, from Maughold Head to S.t Bees Lighthouse E.N.E. ¾ N. 30 miles, from Douglas to the N.W. Bay at Liverpool S.E. ¼ E. 80 miles.

N.B. The courses taken from the true Meridian and the distances Nautical miles, The Variation of the Compass 1780 is 2 ¼ points W.

A remarkable and extensive prospect of the Coasts of England, Ireland, Scotland and Wales, to be seen from Snafield. From Alderby in Cumberland to Pile of Foudrey in Lancashire, 45 miles. The Coast of Ireland, from Ardrew Mountains to the Northward of Belfast, 105 miles. The Coast of Scotland from Barrowmore hill to the Crifle Mountains near Dumfries, 54 miles. The Coast of Wales, from Holyhead to Rutland, 45 miles.

Peel Castle
Contrary Head
PEEL TOWN
Knockaloe
K. Patrick
Glenmay
Dalby Point
Orrisdale
Berrins
Glenrushin
Grenaby
S.t Marks & Chapel
B. Cherry
Bradda head
Port Iron
K. Christ Rushen
CALF of MAN
A dangerous Passage
Fistic Marry
Spanish Head
Poal Vash
Bad Anchorage
B. Norris
B. Doole
CASTLE TOWN BAY
Bad Harbour & Bay to name in
Scarlet
These Rocks are covered at high water
Langness Point

Ballaff
B. Cluck
K. Alpeck
Westyallen
Hamilton Bridge
L. Barrool
Fox Dale
Minus
B. Vinch
Shanvaler
Killey
Ken
Newtown
B. Hut
Athol Bridge
B. Sailor
K. Mallow
Dog Meadow
Grayns
B. Wood
B. Hick
K. Morey
Darby Haven
S.t Anns Head
Great Anchorage here and a good Harbour for Vessels that take the Ground except with Strong easterly winds
Mary Voe
Santon